MW00358757

Disciplining English

Disciplining English

Disciplining English

Alternative Histories, Critical Perspectives

Edited by

David R. Shumway and Craig Dionne

State University of New York Press

Elizabeth Wilson, "A Short History of a Border War: Social Science, School Reform, and the Study of Literature," *poetics today,* 9:4 (Winter 1988), pp. 711–35. Copyright 1988, Porter Institute for Poetics and Semiotics. All rights reserved. Reprinted by permission of Duke University Press.

An earlier version of chapter 4 appeared in *Ideological Approaches to Shakespeare: The Practice of Theory* (1992) edited by Robert Merrix and Nicholas Ranson. Edwin Mellen Press.

Chapter 6 originally appeared in *symplokē,* 3.1 (1995). Courtesy of *symplokē* and The University of Nebraska Press.

Published by
State University of New York Press, Albany

© 2002 State University of New York

All rights reserved

Printed in the United States of America

No part of this book may be used or reproduced in any manner whatsoever without written permission. No part of this book may be stored in a retrieval system or transmitted in any form or by any means including electronic, electrostatic, magnetic tape, mechanical, photocopying, recording, or otherwise without the prior permission in writing of the publisher.

For information, address State University of New York Press,
90 State Street, Suite 700, Albany, NY 12207

Production by Dana Foote
Marketing by Michael Campochiaro

Library of Congress Cataloging-in-Publication Data

Disciplining English : alternative histories, critical perspectives /
edited by David R. Shumway and Craig Dionne.
p.   cm.
Includes bibliographical references and index.
ISBN 0-7914-5365-0 (alk. paper) — ISBN 0-7914-5366-9 (pbk. : alk. paper)
1. English philology—Study and teaching.   2. English philology—Study and teaching—History.   3. English literature—History and criticism—Theory, etc.
4. American literature—History and criticism—Theory, etc.   I. Shumway, David R.
II. Dionne, Craig.
PE65 .D54 2002
428'.0071—dc21   2002021187
10 9 8 7 6 5 4 3 2 1

Contents

Introduction

David R. Shumway and Craig Dionne

What does it mean to say that English is a *discipline?* How does the term shift when it is asserted that English has undergone the process of "disciplining"? Who or what has been disciplined? Who or what is the discipline? The answers to these questions will require more elaboration than perhaps seems likely. We members of academic disciplines don't tend to reflect on the fact of our membership very often. When some of us do so, it is often to question our belonging to this or that discipline, or to question whether the entity with which we are institutionally identified or bound is in fact a discipline at all. Rarely do we reflect on the historical specificity of disciplinary knowledge production, in part because to make the connection between knowledge and its social construction is at least potentially to delegitimate the knowledge produced.

Since it is our assumption that all disciplinary knowledges are social and historical constructions, the essays in *Disciplining English* shouldn't be taken to delegitimate the knowledges of English on these grounds. The purpose of the volume is to explore the historical construction and current practices of English: to show that the current practices both have a history and are neither natural nor inevitable, and to explore how and why these practices have developed. Thus, the volume should lead us to question whether the particular practices and objects that English entails are justifiable given that there could be other practices and objects. In order to consider the specific history and practices of English, it is necessary to understand the specific social organization of knowledge of which English is an example. Before taking up the contributions of the essays themselves, we will here try to present an overview of that social formation we call the academic discipline.

Discipline and the Disciplines

When practitioners of English wonder whether their field is really a discipline, they are usually not asking whether it in fact is an instance of this particular historically produced form. Rather, the question typically involves the implication that English does not live up to the standards of "real" disciplines, the most real of which being those in the sciences. Used in this way, *discipline* is an honorific, a rating attained only by some academic fields. It is important that the reader of this introduction understand that the term is not used in this way here. For us, disciplines are historically specific forms of knowledge production, having certain organizational characteristics, making use of certain practices, and existing in a particular institutional environment. When the term is used in this way, any field could potentially be a discipline, even, say, astrology, if it had the requisite professional association, peer-reviewed journals, and institutional recognition.[1] We define English as a discipline because it meets these tests. To call English a discipline is neither to criticize nor to praise it. Moreover, to identify particular practices within English as more or less "disciplinary," is not to comment upon their validity or value, but to make a judgment about their form and their relative power.

The social form of the academic discipline is dependent on the techniques and strategies of control that Foucault has called "discipline." The convergence of these names may seem like a mere pun, but it is our contention that Foucault's theory of discipline has much to tell us about how academic disciplines work. Chronologically, the two phenomena coincide. Foucault cites the late eighteenth century as the moment of emergence of the disciplinary regime in prisons, factories, and schools. Likewise, knowledge has been produced by academic disciplines only since the late eighteenth century. In the United States, disciplinary knowledge production begins with the emergence of the research university in the late nineteenth century. Of course, divisions of knowledge have been called "disciplines" since Chaucer's era, but they have only much more recently become the sort of enterprises we would recognize today. As David Shumway and Ellen Messer-Davidow have shown, the term was applied to several different conceptions of the division of knowledge. The "disciplines" of seven liberal arts gave way in the late middle ages to "disciplines" dominated by dialectic and philosophy. In both conceptions, knowledge was embodied in lists of books. There was little if any sense that a discipline was an enterprise designed to produce or discover knowledge.

Moreover, these earlier branches of knowledge were little more than a handy taxonomy. They lacked any independent social existence. All educated individuals learned the liberal arts; later they all learned dialectic and philosophy. We honor the lack of specialization that was typical of the learned men of earlier times by our use of the term "renaissance man." The modern disciplines, which are necessarily inhabited by specialists, are social formations, and not merely intellectual categories or bodies of discourse. While they cannot be identified with particular organizations, such as learned societies, disciplines assume the existence of an informal association of practitioners. "A discipline is, above all, a community based on inquiry and centered on competent investigators. It consists of individuals who associated in order to facilitate intercommunication and to establish some degree of authority over the standards of that inquiry" (Geiger 29). In practice, a learned society typically represents this larger ideal community. Such professional associations—the Modern Language Association, the American Economic Association, etc.—make communication possible and serve as arenas where inter-institutional leadership can emerge. The journals they sponsor furnish the means by which scholars' work is evaluated relative to the discipline, and even the fact of publication in these journals indicates a positive evaluation. This apparatus provides the mechanism of evaluation by which disciplines exercise authority over their own ranks.

The apparatus of publication makes possible the anonymous surveillance and judgment of practitioners, since the discipline, rather than individuals, is perceived to be the source of such judgments. These judgments do not rest on the authority of individuals, but on authority vested in an anonymous system of methods, of propositions considered to be true, of rules, definitions, techniques, and tools that may in principle be taken over by anyone who has been trained in them. On the basis of such anonymous systems, academic disciplines are able to create formal restrictions on the discourse produced in their name and on who has the right to speak it. A discipline establishes its own standard form of training which becomes a prerequisite for admission into the discipline, and it determines what forms of examination are to be administered to demonstrate the trainees' competence.

Organized in this way, the academic discipline may be the perfect instance of modern power. Disciplines lack a sovereign or a center. Power is not exercised by an individual or even a legislature. Though sometimes mistakenly perceived to have such power by neophytes or outsiders, organizations such as the MLA cannot normally exercise it directly. Rather, power is exercised through numerous micro-judgments and is enforced through equally numerous micro-rewards and micro-penalties. For example, the decision to publish or not to publish a particular article will not only reward or punish an individual practitioner, but it will also endorse or fail to endorse his or her work as a contribution and a model. Such rewards or the lack of them are ultimately judged by individual departments acting in the name of the discipline in the examinations known as promotion and tenure reviews. Disciplinary power's greatest strength, however, lies in its usually not having to be enforced from the outside at all. The training of graduate students and the mentoring of young professionals disciplines them. That is, they come to internalize the values, norms, and standards that the discipline upholds. Since academics spend perhaps the longest "apprenticeship" of any modern professionals, they may be the most disciplined occupational group—a condition that belies the perception that academics are typically rebels or outsiders.

The primary responsibility for such training, credentialling, and judging academic professionals is carried out by departments. These entities came into existence only with the advent of the research university and the rise of modern disciplines. As with professional organizations, a department cannot be equated with a discipline. For example, departments may contain what are in practice several disciplines, as is rather obviously the case at some smaller institutions where there are departments such as "English and Philosophy." More common combinations, such as French and Italian, are less clear examples since it might be argued that the studies of the two languages are subdisciplines of the same field. Physicists often wonder whether their discipline is physics or the particular specialty they practice.

It may be the heterogeneity of departments that led Jencks and Reisman to argue in *Academic Revolutions* that disciplines are mere administrative conveniences. Departments *are* administrative conveniences to some extent, but they owe their existence to the disciplinary organization of knowledge production.

The nineteenth-century college lacked departments entirely. In these colleges, all students took more or less the same course of study, a model that reflected the presumed unity of knowledge. The advent of the elective curriculum corresponds to the rise of the modern disciplines that divided knowledge into distinct specialties. The departmental organization of the university follows from both of these changes, and it in turn changed the way institutions were administered. The old college had been run autocratically by its president, who could and did hire and fire faculty at will. As Veysey shows, the assumption was that the entire institution would share common beliefs. Departmental organization is a recognition not only of specialization, but also of the heterogeneity of knowledges and of the authority of disciplines as inter-institutional bodies.

Academic folklore has failed to recognize how radical a break the emergence of the research university represents. Just as institutions such as Harvard existed before and after the break, so most people assume that the knowledge taught at such institutions must also have been continuous. This is all the more true because common sense identifies the term *discipline* with the content of an academic enterprise. That content is often understood in terms of subject matters defined by Platonic essences rather than historical or cultural contingency. Many academics assume that there is some kind of unbroken continuity of particular disciplines from, say, Aristotle or Copernicus to the present, and they will cite the concept of a research *tradition* to illustrate the assumption.[2] But even those subjects such as classical languages, which dominated the curriculum of the old college, were very different from contemporary disciplines with similar names. Greek and Latin were taught in the college to inculcate mental discipline in students. The modern discipline of classics produces knowledge about ancient languages and the cultures they represent.

The view that disciplines are traditions devoted to timeless essences makes the social form of the discipline irrelevant to the knowledge produced. It misleads us into thinking that, while the quantity and accuracy of knowledge has changed, knowledge itself has not. The lesson of the last great transition in American higher education, however, is that knowledge itself can change almost overnight. The nineteenth-century college treated knowledge as something that needed to be preserved and inculcated. The assumption was that the most significant knowledge was already available, having been recorded in "literature," understood not as belles lettres but as learning. The classical curriculum was in part intended to give students access to this learning by teaching them the languages in which much of it was written. The emphasis on rhetoric was intended to enable students to communicate such wisdom effectively. Nothing that happened in the college was designed to discover or produce knowledge. The college treated knowledge as if it were limited to what was contained in a relatively small body of texts, and the knowledge required to produce more texts of a similar (if not equal) kind. The research university, on the contrary, was founded on the assumption that knowledge needed to be actively sought via the scientific method. The university assumed that the scope of possible knowledge was infinite but that the knowledge humans actually possessed was tiny. Under such circumstances, the quest for knowledge came to replace the inculcation of knowledge as the chief goal of higher education.

The modern disciplines take research—the discovery and production of knowledge—as their goal. They are neither bodies of lore, as a religious discipline might be, nor ancient crafts or skills, such as, say, the discipline of the violinist or the potter. In addition to being social formations, academic disciplines are ensembles of practices. In the natural sciences, these practices typically include the elaborate manipulation of tools and materials. In the social sciences, they may involve the manipulation of human subjects. In the humanities, however, disciplinary practice is most strongly identified with the production of particular kinds of texts, academic books and articles. All disciplines produce such texts, but the perception is that, while the sciences do so only after experiments have been performed, the humanities produce only writing. At most, humanists seem merely to gather information before they write. Because of this perception and others—for example, the "two cultures" opposition—the humanities are sometimes not reckoned to produce knowledge. But the humanities disciplines came into existence as sciences, enterprises that claimed to produce knowledge of the same truth-value as any other discipline in the university. And, while the practices of many of the humanities have undergone considerable change, they continue to be knowledge-producing practices.

As social and practical entities, disciplines cannot be equated with the knowledge—the discourse, the statements, the facts—they produce, or with the domain that they study. They are, however, strongly identified with both of these, which could not exist without the discipline. All academic disciplines constitute their own domains or objects of investigation. The object that disciplinary inquiry addresses is not available independently of disciplinary language and practice. At one level, this means that physical things—rocks or muscle fibers or literary texts—are understood differently by practitioners in different disciplines. In a larger sense, each discipline constitutes an idealized object that is the domain of its investigation. A discipline's object has only the properties and attributes that fit the discipline's assumptions. The object of history, for example, has traditionally included war and politics, but excluded much of the rest of what happened in the past. So while historians work most often with texts as their source of evidence, the texts themselves are not the object of the discipline of history. The assumptions of the discipline of history render the text a mere medium for facts or information. If interpretations of historical documents became the preoccupation of historians, interpretations of historical events might well be permanently deferred. In this sense, the object constituted by the discipline *embodies* the assumptions of the discipline, without those assumptions being made available for reflection. The disciplinary object appears to members of a discipline engaged in their normal practice as entirely natural and independent.

And yet, this account of disciplinary knowledge is misleading because it suggests much greater agreement than disciplines typically exhibit. A discipline's object is the starting point for research, not its end. Moreover, there may in practice be conflicting versions of the object. While disciplinary practitioners typically share a set of assumptions, methods, and practices, the knowledge they produce tends toward dispersion rather than unity. Disciplines are not organized in order to solve real world problems or to achieve consensus, but rather to produce more knowledge about their objects. In spite of its exclusions, disciplinarity did not have the effect of reducing the overall quantity of learned discourse. On the contrary, while the demand for evaluation encouraged the repetition of previously successful work, it also required the continual production of such work. Thus, disciplinarity requires the production of increasing amounts of similar work, and disciplines can be conceived as machines for the production of statements. "For a discipline to exist, there must be the possibility of formulating—and of doing so ad infinitum—fresh propositions" (Foucault, "Discourse" 223). Thus, disciplines are structured by problems or questions that are in some way self-reproducing. Since new statements must differ appropriately from previous ones, disciplines tend to produce an increasing quantity of narrowly diverging statements.

For Foucault, disciplines are not unified bodies of knowledge, but dispersed ones. This vision conflicts radically with our expectations, and it should lead us to wonder where the criterion of unity comes from and why it should be applied. The criterion of unity functions socially much more than intellectually. The claim of disciplinary unity naturalizes the discipline's boundaries and legitimizes its right to exclude other disciplines from its territory. A discipline is a professional form, claiming control of a certain kind of work based on the cognitive exclusiveness of its knowledge (Abbott, Larson). In the interest of maintaining such control, disciplines regularly engage, as Thomas Gieryn has argued, in "boundary-work," the production of arguments and strategies to justify, maintain, and construct the divisions of knowledge. Boundary-work serves the interests of the individuals who practice it and their colleagues whom it represents by asserting their authority over a domain of knowledge, and, therefore, over the right to perform certain kinds of work. For purely academic disciplines, this work is typically the production of knowledge itself, but it also includes the teaching of information, skills, and ideas related to that knowledge. Thus, the discipline of mathematics controls the teaching of elementary mathematics to college students, and, at a distance, the teaching of arithmetic and mathematics to lower level pupils. As Abbott has shown, the academic knowledge produced by a professional group serves to shore up public confidence in that group's ability to perform the services it controls, and such knowledge production is only indirectly related to the performance of the service. Most academic disciplines reflect this disjunction in the separation of teaching and research. Undergraduates are typically not producing knowledge. At the most, they are learning to do so; at the least, they are learning useful skills or information that are tangential to the discipline's research but for the teaching of which society is willing to pay.

To understand disciplines as professions is to recognize that they exist in the real world and not in the proverbial ivory tower. That means that disciplines are subject to the demands of the larger culture and society just as other social formations are. The research university emerged at the same time as the corporate or monopoly stage of capitalism. It would be a mistake to understand this institution as a mere creature of the economic developments of the late nineteenth century, but it would be a mistake of at least equal proportions to discount the connection. The new economic order, much more dependent on professionals and managers, on the mass media and advertising, and on product innovation and production efficiency, needed a corps of workers trained in ways that the classical curriculum did not seem suited to enable. Disciplines did not in the main train students directly for such corporate tasks, but disciplinary study did teach problem solving rather than mere memorization. We may be on the verge of a new shift in higher education, one that will make disciplines as obsolete as the old classical curriculum. If the university continues to perform direct corporate service, such as product design or testing, rather than disciplinary research, then disciplines will be replaced by other forms of knowledge production.[3]

English as a Discipline

Just as people often assume that there have been disciplines ever since Aristotle, they also seem to think that there has been a discipline of English at least since the Beowulf poet was composing his epic. But since there were no disciplines until the late nineteenth century, English could not have been one until then. In fact, the name *English* doesn't begin to appear in connection with higher education until precisely this moment. In Jack London's *Martin Eden* (1912), the eponymous hero is mystified when his bourgeois girl friend tells him that she has been taking courses in English at the university. Patricia Harkin in this volume refers to a historical event that is often taken to mark the emergence of English, Boylston Professor of Rhetoric Francis James Child's becoming the first professor of English at Harvard. It is important to insist that Child's new appointment reflects the emergence of a new discipline, and not the change of an old one. As professor of rhetoric, Child didn't practice a discipline in the modern sense. Grammar and rhetoric, which were taught in the old college, were not English. Thus, *Disciplining English* is not about how a preexisting object or field, English, became disciplined, but rather about the way the new discipline constructed its object, defended its boundaries, and trained and examined its practitioners. The essays presented here are concerned both with, on the one hand, what these practices have prohibited, excluded, and limited, and, on the other, what they have encouraged, included, and produced.

We have already argued that disciplines are typically not the unified bodies of knowledge they sometimes represent themselves as being. But even if the divided character of most disciplines is recognized, English may still seem unusually fragmented. Looking only at the dominant practice within English, the study of literature, one sees a field more fraught by differences of theory and method than most others. The history of English studies is often told in narratives that recount the struggles over how literature should be taught and studied (Graff; Ohmann; Shumway, *Creating*). Indeed, until recently, the history of English was often treated as identical to the history of criticism, which was mainly told as a history of ideas. Battles among warring camps of critics have been portrayed as having winners and losers, but unlike the stories of other disciplinary histories, it seems that in the case of English literature the losers never quite disappear. The new "paradigms" continue to be contested by the old, even as yet newer conceptions of literary study emerge and challenge the dominant. And though proponents of each new approach triumphantly claim their model represents an advance over the last, it is hard for them to write a convincing narrative of progress in the larger history. The current practice of literary study is far too divided for any one narrative to gain widespread acceptance.

English was not always so divided, however. At the outset, early practitioners of English established disciplinary boundaries and a standard practice within them, naturalizing literature as a seemingly independent object of study from which the discipline derived its identity and its unity. But if literature gave English its identity and became its object of research, English was from the outset as well in control of the teaching of writing. Thus, rhetoric was absorbed and transformed by English into the teaching of composition, a service that literature teachers claimed to be the most fit to provide. There were those within English departments who conceived of the field mainly in terms of teaching, and especially instruction in writing and rhetoric. Similarly, English departments often included literary journalists, critics, and others who conceived of the mission of English as the preservation and transmission of liberal culture. To teach writing or to celebrate culture, however, was not to practice the discipline, as it became increasingly clear. Criticism, rhetoric, and pedagogical matters of all sorts were not disciplinary practice; that was research in philology and literary history. In his contribution to the volume, David Russell describes the exclusion of these other activities as a process of *purification*. The disciplinary object and the practices devoted to it were narrowly defined, so that much of the labor that was performed under the name English was not disciplinary.

The designation by early English departments of rhetoric and criticism as "extradisciplinary" reveals the arbitrary character of disciplinary boundaries, objects, and practices. The existence of these disparate activities within the same faculties has historically been a cause of dissension. While these conflicts go back to the beginning of the discipline, they have become intensified in recent years as practices other than literary studies have developed according to different narratives into either subdisciplines or distinct but captive disciplines. In the 1930s and 1940s, criticism began to rival literary history as the dominant research practice. This in itself intensified conflict within literary studies. More important for purposes of this volume, however, are conflicts among contingents devoted to literature, composition and rhetoric, and creative writing. The 1930s and 1940s are also the watershed years for these developments. In 1936, the New Humanist critic and American literature scholar Norman Foerster founded the Writer's Workshop at the University of Iowa. In 1949, the Council on College Composition and Communication had its first meeting. Since then we have seen the proliferation of M.F.A. programs that train and credential creative writing teachers, and the steady growth of creative writing courses for undergraduates. Similarly, there has been a proliferation of rhetoric and composition tracks within English Ph.D. programs— along with a few Rhetoric Ph.D. programs—and a burgeoning set of research practices ranging from quantitative social science on the one hand, to rhetorical theory on the other. As a result of these changes, English departments now consist not only of people with conflicting literary theories, but also of people who have no affiliation with literary study whatever. Moreover, these more recently disciplined practices, especially composition and rhetoric, are themselves riven by theoretical and methodological divisions.

The essays in *Disciplining English* reflect the vast and unruly dispersion of knowledges that is English. Such dispersion has produced the paradox that within the field of English heterogeneity and hegemony exist simultaneously. The disunity of English does not mean that anything goes; rather, there exists a constant struggle among different groups distinguished by conflicting boundaries, practices, objects, and assumptions, but such conflicts always take place within a structure of dominance. The most entrenched hegemony is not that of a particular theory, but of mundane assumptions and routine practices that are seldom noticed let alone questioned. It is only by stepping back from such normal practice that we can begin to become aware of what the discipline takes for granted. *Disciplining English* is an exercise in this reflection. Its contributors share neither a particular theoretical perspective nor a single disciplinary practice. (Indeed, they may well disagree with many points we argue in this introduction.) What the essays do share, however, is a common attitude toward their material. They all recognize the historically contingent character of the current arrangement of English. *Disciplining English* is genealogical in that it questions the idea of "disciplines as seamless, progressive, or naturally 'about' certain topics." Each of the essays begins with the premise that English is a "historically contingent and adventitious" assembly of "various ideas and practices" (Messer-Davidow, Shumway, and Sylvan 4). The contributions help us understand the historical changes that have produced the current discipline, and the contemporary conditions that are themselves in flux. The volume seeks to make visible the background conditions of English under the assumption that understanding this usually unexamined background can help promote desirable changes, rather than mere change, which is inevitable in any case.

Some of the essays in this book are concerned mainly with the ways in which the discipline of English has differentiated and bounded itself. How, for example, did it incorporate certain types of knowledge and exclude others? How, as a new discipline, was it assembled from bits and pieces of other practices? How was expertise attributed to individuals pursuing certain kinds of work, while those pursuing other kinds were stigmatized as unscientific or unscholarly? Other contributions seek to reveal the connections between the discipline and larger social forces and conditions. What ideologies are embodied in the objects English has constituted, or in its research and teaching practices? How has the discipline fit into the social and economic order that has nurtured it? How are the discipline's own oppressive conditions reflective of more general social inequities?

Part I: Episodes in the History of English

The essays in the first part of the book, "Episodes in the History of English," focus on the internal and external forces that enabled the discipline of English to constitute its own idealized object as a domain of investigation. They examine the historical development of the discipline's boundaries and of the practices and features that they contain: the distinction between "composition" and "literature"; important historical personages and key intellectuals that embodied for their time new disciplinary standards; the constitution of specialties and subdisciplines, such as the Renaissance, American Literature, and theory. Hence, many of these essays are engaged in recovering and reframing the textual remains of these frequently forgotten histories, revealing in often startling images the arbitrary and constructed boundaries that constitute the field we take for granted today.

The history behind how the discipline of English came to credit some forms of labor over others is a complex one, and it is more often than not a story that centers on key individuals from our past who come to stand for and embody the important objectives that were eventually deemed necessary for the advancement of the profession. According to Patricia Harkin, one figure, Francis James Child who in 1876 became the first professor of English at Harvard, has been invoked time and again to mark the emergence of English. In her "Child's Ballads," Harkin analyzes narratives that represent Child from different perspectives within the discipline, and she shows how Child's story is used to support a variety of different interpretations of the history of the discipline. Thus, Child has been seen both as the exemplum of professional objectivity and productivity, setting a perfect standard of scholarship, and as a professor whose intellectual acumen precluded his investment in teaching oratorical and writing skills. "All of the narratives," in Harkin's reading of them, are "about labor—about how academic work has been described, analyzed (into binary oppositions), evaluated and made exemplary." Child reflects a shift in how the role of the professor is constituted. In the nineteenth-century college, it was a vocation or calling; in the research university, it is professionalized and becomes a career. Moreover, Child's preference for pursuing literary research over the teaching of rhetoric is emblematic of the discipline's values. But most importantly, Child "changed the conditions of academic labor."

Harkin's essay observes the birth of long-standing but arbitrary hierarchies that privilege literature over rhetoric and research over teaching. David Russell's essay, "Institutionalizing English: Rhetoric on the Boundaries," also examines the establishment of literature as the disciplinary object of English and the resulting boundary that deemed rhetoric and composition outside of the discipline. Russell shows that, as a disciplinary formation, English needed to "purify" itself of any activities extraneous to the object of its research. Professors of rhetoric had taught in institutions that had privileged oral communication. In the new research university and in the emerging disciplines, writing displaced oratory and "rhetoric was discredited." Rhetoricians thus had to either disavow their former field or try to find a new role for it. What came to be known as composition resulted from both of these strategies, its lowly status resulting from its association with sophistic knowledge in a university that privileged abstract knowledge over skills, truth over rhetorical ability. Yet, English needed composition as what Russell calls a "mediating" function, one that could be used to defend the importance of the discipline as a useful field of study. The discipline was able to capitalize on the "social credit" this position earned for itself in the eyes of the university, and to spend this credit by freeing itself to found literature as a bona fide research-driven discipline.

If both Harkin and Russell are concerned mainly with the demarcation of English from older practices and the establishment of internal boundaries, Elizabeth Wilson describes struggles over an external one, the boundary between English and the social sciences. In "A Short History of a Border War," she shows how the pragmatic pedagogical concerns of the social sciences in the new university shaped the context for the ensuing debate between literary historians and critics in English literature. Wilson's essay points to the broader cultural context that shaped the political content of pedagogy in the university of the 1920s through the 1940s. By focusing on Dewey's definition of progressive education—where "a student might focus on a specific project—building a boat or running a mock farm"—

Wilson is able to uncover the political antagonisms that surfaced when the profession adapted residual Arnoldian conceptions of culture to counter the pragmatic emphasis on education. Wilson's narrative helps us recover the progressive ideology that once defined the contours of these *social* sciences in the new university, where the study of classical literature was seen as an aristocratic privilege.

While the first three essays deal with disciplinary boundaries, the next three are focused on the construction of the object of English, including the tools and practices that helped to produce and maintain it. That object was, of course, literature, but it was "literature" as the discipline conceived it. In "Period-Making and the Discipline: A Genealogy of the Idea of the Renaissance in *ELH*," Craig Dionne examines the idealized vision of the period that that journal helped to promote. *ELH* began as an organ of Johns Hopkins' prestigious Tudor and Stuart Literary Club, which was founded to both to encourage the study of English literature of the period and to promote "fellowship and the love of literature." But the academic journal emerges as a necessary feature of a larger disciplinary program intended, in the words of Ira Remsen, president of Johns Hopkins in 1903, "to keep the body of workers in line." Dionne reads *ELH*'s idealized view of the early modern period in the context of the newly forming research model at Hopkins, which was among the first to employ intensified, programmatic standards to its graduate degree to ensure the "progress" of its students. Growing out of this immediate setting, the journal's view of the "Renaissance" is a reified image of a world free from what one president of the Tudor and Stuart Literary Club described as "the modern vices" of "today's factory, polling booth, and laboratory." For Dionne, the literary historian's fetish for the past is constructed out of the modern "master narrative of 'Renaissance order-Modern disorder,'" a narrative that asks the contemporary humanist to "celebrate and retrieve what it is we lost from the distantly abstract and spiritual life" of the Renaissance "and set it into play."

In "Emerson and the Shape of American Literature," David Shumway examines the invention of an American tradition. Where previously American writing had been represented as a shapeless chronology, the new subdiscipline of American literature constituted a new object with Emerson at its center. This "tradition" was built by a new kind of arbiter of cultural taste, the academic, who saw his mission not as political or social criticism, as had his predecessor, the literary intellectual, but as the maintenance of an ideal order of aesthetic quality. The academic turned to Emerson and represented him as the "father of our culture" to ensure what Shumway calls the "discursive regularity" of an idealized American tradition. Shumway is not addressing the usual canon debates over exclusion and inclusion, but rather seeks to explain the positive function of a literary tradition in maintenance of cultural hegemony. Thus, he examines how Norman Foerster and other founders of subdiscipline harnessed Emerson's idealism to affirm humanist "truths" and invented his "centrality" to fill "a need for a native, cultural elite...which presented itself in the rhetoric of radical individualism and democracy." Shumway's argument demonstrates the arbitrariness of this shape that Americanists gave to their object. Only by conceiving American literature "as a field traversed by many different figures and groups, some of which converge and many of which conflict," Shumway argues, can we move away from a monolithic view of culture that continues to shape the critical debates for and against the canon of American literature today.

In the beginning, the dominant practice of English was philology and literary history. By 1950, it had shifted to become criticism, marking a change in the way the discipline typically understood its object. In the 1970s and 1980s, a new practice, termed "theory," came to rival criticism for dominance within the discipline, and it too has produced a reconstruction of the disciplinary object. The final essay in this section, Jeffrey Williams's "The Posttheory Generation," looks at the intellectual situation of scholars who entered the profession after theory. Thus, it presents a history of the very recent past, tracing the "dispersion or breakdown of the paradigm of theory." It relates this shift in the disciplinary object to "a drastically reconfigured job market, pinched in the vise of a restructured and downsizing university," connecting intellectual changes in English to its current social and economic conditions, which will be addressed again by Cary Nelson in the next section.

Part II: The Current Arrangements

The second part of the book focuses on ideologies, conditions, and practices current in English at the start of the new millennium. These essays remind us that, in spite of poststructuralism, literary theory has failed to deliver us from the intellectual baggage of earlier practices, and that, in spite of the rise of creative writing and rhetoric to disciplinary status, English remains dominated by literary studies. Moreover, neither new theories nor new practices have fundamentally altered the role of English in American society. "The school functions," John Guillory reminds us in his *Cultural Capital,* "as a system of credentialization by which it produces a specific *relation* to culture . . . it reproduces social relations" (56). The more specific training of candidates for corporate management that Evan Watkins and Richard Ohmann have shown is part of the history of English is still a part of its mission. These facts exist in contradiction with more recent attempts to teach oppositional or resistant modes of rationality with names such as "critical thinking," "strong reading," and "resistant reading." This contradiction inhabits the most mundane routines of professional life: not just teaching "style" in our writing class or ascribing authority to a critic whose work we admire, but also the simple act of assigning grades. Whatever the discipline's claims, it reproduces the conditions of a class-structured society at nearly every level: in graduate training, in the job "market," in promotion and tenure practices, in publishing and funding.

Some of the essays in the last half of *Disciplining English* examine how largely unspoken ideas of universal experience and romantic conceptions of authorship get codified in important institutional "sites" where dominant cultural perspectives are explicitly and tacitly transmitted: different types of classroom settings, in textbooks, through one's "voice" in one's research writing, and in the self-fashioning of academic careers. These essays examine what Louis Althusser identified as the central project of the ideological apparatus, the production of systems of representation that naturalize the subject's place in the social hierarchy. In this case, the "subject" is the working academician—the teacher of a composition class, the celebrity critic, the creative writing professor, the beginning English major, the bibliographic specialist—whose professional identity is the product of an elaborate set of teaching strategies, and institutional technologies, from research manuals to handbooks. The production of intellectual power, in the form of credibility, authority, and authenticity, is inscribed in professional practices that help naturalize the very practice of "English" not only by legitimizing traditional canonical formations but by empowering an institutionally inscribed subject, "the specialist," "the teacher," or "the critic," to speak with social and political authority and wield cultural capital.

Other essays deal with the actual social relations of the discipline. It is not enough to examine how strategies of the institutional apparatus produce a subject who works within dominant social relations. "No institution is . . . reducible to its social function," Guillory adds. "Institutions of reproduction succeed by taking as their first object not the reproduction of social relations but the reproduction of the institution itself" (57). Such social positions as "critic," "teacher," and "specialist" are spaces where professional identities are formed to reproduce the semi-autonomy of the discipline. These distinctions are based on residual notions of authority that date back to earlier historically specific social formations, such as those of the master-apprentice relations within guilds, military distinctions of rank, and outmoded romantic conceptions of a radical individualism necessary for frontier expansion—all of which have a rather unstable relation to the dominant forms of social production today. The essays in the second half of the book examine how the internal, semi-autonomous forms of labor within the discipline of English ultimately maintain an ambivalent and contradictory position in relation to larger social and political interests.

Members of the discipline of English gain entry by taking graduate courses. While such courses obviously teach the content of the discipline, they also expose students to the conventions of disciplinary practice. In his "Composing Literary Studies in Graduate Courses," John Schilb examines the important but usually unmentioned activity of teaching writing to graduate students. The lack of discussion of this issue is perhaps not surprising given the fact that the professoriate still tends to believe that college students should have learned to write before they enrolled in college. Beginning with David Bartholomae's influential notion that novice students of writing need to learn to "invent the university" by assimilating the conventions that constitute knowledge, Schilb argues persuasively that graduate education must be seen as a continuation of this process. Writing is the task that will be most decisive for the careers of graduate students in English, but, much like another important task, teaching, writing is almost never directly taught. Schilb proposes that graduate students should be asked to focus on their own writing and that the conventions of writing in the discipline should be made explicit. Thus, Schilb suggests that teachers of graduate students need to help them read the discipline's research in terms of its rhetorical strategies and understand the issues that the discipline currently regards as significant. Yet Schilb also recognizes the potentially conservative character of these proposals, so he also calls for a recognition of conflicts within the discipline and between the discipline and the larger society.

Teachers in traditionally defined English courses face an even more daunting task of challenging discursive boundaries in ways that patently contradict the very professional knowledge it is their job to impart. Molly Hite's "Inventing Gender: Creative Writing and Critical Agency," is a critique of the ideology inherent in the dominant form of the creative writing workshop. This bourgeois-humanist ideology was once dominant in the discipline as a whole, and it continues to exert influence in both academic and nonacademic literary criticism. As Hite observes, what differentiates creative writing is that the theories which made ideology a central question for criticism were largely ignored. Thus, the creative writing workshop has an ideology that "denies it is one." This makes it hard for ideological issues to surface in workshops, and it legitimates an unacknowledged bias against politically committed writing. Hite offers an alternative conception of the workshop that takes contemporary theory into account in the teaching of fiction writing. It asks students not to represent gender as natural, but to "invent gender": to participate discursively in remaking sexual difference.

On the surface, research appears to be that form of intellectual labor that is most free from the institutional restraints that determine the type of work one does in the classroom; common sense provides an illusory vision of research as the place where critics are afforded a limited form of freedom to challenge the discursive perimeters that constitute intellectual labor. However, it is in research where we are asked to model the tacit standards of professional aptitude and zeal. As Laurie Finke and Marty Shichtman point out in "Profiting Pedants: Symbolic Capital, Text Editing, and Cultural Reproduction," when old literary history was dominant, textual editing was among the most visible and prestigious activities within English. Their essay traces the decline and possible resurrection of the disciplinary value of this practice by focusing on medievalism as a subdiscipline. Finke and Shichtman examine the institutional mechanisms that confer prestige to textual editing as a disciplinary practice. Before World War II, editing was a certain route to tenure and a valid mode of acquiring professional status. But the disciplinary contexts of research in English changed dramatically, and "symbolic capital ceased to accrue to the editors of texts." Finke and Shichtman focus on the interplay of forces that legitimate some modes of research over others, explaining why in the next decade "digital reproduction and transmission will once again recenter the academic enterprise making text editing a profitable means of career advancement."

These technical innovations are not the only changes effecting the discipline of English. In "A New Kind of Work: Publishing, Theory, and Cultural Studies," Ronald Schleifer takes up the contemporary practice of theory, its relationship with cultural studies, and the impact of them both upon scholarly publishing. Schleifer observes that theory has called into question assumptions about knowledge that the disciplines and their publishers have taken for granted. Theory and its intellectual offspring, cultural studies, have meant not merely new methods of literary criticism, but a much more fundamental "critique of the concept and phenomenon of knowledge itself and the *cultural conditions* for that knowledge." This critique, however, has put theory and cultural studies at odds with the traditional mission of scholarly books and journals, the preservation of truth. Presses and journals committed to publishing in cultural studies need to reflect conflict rather than agreement, and this has begun to happen in periodicals such as *Genre* and in certain book series that in their very form represent knowledge as essentially incomplete.

If Schleifer is concerned with how intellectual trends effect material practices in the profession, Cary Nelson contextualizes the discipline in the material practices of the contemporary university. "What Hath English Wrought: The Corporate University's Fast Food Discipline" begins with the reality of the job crisis, a reality that the Modern Language Association has only within the past few years deigned to recognize. Nelson sees trends in the hiring policies of English departments that may well forecast where the university as a whole is headed. Noting the rapid increase in the use of part-time teachers by English departments, Nelson suggests that this could well be the model other departments will be forced to follow as corporatization turns the university from a place where knowledge is produced and shared to one where information and students are both turned into commodities. Thus, Nelson sees the corporate university as profoundly anti-intellectual. His essay suggests that, in spite of the very real restrictions of the discipline of the research university, there are worse forms of discipline with which English is already having to cope.

The final section of the volume consists of comments by Richard Ohmann, whose book *English in America* was the first major study of the institution of English in American universities. Following the critical trajectory of Ohmann's earlier work, published in 1976, we hope that this latest contribution continues to invite the critical self-reflection needed to begin to think about change.

Notes

1. That it would be unlikely to receive such recognition is a significant issue. Disciplinary status is partly related to boundaries that define large categories of discourse, for example, science and nonscience, knowledge and superstition.

2. For an example of theory built on such a conception see Toulmin whose use of

the term *genealogy* reinforces the sense of historical continuity implicit in *tradition*. When *genealogy* refers to the lineage of a species or a people, it has historically been essentialist, the current generation being understood as the embodiment of a set of essential characteristics. Moreover, the metaphor suggests that intellectual change occurs gradually in the manner that traditional evolutionary theory asserted of species change. A more useful conception of the genealogy of knowledge comes from Nietzsche via Foucault. Like more recent renderings of Darwin's theory, this genealogy regards the history of knowledge as discontinuous and random. Only by beginning with this assumption can we recognize the radical implications of historical and future changes in the university.

    3. For a longer discussion of where the university may be headed, see Shumway, "Disciplinarity, Corporatization, and the Crisis."

Works Cited

Abbott, Andrew. *The System of the Professions*. Chicago: U of Chicago P, 1989.

Althusser, Louis. "Ideology and the Ideological State Apparatuses." *Lenin and Philosophy and Other Essays*. Trans. Ben Brewster. New York: Monthly Review, 1971. 127–186.

Foucault, Michel. *The Archaeology of Knowledge*. Trans. A. M. Sheridan Smith. New York: Pantheon, 1972.

———. *Discipline and Punish: The Birth of the Prison*. Trans. Alan Sheridan. New York: Pantheon, 1978.

———. "The Discourse on Language." Trans. Rupert Swyer. Appendix to *The Archaeology of Knowledge*. New York: Pantheon, 1972.

Geiger, Roger L. *To Advance Knowledge: The Growth of American Research Universities 1900–1940*. New York: Oxford UP, 1986.

Gieryn, Thomas F. "Boundary-Work and the Demarcation of Science from Non-Science: Strains and Interests in Professional Ideologies of Scientists," *American Sociological Review* 48 (1983): 781–95.

Graff, Gerald. *Professing Literature: An Institutional History*. Chicago: U of Chicago P, 1987.

Guillory, John. *Cultural Capital: The Problem of Literary Canon Formation*. Chicago: U of Chicago P, 1993.

Jencks, Christopher, and David Riesman. *The Academic Revolution*. Garden City, NY: Doubleday, 1968.

Messer-Davidow, Ellen, David R. Shumway, and David J. Sylvan. "Disciplinary Ways of Knowing." In *Knowledges: Historical and Critical Studies in Disciplinarity*. Ed. Messer-Davidow, Shumway, and Sylvan. Charlottesville: UP of Virginia, 1993. 1–21.

Ohmann, Richard. *English in America: A Radical View of the Profession*. Hanover, NH: Wesleyan/UP of New England, 1996 [1976].

Shumway, David R. "Disciplinarity, Corporatization, and the Crisis: A Distopian Narrative." *Journal of the Midwest Modern Language Association* 32 (Winter/Spring 1999): 2–18.

————. *Creating American Civilization: A Genealogy of American Literature as an Academic Discipline.* Minneapolis: U of Minnesota P, 1994.

Shumway, David R., and Ellen Messer-Davidow. "Disciplinarity: An Introduction." *Poetics Today* 12 (1991): 201–25.

Toulmin, Stephen. *Human Understanding: The Collective Use and Evolution of Concepts.* Princeton: Princeton UP, 1972.

Veysey, Laurence R. *The Emergence of the American University.* Chicago: U of Chicago P, 1965.

Watkins, Evan. *Work Time: English Departments and the Circulation of Cultural Value.* Stanford: Stanford UP, 1989.

PART I

EPISODES IN THE HISTORY OF ENGLISH

One

Child's Ballads:
Narrating Histories of Composition
and Literary Studies

Patricia Harkin

My focus in this essay is not on the ballads that Francis James Child collected, but rather on stories about him. I shall be concerned specifically with the ways in which narratives about Harvard's Professor of Rhetoric and, later, of English Literature serve as grounds for claims about the current state of English Studies and about how a future for the profession should be imagined. Since an individual reader's willingness to accept a judgment about the present—or a plan for the future—will be a function of her belief in a particular plotting of the past, it seems prudent to remember the rhetoricity of these arguments and—especially—of the narrations that serve as their grounds.

The several states and witnesses of "Child's story" recount substantially the same events. Francis James Child, the son of a sail maker, came to Harvard as a student in 1842. After graduation, he taught mathematics, then political economy and history. In 1854, he became the fourth Boylston Professor of Rhetoric.[1] At that time, he requested and received leave to study at Göttingen, where he learned philological method. From it, he fashioned disciplinary ways of collecting, establishing, and reading literary texts—methods that became paradigmatic. Back at Harvard, he lectured on Shakespeare and Chaucer as well as on Quintilian and Aristotle, while also correcting the weekly themes that Harvard required of its undergraduates. In 1876, Johns Hopkins offered him an appointment as Professor of English Literature. Harvard met the offer and Child became the first Professor of English Literature at Harvard. Adams Sherman Hill, who had been Child's assistant, became the fifth Boylston Professor, taking over the responsibility of reading the weekly themes.

But if the narrative verses of these ballads about Child are similar, their choruses—the commentaries on these events—differ significantly. Varying characterizations of the protagonist, plottings of these events, and generic characteristics of narration offer varying meanings for the "story" of Francis James Child. All of the narratives that follow are, in my reading, about labor—about how academic work has been described, analyzed (into binary oppositions), evaluated, and made exemplary. The stories show English Studies in transition from a relatively undifferentiated set of individual "tastes" to an institutional formation striving to become a discipline.

I turn first to a eulogy delivered by Charles Eliot Norton at a meeting of the

American Academy of Arts and Sciences, in May 1897, shortly after Child's death. When Child arrived at Harvard as a student in 1842, Norton observes,

> Josiah Quincy was approaching the close of his term of service as President of the College, and stood . . . as the type of the great public servant, embodying the spirit of patriotism, of integrity, and of fidelity in the charge of whatever duty he might be called upon to perform. (334)

Like Josiah Quincy, Child was a student whose "excellence was not confined to any one special branch of study" (334). In the "predisciplinary" Harvard of 1842, academic "advancement" consisted simply in an individual's change from the role of student to the role of teacher, without particular attention to specialization. But change came quickly; when Child was appointed Boylston Professor on the resignation of Edward Tyrrell Channing in 1851, he was awarded a "leave of absence for study in Europe, before assuming the duties of the position" (335). Child used the time to learn the principles of philological study—and earn the Ph.D.—at Göttingen. When he returned to Harvard in the autumn of 1854, he had become a professionalized philological scholar. Although, as Norton explains, "a great part of his time was employed in the teaching of English Composition, and the drudgery of correcting students' exercises, . . . he had an indefatigable industry and a steady ardor of learning, and he found time to carry on his own special studies" (335). In the time that remained after this "drudgery," Child superintended a series of the works of the "chief British poets," for which he "himself prepared . . . the edition of Spencer" *[sic]*, a Collection of Ballads in eight volumes, and a treatise entitled "Observations on the Language of Gower's Confessio Amantis." Norton then describes Child's magnum opus, an edition of The English and Scottish Ballads, giving emphasis to its apparatus:

> The character of the undertaking was set forth in a prospectus. The popular Ballads existing in the English language had never before been collected into one body; a large portion of the remains of the ballads was unprinted; the text of much that was in print was vitiated by editorial changes; it was now proposed to publish all in their entirety and their purity; to include every independent version of every ballad, and to record all important variations of different copies, both printed and manuscript; each ballad was to have a proper Preface, and in the case of those ballads which the English have in common with other nations an account was to be given of related traditions. The work was to be completed by a general introduction, a glossary, and indexes. (336)

In (genealogical) retrospect, Norton's account of Child's project makes legible the precise formulation of the question and the emphasis on regular method that other contributors to this volume see as constitutive of disciplinarity. What it also shows is that Norton and his contemporaries regarded this disciplinary work as commendable *because* it was laborious. But labor alone would not suffice. Norton also praises Child's "taste": the task "demanded . . . fine critical acumen and poetic appreciation,—the gifts of taste and culture as well as of scholarship" (337). One can learn to work hard, but the innate ability to "appreciate" texts, in Norton's world view, is a (class-based) "gift." After a sympathetic account of the "drudgery involved" in the task of preparing the apparatus for the Ballads, Norton turns to Child's teaching.

> For far too many years far too much of his time was occupied in the correction of students' themes. He never shirked this wearisome drudgery. . . . Even the dullest and most careless undergraduate could hardly fail to be quickened and improved by such teaching as Mr. Child's. Here was a master of most accurate and extensive learning, a scholar of unwearied diligence and exact method, with the faculties and sympathies which enabled him to impart his learning to his pupils, and to inspire in the more capable among them something of his own enthusiasm for the best in literature and life. . . . He was a lover of nature, of poetry, of roses, of all that was sweet and good; above all he was a lover of his fellow men. When he died the world lost much more than one of its great scholars. (339)

Norton's rhetoric marks the changes Laurence Veysey and Burton Bledstein describe in their accounts of the American university system in the nineteenth century.[2] In the old college, a professor's work was understood as a vocation to pursue an ideal whose reward was spiritual. In the new university, a professor instead fashioned a career whose reward was material. Notice that Norton uses the word *drudgery* to describe *both* the reading of themes and the preparation of a scholarly apparatus. He seems to value both teaching and research and to think of them both as "work"—in opposition with the leisurely (and gentlemanly) activity of tending a rose garden. His emphasis is on Child's faithful performance of his duties as a teacher of undergraduates rather than on the undergraduates' dullness. Interestingly, Norton also sees what more recent university administrators might call "service to the community" as *opposed to* Child's "calling":

> With the highest sense of the duties and the privileges of his calling, he did not regard them as exempting him from the discharge of the common duties of a citizen. He did not bury himself in his books, and he had nothing of the indifference of a recluse to the affairs of the community in which he lived. . . . He took the part of a good citizen in local politics; he was for many years an active member and officer in local charities, and he served his term as a member of the School Committee. (338)

Norton's remarks characterize Child as a nineteenth-century scholar who was called to serve his community in a number of ways. His effusive account of Child's scholarly research is evidence that such research was highly unusual in the academy but he gives no fewer accolades to Child's inspiring work as a teacher.

A very different tone is apparent in the rhetoric of Child's student and protégé, George Lyman Kittredge. Although the two documents are separated in time by only a few months, Kittredge's account of Child's life describes the opposition between research and teaching that characterizes the new university. The younger scholar (who uses the term *career* instead of *calling*) realizes that the old ways are over and feels no grief for their passing. He notes that Child "entered the service" of Harvard College as a tutor in mathematics immediately after his graduation in 1846. After describing Child's "request" to be "transferred" to a tutorship in history and political economy, "to which were annexed certain duties of instruction in English," Kittredge draws an opposition between work and (leisured) taste. He explains that

> the tutorships which Mr. Child had held were not entirely in accordance with his tastes, which had always led him in the direction of literary and linguistic study. The faculty of the college was small, however, and it was not always possible to assign an instructor to the department that would have been most to his mind . . . and Mr. Child, whose preference for an academic career was decided, had felt it was wise to accept such positions as the college could offer, leaving exacter judgments to time and circumstances. Meanwhile he devoted his whole leisure to the pursuit of his favorite studies. (xxiv)

While Norton praised the breadth of Child's interests and competence, Kittredge sympathetically reports that his tutorships were not in accordance with his "tastes." Norton construed both collecting ballads and reading themes as drudgery—and saw tending a rose garden as a leisure activity; Kittredge, writing at the same time, completely excludes both gardening and service to the community from his discussion and instead laments that Child was forced to devote his leisure (rather than salaried) time to the studies of Chaucer and Shakespeare. Aware that the opportunity to advance by following one's "tastes" is recent, Kittredge is candid about the circumstances that surrounded the Boylston Chair in 1851.

> The . . . Professorship of Rhetoric and Oratory . . . was no sinecure. In addition to academic instruction of the ordinary kind, the duties of the chair included the superintendence and criticism of a great quantity of written work, in the nature of essays and set compositions prepared by students of all degrees of ability. For twenty-five years Mr. Child performed these duties with characteristic punctuality and devotion, though with increasing distaste for the drudgery which they involved. (xxv)

Kittredge's use of the word *taste* carries a semantic charge that differs sharply from Norton's. Whereas for the older scholar, "taste" is a marker of innate class-based refinement, Kittredge's use of the word suggests that "taste" names the predilection of the new professoriate. And he openly celebrates the changes that Bledstein describes:

> Harvard . . . had developed from a provincial college into a national seminary of learning, and the introduction of the "elective system"—corresponding to the "*Lernfreiheit*" of Germany—had enabled it to become a university in the proper sense of the word. One result . . . was the establishment of a Professorship of English, entirely distinct from the old chair of Rhetoric. This took place on May 8, 1876 and on the 20th of the next month Mr. Child was transferred to the new professorship. His duties as an instructor were now thoroughly congenial, and he continued to perform them with unabated vigor until the end. In the onerous details of administrative and advisory work, inseparable, according to our exacting American system, from the position of a university professor, he was equally faithful and untiring. (xxv)

Kittredge applies the term *drudgery* to the reading of papers; administrative and advising duties are "onerous"; the entire American university system is "exacting"; but the "study of the English language and literature" is something to be "pursued with unquenchable ardor" (xxvi). Kittredge then gives a full and admiring account of the process by which, with Child's work as the paradigmatic instance, English Studies became a profession with disciplinary aspirations.

> It is difficult at the present day to imagine the state of Chaucer philology at the moment when *[Observations on the Language of Chaucer's Canterbury Tales]* appeared. Scarcely anything, we may say, was known of Chaucer's grammar in a sure and scientific way. Indeed the difficulties to be solved had not even been clearly formulated. . . . Mr. Child not only defined the problems, but provided for most of them a solution which the researches of younger scholars have only served to substantiate. He also gave a perfect model of the method proper to such investigations—a method simple, laborious, and exact. (xxvi)

Belonging to a generation and a class for whom the German model had become commonplace, Kittredge is especially careful to delineate the differences between the climate for scholarship in Göttingen and that in Cambridge.

> In the three or four decades preceding Mr. Child's residence in Europe, Germanic philology (in the wider sense) had passed from the stage of "roman-

tic" dilettantism into the condition of a well-organized scientific discipline
. . . . (xxv)

For Kittredge and his contemporaries in literary studies, Child had become the
very model of a modern major professor.

A decade later, the ideals of service and teaching are even more fully separated from those of research. Although Francis Gummere's unabashedly laudatory
1909 *Atlantic Monthly* essay, "A Day with Professor Child," praises Child's service
and teaching, most of his admiration is reserved for the older man's research. As a
description of Child's attitude toward scholarship, Gummere quotes him as advising younger scholars how to build a discipline: "Do it so it shall never have to
be done again" (422). Again in Gummere's rhetoric, English Studies as discipline
is constituted by a rigorous method energetically deployed on an agreed-upon object. The exhortation to do it so that it will never have to be done again presupposes that such a thing is possible: that the philological method, appropriately applied, will enable a monumental work that cannot be superceded. Clearly,
Gummere had absorbed a sense of disciplinarity from Child.

Gummere describes his mentor as ambivalent toward teaching, however, or
more precisely, as a person who loves the texts he teaches but finds his students
somewhat unappealing. Nonetheless, he reports that Child generously volunteered
to read Chaucer and Shakespeare aloud to undergraduates.

> Some of those hearers can never forget . . . the quiet but effective tones, the
> comments, the sympathy which made Chaucer so fresh, so rich, such "God's
> plenty" indeed; and above all, the pause and the slow wiping of spectacles
> after the "And so I am, I am" of Cordelia to Lear. (423)

On the other hand, here is Gummere's account of another aspect of Child's attitude toward teaching:

> When it was proposed to reinforce old ways of teaching by modern appli-
> ances in the classroom, Mr. Child is reported by his colleagues to have asked
> the authorities for an aviary.—
>
> "An aviary?"—"Yes, and a boy with a pole. When we come to mention larks
> and nightingales, exotic for my classes, I shall say, 'Boy, the lark!' or 'Boy, the
> nightingale!' with edifying results." (425)

In Gummere's narration, Child sees "modern appliances" as a kind of crutch for
underprepared students, helpful only for teaching *Romeo and Juliet* to someone
who has never seen either a lark or a nightingale. The discipline that Child is in

the process of founding is based on a notion of a solitary researcher, alone with his texts, who has no time for gadgets. This story is intensified by another, more revealing anecdote:

> "Do you know,"[Child] said solemnly, placing his foot on a light chair in front of him, "that I corrected themes in Harvard College for twenty-five years?" It has been remarked that Mr. Child never lifted his voice unduly; but some sort of physical emphasis was imperative, and this was furnished by the chair. As he pronounced the "twenty-five years" with most exact and labored utterance, his foot was released, and the chair found a new site halfway across the room. (423)

Gummere's story about a preference for scholarship over teaching, especially the teaching of writing, concludes with the judgment that Child's "fame" is "secure" because he "chose the right path in his determination to set high standards for American scholarship" (425).

In 1930, in Henry James's Pulitzer Prize–winning biography, *Charles William Eliot* uses Child and his "career" as evidence for a judgment about the Harvard president's administrative vision. James describes the time before Eliot's presidency as one in which literary study in English was virtually ignored.

> A student might read the literature of our own language privately, but it was not a subject of instruction. The Harvard Catalogue of the year 1868–69 shows that one elective study was offered under the heading "English" in each of the Sophomore, Junior, and Senior years. (I:211)

James observes further that

> when Eliot became president, Child was a man to whom advanced students would have been flocking if conditions had been what they are today. In 1867–68 his chief duty as a teacher was to conduct the classes in "composition" that all sophomores and juniors were made to attend. So he had to spend hours and hours in correcting their boyish and *ill*-written exercises. It was an occupation that his spirit loathed. With an unconcealed note of bitterness, [Child] . . . remarks that in . . . [1868] for the first time, he had had an elective section of the Junior class assigned to him. The men who chose that "elective" studied old English and read part of the *Faerie Queene* under his inspiriting guidance, and during the second term, they went on with him to Shakespeare. No other course in English literature was offered to any class that year. In short, until then, and so far as the students of Harvard College were concerned, Child's unusual knowledge and gifts were largely wasted. (I:257)

But Eliot's interest in the elective system gave Child an opening. By 1872–1873, according to James, Child's "labors as a teacher of Rhetoric had been cut down to part of a half course." Moreover, he offered electives in Anglo-Saxon, History and Grammar of the English Language, English Composition, and English Literature.

> The next year he substituted for the last of these courses a new elective on Chaucer, Shakespeare, Bacon, Milton, and Dryden in which thirty-three Seniors and twenty-seven Juniors enrolled. A significant and promising consequence of all things taken together was that Harvard College began straightway to be an institution with which teachers of scholarly taste and ambition could more easily be persuaded to ally themselves. (I:259)

James gives a much fuller account of the Hopkins offer—and of the motives of all three men involved—than does any earlier commentator.

> Child declined the Johns Hopkins invitation for domestic reasons, but went on to tell [Hopkins president] Gilman that it had helped as well as pleased him because it had led to his being wholly relieved at last from the burden of correcting undergraduate compositions. He had been Eliot's neighbor, colleague and friend since the fifties and his house had been one of the few to which the President had enjoyed going during the sorrowful years of his widowhood. His [Child's] state of mind about student themes must have been as well known to Eliot as was the fact that he was a rare scholar. But until Gilman's invitation providentially brought both men to a just apprehension of the situation, Child had been compelled to let his Chaucerian studies and his researches in ballad literature suffer the interference of what he chafed against as a loathsome chore. (II:15)

James is the first to stipulate the portentous economic consequences of what Gerald Graff describes in *Professing Literature* as perhaps "the first case of an 'outside offer' improving an English professor's lot" (41).

> Eliot took occasion to remark in his Annual Report [1876–1877, 20] that the Corporation "are disposed to relieve professors of such routine work as can be equally well done by persons whose time is less valuable."

"This incident," Graff writes, "showed the way professionalization would change the curriculum" (41).

By the time William Riley Parker's *College English* essay, "Where Do English Departments Come From?" appeared in 1967, those changes and their consequences were fully institutionalized. It had become commonplace to see the teaching of literature as more valuable, by every measure, than the teaching of writing. Parker's explanation of these circumstances is unusual however. Whereas others see literary studies as evolving historically (if contingently) from rhetoric, he offers an elaborate kinship narrative to explain the genealogy of English departments and to lament the fact that they have no clear disciplinary object. Parker describes "composition," a service that he sees as unrelated to literary studies, as an instance of a kind of retrospective imperialism whereby English departments, having broken from rhetoric, return to annex rhetoric's "service," now severed from its research component, as a way to increase their own institutional power.

> Surprising as the idea may first appear . . . there was. . . no compelling reason at the outset why the teaching of composition should have been entrusted to teachers of English language and literature. Teaching the language meant teaching it historically and comparatively, according to the latest methods of scientific philology. . . [whereas] composition was a branch of rhetoric, a subject which had been a basic part of the college curriculum since medieval times. . . . [C]omposition involved oratory in addition to writing intended only for silent reading. . . . In 1876, when Francis Child became Harvard's first professor of English, his post as professor of rhetoric was immediately filled by someone else, and naturally so . . . written composition [being] chiefly identified with that dismal, unflowering desert, freshman theme writing. (347–49)

Parker's condescension was commonplace in the academy of the sixties and seventies, but became problematic during the Reagan/Bush era when a "literacy crisis" evoked demands for "more effective" teaching of writing in the nation's schools and colleges.

Phyllis Franklin's accounts of the beginnings of English Studies in America were written to celebrate the centennial of the Modern Language Association in 1983. Her epideictic rhetoric maintains Parker's hierarchy without the arch tone. "When Child became Professor of English in 1876 and stopped grading themes to teach literature," she writes in "English Studies in America," "it was not because it suited him, but because it suited others" (22). Franklin delineates complex descriptions of these "others" and their agendas, but it suffices here to mention Charles W. Eliot, whose "special preference for the teaching of English" (22–23) emerged, according to Franklin, from a desire to make literary studies available to everyone.

I suspect that it is a gentlemanly disinclination to put himself forward that Phyllis Franklin admires in Child. If the professor is passive—fulfilling the desires of "others" rather than his own—then his preference for literary studies becomes a kind of *noblesse oblige:* a person of superior taste who shares his "tastes" with the less discerning. Moreover, Franklin stresses the vision of the early literary scholars—rather than their career ambition—as they persuaded the world that the study

of English literature should be thought of as "a discipline suitable for the undergraduate college curriculum." She describes Child as a person "drawn by a passion
for philology and English studies [who] first thought to master a new field and become [a] scholar. Interestingly, she then asserts that "[p]assion is not too strong a
word here" (356). Indeed, insofar as the noun *passion* is both the antonym of action and the mark of emotional commitment, it might be said to be exactly appropriate. "Passion" echoes "unquenchable ardor" (Kittredge) and "steady ardor"
(Norton) to describe Child's emotions as he devoted his "leisure" time (wrested
from the "drudgery" of paper grading) to the study of literature. But the word *passion* also connects Child's literary pursuits with quietude and leisure. Franklin remarks that Child's "view of the discipline . . . his attitude toward teaching, especially the teaching of writing, and his quiet commitment to scholarship—and his
rose garden—became ideals" (356). Enthusiastically continuing the process of idealization, she describes him as "curly haired and short" and known "for his sense
of humor," citing Gummere's story of the aviary by way of example (365). Still,
Franklin mentions those details of Child's life that paint him as ambivalent about
students, especially student writers:

> [T]hough he was known as a fine teacher, he was not committed to teach-
> ing in the way [Francis Perkins] March [at Lafayette College] was. . . . In
> time, Child concluded that writing was not an appropriate college subject.
> As for teaching in general, perhaps it was whim that led him to write two
> lines in Provençal in his copy of the early edition of the ballads, which is in
> the Houghton Library. Here is a translation:
>
> > He who wishes to learn must love
> > Because never through a teacher will one learn anything. (367)

Perhaps it was whim, but the sentiment was already being institutionalized as a
professional attitude toward teaching.

"At Child's death," Franklin concludes, "all agreed that he had created for
himself a lasting 'monument' through the Ballads. And when they said this, . . .
they assumed that the creation of such a monument was a scholar's natural goal"
(366). Her use of the word *natural* clarifies and emphasizes what has become the
case: Child's biography has been *naturalized* as a goal to be attained by professors
of literary studies.

A very different story is told by scholars whose institutional allegiance goes
to rhetoric. In a 1959 history of the Boylston professors for the *Quarterly Journal
of Speech*, Ronald F. Reid describes an opposition between "composition and criticism" (250) which he links to an opposition between teaching and research. After quoting Albert Bushnell Hart's reminiscence that "Francis James Child used to
say with a disarming twinkle that the University would never be perfect until we

got rid of all the students." (64, qtd. in Reid 250), Reid writes that "Child's victory over rhetoric [as composition] came into sight in 1869, when Charles William Eliot became president of Harvard, after which, according to Reid, "within twenty years Harvard resembled a German university" (251). Reid's observation that Eliot's commitment to the elective system "was tempered by his belief in teaching students to express themselves clearly and effectively," (252) helps to resolve an apparent disparity between James's and Franklin's readings of the president's attitude toward English Studies. In Reid's view, the president saw composition (a part of English Studies) as a service to Harvard's new clientele, the sons of an industrial bourgeoisie. In his *Atlantic* papers, Eliot declared that

> No men have greater need of the power of expressing their ideas with clearness, conciseness, and vigor than those whose avocations require them to describe and discuss material resources, industrial processes, public works, mining enterprises, and the complicated problems of trade and finance. In such writings embellishment may be dispensed with, but the chief merits of style—precision, simplicity, perspicuity, and force—are never more necessary. (359, qtd. in Reid 252)

In the context of Eliot's sense of his mission to prepare the new professional managerial class, correcting the weekly themes, occasions for students to practice precision, style, perspicuity, and force, might have seemed an important enough use of Child's time. The Hopkins offer changed the economic frameworks, and Eliot's new judgment was that Child's teaching literature would make Harvard competitive with Johns Hopkins.

Donald Stewart's "Two Model Teachers and the Harvardization of English Departments" contrasts the careers of Child and Fred Newton Scott (at the University of Michigan) to demonstrate that "a large segment of our profession has venerated the one and forgotten the other. . . . That mistake . . . is deeply symptomatic of what has been wrong with our profession for many decades" (119). As Stewart turns the romance narrative(s) of his sources into a tragedy in which Child's careerist hubris led him to shirk and even ignore his duties as a teacher (of writing) and reject rhetoric as a foundation for English Studies, he creates eerie echoes. What for Kittredge was Child's willingness to "leave exacter judgments to time and circumstances" becomes in Stewart's rendering a cynical opportunism:

> Although Child served as Boylston Professor from 1851 until 1876, I can find no evidence that he took his job for any reason other than his desire for a position at Harvard and his trust that time and Providence would provide something better. (119)

Gummere's sychophantic admiration is transformed in this one:

Providence, as I have noted, took its time. A story circulates that on one occasion Child angrily kicked a chair across a room, complaining bitterly about
the years he was wasting correcting student themes. . . . [A]s the years passed,
he increasingly questioned the legitimacy of oratory and composition as university subjects, because they were too elementary, but one might point out
that he made little effort to raise the level of this work to that of a true university discipline. (120)

Stewart attributes part, at least, of Child's distaste for rhetoric to the fact that the
short, curly-haired, jovial man was "neither by temperament nor by physical appearance an orator" (120). Writing in the early '80s, Stewart seems fully to accept
the nineteenth-century notion of "calling," accepting and finding dignity in the
teaching of both writing and literature and in both service and research. He believes that, but for the Child/Harvard influence, the two inquiries would now be
seen as coequal parts of the mission of English departments. With Child and his
career as models, however, Stewart asserts, "the Harvard English Department, with
its increasing emphasis on literary-critical scholarship, significantly helped cause
the reduction of rhetoric and composition to second rate status" (121) (a status
reflected in William Riley Parker's use of the words "unflowering desert" and "slave
labor"). In contrast to the narratives of Norton, Kittredge, and Gummere, Stewart stresses Child's (and therefore Harvard's) lack of interest in writing. "By
1895–96," Stewart writes, "some elective courses in composition were offered, but
they were at lower levels and none even faintly suggested that truly advanced work
in this field was taking place" (121).

In his exhaustive study of Rhetoric in American Colleges, Albert Kitzhaber
writes simply that "Francis J. Child . . . was anxious to be relieved of the chore of
correcting compositions so as to be free to pursue literary research" (99). Patricia
Bizzell and Bruce Herzberg, in *The Bedford Bibliography for Teachers of Writing*, reproduce Stewart's narrative and sentiments:

Francis J. Child . . . [was] determined to turn the study of English from rhetoric to literature. Child bitterly resented the time he had to spend correcting student compositions. He delegated as much of this work as he could to
faculty underlings and concentrated on enlarging Harvard's offerings in literature. In 1876, to keep Child from moving to Johns Hopkins . . . Harvard
created the first Profesorship of English for him, and Child spent the next
twenty years developing the English literature curriculum. (2–3)

In *Rhetoric and Reality*, James A. Berlin invokes the by now familiar story of the
Hopkins offer as evidence for his assertion that "literature was now on its way to
becoming the dominant concern of the new English department" (23). Unlike

Bizzell and Herzberg, Stewart, and Kitzhaber, however, Berlin is explicit about the class relations that this "dominance" embodied:

> In 1874, Eliot introduced a test of the student's ability to write in English as part of the university's entrance requirement. . . . [T]he test in English ensured that the new open university would not become too open, allowing the new immigrants, for example, to earn degrees in science or mathematics without demonstrating by their use of language that they belonged in the middle class. However, establishing the entrance test in composition suggested that the ability to write was something the college student ought to bring with him from his preparatory school. . . . Eliot probably . . . [hoped] to cut costs in the English department. The fact that no freshman class had ever been able to write in the manner thought appropriate for college work and that additional writing instruction had always been deemed necessary for college students seems not to have been noticed by either Eliot or the staff of his English department. (24)

As Susan Miller and Lester Faigley have since demonstrated, English Studies in general and the teaching of writing in particular had become disciplinary mechanisms for the production of what Richard Ohmann calls the professional managerial class.

In these disparate narrations, Child's story has been invoked to link an opposition between literature and composition with oppositions between research and teaching, between criticism and rhetoric, between reading and writing, between attention to texts and care for persons, between intellectual "passion" and onerous "drudgery," between leisure and work, between work and job, between work and service. The Boylston Professor turned literary scholar has been a hero to the MLA and a villain to the CCCC. In some tellings, "the" history of English Studies is plotted as quest romance in which the heroic Child goes forth to Germany and returns with the grail of philology. In others, he is represented as a Herculean free agent, teaching us all how to improve our lot through "outside offers." In still others, he is a comic protagonist who connects Randy Rhetoric with pretty Polly Semous to establish a new world order. To some readers, he is tragic *Homo Academicus,* blinded and exiled, commending his two daughters, Beauty and Truth, to the care of an avuncular brother-in-law while his two sons, Discipline and Profession, energetically strive to do each other in.

What these stories demonstrate is that, even now, academic apprentices are disciplined, both tacitly and explicitly, not only to read, write, research, and teach like the professors they admire or envy, but also to dress, act, talk, smoke a pipe or a cigarette or a cigar, wear tweeds or leather or a skirt made of neckties, use their leisure, engage issues of power, in fact, to model their lives on the life of a "master."[3] Such a character constitutes a kind of Originary Presence, who is presumed to embody the profession, not only as a way of reading and writing and research-ing, but also as a way of life and (implicitly) a source of agency. Consequently, in the discursive economy of English Studies, what had been an opposition between the teaching of writing and the study of literature is now contained within a sin-gle term, *job,* that designates not only teaching but also all the other kinds of serv-ice that are now seen as onerous drudgery. "Work," on the other hand, is now the privileged term for designating "passionate ardor" for research into writing, read-ing, cultural studies, assessment, WAC and WID programs—any and all of the ac-tivities that advance a career. Activities that serve social and communal ends now go by the name of "job," while "work" names activities that produce the profes-sional "self" that competes, advances, gets, and spends.

In the process, narratives such as the ones about Child that I have just ex-amined have engendered scores of professors who reject today's "modern [techno-logical] appliances" in the belief that no web site, listserv, MOO, or MUD could possibly replace the "God's plenty" of an individual reading of *Lear;* generations of graduate students who seem to think that somebody, somewhere promised them a rose garden; and a culture of teachers and students who hold to a "perhaps whim-sical" sense that, since "never through a teacher can one learn anything," it is finally foolish to waste time on teaching.

Such a state of affairs is, of course, unfortunate, and I think, neither in-evitable nor immutable. Other readings of the life of this *Magister* and others are, I believe, possible. The "users" of the narratives I've recounted have attended more to what Child taught to whom than to his structural relation to the institutions and ideologies that sought to discipline him. But it's possible to read "Child's Bal-lads" in other ways. In his refusal to limit himself to institutional exigencies, for example, Francis James Child may be said to have engaged in what Foucault would have called "revolutionary action" by agitating both the (classist) ideology and the (curricular) structures of the nineteenth century academy. The result was a new sense of English Studies more suitable to his time than were lectures on Aristotle, Quintilian, and Cicero supplemented by weekly themes. It's worth noticing that Child did what he wanted to do—what (from collecting ballads to tending roses) he thought important to do—rather than what the institution expected. In the process, he changed the conditions of academic labor. If we (must) take him as a *"magister,"* let it be for showing us how (in a capitalist economy) to do that.

Notes

1. The Boylston Professorship of Rhetoric in Harvard College was established in 1771 by a bequest of £1,500 from the estate of Nicholas Boylston. The terms of the bequest required the holder of the chair to "deliver to the resident graduates and undergraduates a series of lectures on rhetoric and oratory, based upon the 'models of the ancients'" (Adams,

"Introduction" np.) Harvard put the money out to interest and it was not until 1804, when the endowment had grown to $23, 200 of the new republic's dollars, that the university, under threat of a lawsuit from Ward Nicholas Boylston, finally made an appointment, Boylston having agreed to withdraw his suit if a family member, John Quincy Adams, became the first occupant of the chair. Adams served from 1806–1809, after which he was succeeded by Joseph McKean (1809–1818), Edward Tyrrell Channing (1819–1851), and, in 1851, Francis James Child.

2. In *The Emergence of the American University,* Laurence Veysey explains that three predominant rationales—humanism, service, and research—were invoked to justify the university system to the public. These rationales can be analyzed in the context of what we now know as English Studies. In the terms of the first, the secular humanist needed to be a citizen rhetor in order to bring the sort of "civil" deliberation and exhortation characteristic of the privileged classical rhetor to the new democracy. Next, the university was expected to serve the citizenry by furnishing expert advice of all kinds. The study of English provided not only the "literacy" prerequisite to democracy but also the familiarity with literature that was construed as part of gentle acculturation. Within the rationale of research, the study of literature, with philology as its principal method, was seen as the scientific and disinterested accumulation of objective knowledge. In *The Culture of Professionalism: The Middle Class and the Development of Higher Education in America,* Burton Bledstein asserts that the idea of a career emerged in the nineteenth century concomitantly with the rise of the professions. A career involved "a pre-established total pattern of organized professional activity, with upward movement through recognized preparatory stages, and advancement based on merit" (172). This notion of a career, according to Bledstein, stood in contrast to that of the older learned professional life of the eighteenth and early nineteenth centuries. In the earlier period such external attributes of gentlemanly behavior as benevolence, duty, virtue, and manners circumscribed the professional experience. Competence, knowledge, and preparation were less important in evaluating the skills of the professional than were dedication to the community, sincerity, trust, permanence, honorable reputation, and righteous behavior. (173)

3. Paul Bové, for example, calls them "sublime masters," David R. Shumway writes of "the star system," and James J. Sosnoski invokes the name "*magister implicatus*" for the ideals that, as a technique of schooling, academicians are subtly trained to imitate. As a part of this process, individual biographical narratives become models of ideal "careers" against which critics measure themselves and are measured by the academic system of rewards and punishments.

Works Cited

Adams, John Quincy. *Lectures on Rhetoric and Oratory Delivered to the Classes of Senior and Junior Sophisters in Harvard University.* Cambridge: Hilliard and Metcalf, 1810.

Berlin, James A. *Rhetoric and Reality: Writing Instruction in American Colleges, 1900–1985.* Urbana: NCTE, 1987.

Bizzell, Patricia, and Bruce Herzberg. *The Bedford Bibliography for Teachers of Writing* 3rd. ed. New York: St. Martin's P, 1991.

Bledstein, Burton J. *The Culture of Professionalism: The Middle Class and the Development of Higher Education in America.* New York and London: W. W. Norton & Company, 1976.

Bové, Paul. *Intellectuals in Power: A Genealogy of Critical Humanism.* New York: Columbia UP, 1986.

Douglas, Wallace. "Rhetoric for the Meritocracy." In Ohmann, Richard. *English in America: A Radical View of the Profession.* 97–132.

Eliot, Charles Williams. "The New Education, Its Organization II" *Atlantic Monthly* 23 (March 1869): 358–367.

Faigley, Lester. *Fragments of Rationality: Postmodernity and the Subject of Composition.* Pittsburgh: U of Pittsburgh P, 1992.

Franklin, Phyllis. "English Studies: The World of Scholarship in 1883." *PMLA* 100 (1983): 356–70.

———. "English Studies in America: Reflections on the Development of a Discipline." *American Quarterly* 30 (1978) 21–38.

Graff, Gerald. *Professing Literature: An Institutional History.* Chicago: U of Chicago P. 1987.

Gummere, Francis B. "A Day with Professor Child." *Atlantic Monthly* (March 1909): 421–25.

Hart, Albert Bushnell. "Ten Years at Harvard." *Harvard Graduates Magazine* XI (September 1902).

James, Henry. *Charles William Eliot.* 2 vols. New York: 1930.

Kittredge, George Lyman. *Atlantic Monthly,* December 1896, rpt. in *The English and Scottish Popular Ballads.* Ed. Francis James Child. New York: Dover Publications, Inc., 1965.

Kitzhaber, Albert R. *Rhetoric in American Colleges 1850–1900.* diss. Univ. of Washington, 1953.

Miller, Susan. *Rescuing the Subject: A Critical Introduction to Rhetoric and the Writer.* Carbondale: Southern Illinois UP, 1989.

Norton, C. E. "Francis James Child." *Proceedings of the American Academy of Arts and Sciences* 32 (1897): 334–39.

Ohmann, Richard. *English in America: A Radical View of the Profession.* New York: Oxford UP, 1976.

Parker, William Riley. "Where Do English Departments Come From?" *College English* 28 (1967): 339–51.

Reid, Ronald F. "The Boylston Professorship of Rhetoric and Oratory, 1806–1904: A Case Study in Changing Concepts of Rhetoric and Pedagogy." *Quarterly Journal of Speech* 45 (1959): 239–57.

Shumway, David R. "The Star System in Literary Studies." *PMLA* 112 (January 1997): 85–100.

Sosnoski, James J. *Token Professionals and Master Critics: A Critique of Orthodoxy in Literary Studies.* Albany: State Univeristy of New York P, 1994.

Stewart, Donald C. "Two Model Teachers and the Harvardization of English Departments." *The Rhetorical Tradition and Modern Writing.* Ed. James J. Murphy. New York: Modern Language Association, 1982.

Veysey, Laurence R. *The Emergence of the American University.* Chicago: U of Chicago P, 1965.

Two

Institutionalizing English:
Rhetoric on the Boundaries

David R. Russell

By the 1910s, the discipline of English emerged as two distinct activities, composition and literature. Composition has always had the most students; literature has had most of the prestige (all the prestige for several decades, though composition has gained a bit in the last three). Any comprehensive explanation of the professionalization of English as a whole must address this split.[1] Historians of the profession—Berlin, Ohmann, Miller, Scholes, and others—have usually explained the disciplining of English by looking first outside of the academy, to class, gender, and race, and industrial-economic transformations, to which English responded and which in turn it helped create. Other historians have understood the disciplining of English as occurring mainly within the English department, as in Graff's account of faculty talking past each other while all finding shelter under the umbrella of a "humanist myth." While both these approaches are useful (and in many ways complementary), I want to examine the disciplining of English into composition and literature by looking at relations English had with other disciplines, both within the new university, in that most defining feature of it, the specialization of disciplinary activity, and, indirectly, beyond the new university, in various social practices with which English and its neighboring disciplines interacted. Composition, I will argue, mediated those interactions in such a way that English was quite successful in its professionalization, in large part because composition was marginalized in crucial ways.

To get at this middle ground, between English departments and wider social practices or "forces," I conceive of English and the other emerging academic disciplines as specific but intersecting and highly elaborated networks of activity and influence. In other words, I look at what Michael Warner calls homologies between disciplines. The French sociologist Bruno Latour analyzes modern professions (like other phenomena) as networks of humans and nonhumans mediated by various technical means (among them inscriptions, tools, machines). In the modernist project, he argues, the messy networks of human and nonhuman actors are officially divided up and marked off or *purified*—into disciplines and professions, for example. In the process, the mediation that makes up the work of the discipline or profession, and its complex, shifting relations with other disciplines and professions, seems to disappear. Large-scale professionalization is a characteristically modern phenomenon, where the ongoing *work of mediation*[2] in one network is marked off through the *work of purification:* boundaries with other networks are established and maintained to delineate and defend some object as a profession's legitimate domain, while officially ignoring the complex networks of interactions with others through which the discipline's work gets done.

I will argue that English purified itself by constructing literature and composition as two separate activities, one professional, the other not. The teaching of rhetoric, the heart of the old nineteenth-century college curriculum, was gradually reduced from a four-year course to a single first-year course in what came to be called "composition." Under the institutional pressure to purify disciplines, composition became distanced from rhetoric and, as we shall see, from the emerging object of "English," the teaching and research of what came to be called "literature." To have reconceived rhetoric as written mediation of specialized inquiry and activity in a range of social practices, and taken it as their disciplinary object, the emerging profession of English would have had to break the ranks of the new modern institution, the comprehensive university organized by discrete, purified disciplines, and study the work of mediation in all disciplines—and in doing so radically transform the study of rhetoric (and the discipline) into a social science. English might have chosen to remake rhetoric into the study of textual mediation in society, and adopted social science methods or created its own. But just as the modern project of purification, the drive toward specialization, made old rhetoric impossible, such a new rhetoric of written, discipline-specific mediation, tied to the new purified practices of the new professions, would have challenged the modernist project of purification that drew lines and ignored the messy work of mediation—written, mainly—through which disciplines built their long and powerful networks.

The work I am doing was actually begun by others who have sketched the boundary work (Gieryn's term) the discipline of English did in negotiating its professional territory with other social practices, including academic disciplines. Elizabeth Wilson (in this volume) has persuasively sketched how the rise of the social sciences restricted the claims of English professors to study civilization in general, and led to a much narrower construction of English's object as "literature" defined in aesthetic terms and focusing—particularly with the rise of new criticism in the 1930s—on hermeneutics rather than history, with history and culture relegated to "background." She also analyzes the retreat of English from the massive school reform projects of the early twentieth century, where it might also have had a direct influence.

Similarly, David Shumway has persuasively argued that English professors failed to gain and exert much control of the network of literary journalism and publishing, out of which many of them came and to which many continued to contribute. Even in the first two decades of the twentieth century, when English was solidifying its identity, the publishing industry and the old network of "men of letters" came to distrust academics. And in the 1920s and beyond, the industry proliferated and diversified to such an extent and in such a variety of media that the standard authors studied by academics became a relatively small part of it.

This essay expands these arguments in the direction of composition to ana-lyze the boundary work English did in relation to other academic disciplines in terms of written discourse. Those professors of rhetoric, belles lettres, and moral philosophy who would come to be known as English professors constructed a cur-ricular space for themselves in the highly competitive environment of the nascent modern university, and—only very weakly and indirectly, as it turned out—con-structed alliances beyond the university in various other social practices.

English retained a great deal of cultural capital from its association with old networks of power in the Northeast, and familiarity with elite culture (what Vey-sey calls "liberal culture") continued to be a ticket to acceptance within the pro-fessional-managerial class. In contrast to the newly emerging professional fields such as engineering, which created secure professional pathways out of academia into other social practices enlisted by the discipline, English's influence on the emerging networks of social practice, in and outside the emerging university, was largely indirect—apart from reproducing itself in higher education and, as Wilson argues, maintaining an ever-diminishing influence over secondary school instruc-tion. But English, unlike the other humanities, was able to construct itself through composition as a service to other disciplines within the university and indirectly to the emerging corporate economy—and thus gain credit and resources that, say, history and philosophy did not.

The Speaking Student as Object/Motive: Rhetoric and Its Teachers in the Old College

From the Renaissance humanist revival of classical education to the late nineteenth century, the object of higher education—the raw material on which the professor and the institution focused their activity—was the speaking (and, to a lesser ex-tent, writing) student. Rhetoric, along with the Latin and Greek languages through which they studied rhetoric, was the center of the curriculum. Rhetoric was typi-cally the only course students took all four years—and the heart of the extracur-riculum also, as we shall see. In America, the oratorical college, as it has been called, was most firmly linked to networks of institutional religion because it prepared and (for many denominations) credentialed young men for the ministry, and to the families of the wealthy, because they sent their sons (often the less promising sons) and a few daughters there as a kind of finishing school before assuming adult re-sponsibilities. The motive of the college was to form the speaking students into "a cast of trained 'college men,'" as Edmund Wilson put it, who would maintain and extend networks of powerful families and institutional religion.

The old college attempted to produce students who were capable of inter-acting successfully in *oral*, face-to-face interactions among the powerful family net-works (in "literary" discussions) and in public meetings (speeches, debates, sermons) where their power would be exerted, the boundaries drawn. The college acted, officially, *in loco parentis,* as an extension of the family networks around which privilege was organized and power exerted. The writing demanded of the class was preparation for speaking or, much less frequently, formal communication by letter as an extension of face-to-face interaction (letters were frequently dictated).

In the old college, literature was constructed in the eighteenth-century *belle-lettres* sense of important texts from any social practice of the upper class, and was a *means* of forming the speaking and writing student, not the *object* of the professor's activity, as it would become in the new professional discipline of English. Professors of rhetoric spent most of their working day interacting with students: listening to and critiquing their speaking in recitation and oratorical performances, as well as reading the writing students did to prepare for those performances. Within the old liberal curriculum, students learned to read, speak, and write the classical languages—and indirectly their native language—through the infamous recitation method, the standard pedagogy for all subjects. Despite its faults, the nineteenth-century classroom was a performance-centered, interactive place by comparison with the modern lecture classroom. The hour was taken up with students speaking, so much so that faculty complained that they had too little time for their own pronouncements. Students also learned through the public oratorical performances (rhetoricals) central to the life of the college community—debates, orations, declamations, forensics, and so forth. And they learned through extracurricular literary societies in which students (often without a professor's supervision) read, wrote about, and discussed vernacular literature, as well as politics, religion, and other issues. Though recitation, rhetoricals, and performances in literary societies were almost always oral, they necessitated much writing—but as preparation for orally mediated public *speaking,* not for specialized inquiry mediated by writing (Halloran).

The subjects of rhetorical exercises and teaching, whether in class, in the required rhetorical exercises, or in the literary societies, reflected the whole range of studies in the curriculum—no great feat since that range was quite limited. Though subjects of student rhetoricals ranged from classical to modern literature, morals, philosophy, grammar, and natural history, they were all drawn from a common *public* store of knowledge and received ideas, a shared tradition. This was the human*ist* tradition, and it had to be radically modified to construct the purified, professionalized disciplines of the human*ities* that evolved in the late nineteenth-century university (for the distinction, see Grafton and Jardine).

In the old college, professors of rhetoric typically taught other subjects as well: Latin, Greek, history, logic, moral philosophy, elocution, evidences of Christianity—everything, in short, except the natural sciences, which were never a large part of the old curriculum since they did not play a large part in the activity of the religious and family networks students would enter (Parker 346). Latin and, to a lesser extent, Greek were not primarily taught because they were the languages of international scholarship, but as "mental discipline," at least after the reforms of the 1820s (Rudolph). French was the only "modern language" widely taught (including English)—and this was a matter of cultural refinement, not scholarship. There were no departments, since colleges were small, teaching duties among courses shared, and the networks of religion and family students would be a part of were religion and family-network specific (religions and classes did not share a college as disciplines shared universities).

Under the influence of the Scottish Enlightenment—notably in the most influential textbook in nineteenth-century American education, Hugh Blair's *Lectures in Rhetoric and Belles Lettres*—the criticism of English poems and poetic drama became an important pedagogical technique within early-nineteenth-century rhetoric courses. As in the ancient rhetorical tradition, students studied these texts as models of excellent expression (both stylistic and moral) to be imitated in their own speaking, writing, and other kinds of conduct. Beginning in the 1820s, some professors of rhetoric began to offer series of lectures on those texts, lectures that aided the students' reading and criticism of vernacular texts in their literary societies (Parker 343). By the 1840s, titles of these professors began to reflect this: for example, Professor of Rhetoric and Belles Lettres, Professor of Rhetoric and English Literature. But these lecture series were never required or sequenced, as were the three or four years of rhetoric courses. And English—old, middle, or modern—was not taught systematically, as Latin, Greek, and (to a lesser extent) French were. Students were presumed to be able to speak and write their own language, though their rhetoric—including their elocution—was the focus of the institution's activity.

Rhetoric and the Ideal of Research: What Shall We Teach (Besides Students)?

From the late 1870s to about 1910, a number of U.S. colleges experienced a sea change and became modern universities. The new aims that emerged to replace oratorical education—utility (service), research, and liberal culture (in Lawrence Veysey's formulation of them)—all required the purification of disciplinary objects and activity—and new genres of specialized written discourse.

Clearly, research was purified, as specialties and subspecialties developed what came to be called "pure research," as distinct from "applied." The ideal of research eschewed the messy mediation of rhetoric and evolved highly specialized genres of inquiry in scientific journals, which researchers considered to be above rhetoric. Yet the ideal of service became purified as well, spurred by the Progressive movement. Government, industry, and even domestic life would be rationalized under the banner of positivist social reform, brought under the control (it was hoped) of technocratic specialists, for the public good. Again, specialized discourse of the social scientist and bureaucrat was thought to be above the messy realm of rhetoric, or would enter it only to correct and purify it. Liberal culture was purified as well, though under the banner of philosophical idealism rather than positivism or empiricism (Veysey 191–94). Although liberal culture attacked science, both pure and applied, as leading to "undesirably narrow specialization" (Veysey 200), and taught "general ideas" (Veysey 194), advocates of liberal culture in English departments gradually evolved a purified notion of general ideas as universal truths, above the messy mediation of mundane affairs, commercial or political, as they evolved a purified canon of texts. The Great Books and the Great Ideas they embodied (which the Great Books movement of the 1930s would attempt to fix and index in volumes of those titles) eventually became the object of the field. And again, rhetoric (along with science) was viewed as an impediment to understanding and appreciating ideal truth and beauty, which were considered largely above the political, the negotiated, the rhetorical.

The object of activity in the new university, then, became not the speaking (and writing) student but a range of specialized disciplinary objects, each competing for curricular space. In terms of teaching, the new modern university divided into discrete departments, split the curriculum into electives, and established specialized majors. In the process, the new university also set up a range of new programs to train and credential professionals for a wider range of activity networks for specialized roles in the emerging networks of techno-science.

Many specialized faculty in new universities were thus enlisted (directly or indirectly, consciously or unconsciously) in long networks of techno-science ("natural" and "social") that were spreading across the land and around the world. Networks of railroads (and the steel mills to build them), networks of telegraph, telephone, and electrical lines, networks of mass circulation publications and advertising, networks of sewers and vaccinations and settlement houses and other public health works, networks of agricultural extension services reaching across every county, national networks of census statisticians, and so on. Even faculty who upheld the ideal of pure research and disdained the aims utility had the fruits of their research taken up by others and applied to extending powerful networks of natural and social science. And English was also subtly enlisted—despite its resistance to utility—through providing a service to other departments and, indirectly the networks of techno-science they served: the teaching what came to be called composition.

The teaching of composition was often justified by English departments as being "practical," as opposed to the old impractical study of rhetoric, and indeed it was in the sense that it concerned written discourse, which was gaining importance. The powerful new networks that were emerging came to be mediated not primarily through oral, face-to-face interaction as in the old family-based institutions, but through *writing at a distance* (Kaufer and Carley), where the network has to guarantee the loyalty of its functionaries across time and space. Specialized written genres proliferated: examinations, certificates, schedules, manuals of procedures, corporate publications, and so on (Yates). The purified intellectual products of the new universities were mediated by long strings of short texts (data files) that quietly extended the disciplinary networks into almost every corner of human activity. Technologies of written communication developed apace: the steam-driven rotary press, the linotype, the typewriter, and the most important of all, the vertical file, which allowed much more precise and rapid control through communication in the amassing of long strings of inscriptions that mediated the new networks. In the 1910s, this allowed Taylorism and Fordism to extend the work of purification by separating the "mind from the hands" in manufacturing, divorcing professional/management work from labor/machinery, decimating craft organizations, and intensifying workers' alienation (and labor uprisings).

Over several decades—and with much dissent from within—the new universities gradually positioned themselves to receive resources and provide resources—people and tools—for these networks, networks far more diverse than the networks of family and religion that the old college had extended—and far longer and thus more powerful, because they enrolled more resources, human and nonhuman. By 1910, research and service had become the dominant aims of the new university, and advocates of liberal culture had become a small but sometimes vocal minority (Veysey 256).

The emerging structure of the new university posed thorny barriers to those professors of rhetoric, Latin, Greek, history, and moral philosophy (many of whom taught all of these) who were looking to hold a place in the transforming institution, an institution that increasingly looked more toward long networks of techno-science for social credit and less toward old networks of family and religion. The specialization (purification) of activity—and of written discourse—necessary for extending networks of techno-science meant that these professors would also have to have an object/motive other than the speaking student. They would have to purify their activity as other disciplines did, to construct a more particular object and move in a direction beyond the oral, face-to-face mediation of family and religion. The solution that evolved was a new construct, "the humanities" (Grafton and Jardine), which would teach to undergraduates a version of the old oratorical curriculum in general and idealized—purified—terms, what Veysey calls "liberal culture," and also pursue specialized research (and graduate teaching) conceived in scientific terms.

As Veysey, Graff, Shumway, and others have shown, English had in the late nineteenth century a complex relationship with the ideal of research. One element in the new English department emphasized a scientifically justified philological research, which gave way by about 1910 to a scientifically justified literary history on a discrete canon of texts and, after World War II, "criticism" of those texts (not justified scientifically, for the most part) which still counted as research in the intellectual economy of the university. But it is important to notice that this purified activity of English departments (whether called research or scholarship or criticism) did not lead to an "applied" field (a longer network of control or influence) beyond secondary and higher education systems, as research in the sciences and social sciences did. Instead, composition provided that service function, but it was composition conceived in technocratic, purified terms, as a discrete, specialized set of skills, to be learned once and for all (by the end of the freshman year) and applied unproblematically in any field to produce "correct" writing, without any regard to the specialization of discourse in all its varied, mediated complexity. Indeed, English eventually became the most successful of the humanities in institutional terms, with larger faculty and, later, graduate programs, than history, philosophy, or any of the other modern languages had. But to do so, English had to give up rhetoric.

It became impossible for English to focus on rhetoric in the old sense, as the old networks it served lost power and prestige. And the drive toward specialization and purification made it impossible for them to refigure rhetoric to study the written mediation of activity in all fields. Yet the social credit of English could be bolstered by transforming rhetoric into composition, by teaching writing "per se," as generalized, purified techniques (general "modes" of discourse [e.g., description, comparison and contrast, narration] and universal standards of written correctness).

In the new secular, specialized university, and in the wider culture, rhetoric was discredited. It was called hollow bombast—hollow because the official discourse that mattered most was now written, based on the long strings of files stored in offices and bureaus, mediating long (powerful) networks of actions that involved large resources. But writing became much more important. Writing was what *counted,* what stored and analyzed and mobilized the data that mediated the long networks. The young discipline of English, by constructing writing as composition, was able to claim social credit for performing the useful service of teaching writing as an adjunct to its main work, while maintaining its purified object, literature.

English professors joined in the discrediting of rhetoric, distancing their purified object from rhetoric and the old curriculum. In doing so, professors of English rejected Isocratic rhetoric for Socratic dialectic, oratory for philosophy, the work of mediation for the work of purification. In an 1885 *PMLA* article, James Morgan Hart of Cornell, for example, echoed Plato's attack on rhetoric in the *Gorgias:*

> To me rhetoric is a purely formal drill. . . . Rhetoric always savors to me of the school bench. It is, if we look into it scrutinizingly, little more than verbal jugglery. . . . And the less rhetoric here, the better—in my judgment. Rhetorical exercises are, of course, useful. So are the parallel bars and dumbbells of a gymnasium. Need I push the comparison further? (qtd. in Graff and Warner 35)

Rhetoric was conceived as the opposite of purification, whether scientific or humanistic, positivist or idealist. If the new profession of English was to teach communication, it would have to be arhetorical, within a clearly demarcated domain that would not interfere with the work of mediation in other fields, including specialized literary study.

Boundary Work with Modern Languages: "Literary Skill" as Composition

Faced with an elective curriculum, what were those professors of rhetoric who wished to construct English to do in the new university? And what was the new university to do with them? One answer was to ally themselves with foreign language teachers in their quest to purify their activity. They continued to teach students rhetoric, but in a very altered form, as basic language learning on the analogy of the modern languages—as composition. This separated them from rhetoric in the old college, which was identified with classical languages, and put them firmly on the side of the "modern"—and helped to form the Modern Languages Association.

Moreover, modern languages, not classical languages, were coming to mediate the scholarly activities of academic disciplines, because those activities were linked to networks of techno-science ("social" and "natural") outside the university. Foreign (written) language teaching became more necessary as networks of techno-science (and the extension of print and transportation networks of which they were a part) made international travel and communication necessary to professional work. U.S. academics traveled to France and Germany to study science, which had been professionalized earlier there, and foreign modern languages thus became necessary to much professional work. At his welcoming address to the first MLA convention in 1883, President Barnard of Columbia, a chemist by training, expressed "his full sympathy with the object of the meeting," lamenting that in his old college (Yale '28) he "had no instruction in the subjects presented at the convention" and was "painfully alone in the two languages, French and German, necessary to unlock the books his profession required him to know" (Watts 139). Written communication also became necessary in ways it never was when the networks were shorter and less strongly aligned (less mediated by specialized written genres). The emerging American university appropriated the genres of German scholarship (thesis, dissertation, scholarly article) and of commerce, the memorandum (or memorial), proposal, and report.

The first problem was to get curricular space in the new university. Courses in English literature in the old college were few and rarely required. Courses in Latin, Greek, and rhetoric were almost universally required, often for all four years. Many professors of modern languages (English now included) began a frontal assault on their chief rival, the classical languages, and the course most closely associated with them, rhetoric. As A. N. Hunt put it in 1878, "The ancient languages have had the field. English now applies for more space in the department—for its rightful place" (qtd. in Graff and Warner 41). Hunt goes on to say that the science faculty were more welcoming to English than the classics faculty, who were "patronizing and cynical." "Any body can teach English," they argued (qtd. in Graff 67–68), for in the old oratorical curriculum, English was merely the mother tongue, learned from childhood in its oral form. But the science faculty needed written French, German—and new written genres in English, particularly the "research paper," which become a staple of the new composition courses. A professional need appeared.

At the first MLA meeting in 1883, English professors were outnumbered by those in foreign language three to one (Watts 139). Professors of English were allying with a stronger network. Early rationales for English emphasize not literature as the study of certain specific kinds of texts (reception) but rather writing (production). As Michael Warner points out, the first MLA members "had in most cases begun their academic careers with little or no interest in teaching literature," and "thought of literary texts as pedagogical tools" (Warner in Graff 68). The first meeting was almost exclusively pedagogical. But of course since all the students already knew their mother tongue, the definition of knowing English had to change. The emerging discipline was to claim expertise in solving some perceived social problem—composition, or as it was first ambiguously termed, "literary skill."

Constructing the Disciplinary Object and Motive: "Literary Skill"

What then would it mean to teach the English language, the mother tongue, as a modern language at the university level? The initial answer, in the 1870s, was the "writing of the mother tongue" or "literary skill." In 1873, ten years before the MLA was founded and, significantly, the same year that Harvard was organized into departments (Graff 66), President Charles Eliot appointed to the newly formed English department faculty a journalist, Adams Sherman Hill, to "familiarize the pupil with the principles that underlie good composition" (Hill, Briggs, and Hurlbut 17). Hill and others embarked on a campaign to show that traditionally educated people were "illiterate" in their mother tongue. In "The Cry for More English" (1879) and other articles in the popular press, Hill, the chief architect of composition and the English department at Harvard, wrote, "So long as people think literary skill easy of acquisition, they will be unwilling to have their children spend time in acquiring an accurate and refined use of the mother tongue" (47). The "average graduate," wrote Theodore Hunt, "can do almost anything else better than express his ideas in clear, vigorous and elegant English" (qtd. in Graff and Warner 39). Criticisms of student writing began to appear in the popular press of 1870s—many of them (like Hill's) written by professors.

The reformers stressed a practical and elementary knowledge of the *written* "mother tongue." Students must learn to write "a simple English sentence" *before* opening a Latin grammar, as Hill argued (51). The nascent departments of English strove to put a general composition course in the freshman year (before, not after, Latin and Greek). Writing was viewed primarily as an elementary skill (as it had been in the old college). Writing amounted to correct transcription of fully formed thought or speech. The oral emphasis of the old college was beginning to fade as writing became dominant, but it left in its wake "the opinion that 'reading and writing' can or should be completely mastered before the main business of education begins," as Susan Miller says (65).

In constructing "literary skill" as something to be learned from professional specialists, professors assumed the role of arbiters and teachers of "literary skill" per se. But "literary skill" was left very ambiguous. Because writing mediates many social practices, professors of English, in responding to the internal contradictions of the emerging institution, had to choose which social practices they would focus on, which genres and uses of writing. They purified their object, changing it from the messiness of students speaking and writing in socially mediated activities of many kinds, to the "pure" study of texts in the realm of ideas (Miller). "Literary skill," in the last three decades of the century, came to mean reading and writing about the texts that professors did research on, and mechanical transcription of oral to written speech—correctness—was a separate and less prestigious activity.

Boundary Work with Secondary Schools and University Administrators

The first and crucial action in purifying the disciplinary object of English was the institution of entrance examinations, enlisting university administrators and secondary school teachers in English's nascent professional network. Professors of the emerging discipline of English finessed the problem of specialization by defining writing in general terms as grammatical and mechanical correctness and limiting its genre to literary history (later criticism). In 1873–1874, the year after the Harvard English department was organized, a separate *written* exam in "English" was first required. Before 1873, the Harvard examination only required *oral* reading of passages from such authors as Shakespeare and Milton, familiar as oral declamation memory pieces. On the new exam, grammatical and mechanical correctness was the *only* criterion mentioned for its evaluation, and literary history the only genre. The year after the written English entrance examination was given, the Harvard catalog warned: "Correct spelling, punctuation, and expression, as well as legible handwriting, are expected of all candidates for admission." Professors of English could not claim to be arbiters of the specialized rhetoric used in all disciplines, the many strategies of argument, criteria of evidence, and other specialized conventions of discourse proliferating in the new disciplines. But they could claim a copy editor's expertise (indeed, Hill was a journalist), now purified into to an academic subject, composition.

The purification of disciplinary activities forced professors of English to choose what kinds of writing the English department had the authority to judge, to set boundaries to the ubiquitous mediation of writing in the powerful new networks being constructed. On that first entrance examination, students were required to write on the "works of standard authors," which became the content of secondary school English (Graff 44 quoting Applebee). It was no longer oral performance of works of standard authors for the enjoyment or edification of a nonspecialist audience—rhetoric or elocution. The students' work was transformed from oral performance for the edification of a nonspecialist audience into *written* texts as interpretation of works of standard authors for specialists in those authors' works—literary history or, later, criticism.

To purify its activity, English claimed as its object texts—but not all texts, only a relatively small set of texts not already claimed by others (e.g., history or philosophy or science). By the 1910s, when a fairly firm canon had emerged (at least in British literature), literary skill became the valuing of "literature," and the marked term in English. This, not composition, was the "literary skill" specialists possessed and taught. English became "literature," not literacy.

By about 1900, composition had become primarily remedial, and took over one function of the old and discredited oratorical curriculum: teaching social refinement, but refinement constructed as an elementary technique, proper writing, not a disciplinary object. Indeed, writing "hospitals" or "clinics" or "laboratories" were created around the turn of the century in high school and university English departments, to provide a cure for poor writing, which had now been constructed in terms that resembled public health campaigns, but it was errors that would be cleaned up, scrubbed from student papers with red ink.

In 1894 a national "Committee of 10," headed by Eliot, issued its profoundly influential report, which formulated the U.S. secondary school English curriculum. It required English for all four high school years for all students, with two goals: composition training and literary appreciation. Though the Committee of 10 insisted the two should "never be dissociated in the mind of the teacher and their mutual dependence should be constantly present to the mind of the pupils," literature came to be dominant in the schools, though never as thoroughly as in the universities. As Ohmann has forcefully argued (*Politics* 26–41), despite the efforts of many secondary school and freshman composition teachers to help students from immigrant and working-class families write "correctly," the emerging discipline did not turn its energies to improving the teaching of writing and did not need to. Composition as correctness—enforceable, countable—allowed for sorting, particularly with the advent of national testing mechanisms such as the College Entrance Examination Board in 1901. Proofreading became one proof of fitness to enter the managerial class. And by constructing composition as a set of discrete mechanical skills and claiming it as its own, English gained social credit as the arbiter of good writing as well as good reading to the wider society. People looked to English professors, not linguists (or professors of rhetoric), to decide issues of correctness and clarity.

Composition provided a service to the university, then, by facilitating selection, gatekeeping. Composition either could or could not be taught, depending on the needs of the institution. It could be taught to some students and not others, depending on the way the institution constructed "remedial" students. Failure rates in composition courses (at times reaching 50 percent at some public institutions) provided a subtle form of postadmission selection at public open admissions institutions, where there was public pressure for access.

Admissions examinations also allowed English professors to enlist the secondary teachers and students in their network of activity. University English departments retained some measure of control over the training of secondary school teachers, though English did not become an active player in the powerful school reform movements of the late nineteenth and early twentieth centuries (Wilson). School textbooks were until recently written primarily by English professors. And almost all of the leaders of the NCTE in its formative years were college professors of English.

Yet because composition was constructed as "remedial"—teaching students a skill that should have been learned in secondary school or before and not developing involvement with social practices that used written discourses—English, like high-status scientific and social scientific disciplines, could separate its own high-status, purified, study (reception) from its low-status teaching and utilitarian service (production), composition. By constructing composition as a practical, remedial service, with no systematic training necessary to teach it and no research expected of those who did, large numbers of courses could be taught by low-paid, part-time staff, usually women (Miller). In institutions large and small this provided a range of material benefits. In large institutions, part-time and graduate students teaching composition allowed time for senior faculty to teach the new, purified object and do research on it. In time, composition also financed graduate training, allowing for more graduate courses and programs than in the other humanities. In institutions without graduate programs, composition provided positions for the new Ph.D.s and allowed English departments to have larger staffs—and greater institutional influence than other humanities departments.

Boundary Work with Stronger Disciplines: The Forensic System

English gained credit within institutions by claiming to teach "practical" writing as a service to other disciplines, and in the late nineteenth century many English departments made attempts to develop students' writing in the disciplines, though these attempts were short-lived. What might "literary skill" mean for university students in the various disciplines, all of whom had been taught elementary reading and writing in primary school, and had indeed often had to pass entrance examinations that demonstrated that?

The transition of English's disciplinary object from the speaking and writing student to a canon of texts was gradual. Professors of English continued to take responsibility for improving students speaking and writing through a *written* version of the old rhetoricals. For a time, professors of English supervised students in the writing (and sometimes oral presentation) of texts on subjects from across the new elective curriculum.

In fact, the many reformers originally saw the freshman composition course as merely the beginning of a four-year program for developing students' writing in the disciplines, a program that retained the essential shape of the traditional rhetorical training. During the 1870s, Harvard students attended lectures and recitation on rhetoric in the last three years (freshmen took elocution), but the catalog also specifically prescribed "themes once every four weeks" for sophomores, "once every three weeks" for juniors, and "four forensics" for seniors (Russell 52).

In 1878, Harvard dropped the junior and senior rhetoric courses (leaving sophomore rhetoric the only composition course) and instead instituted "the forensic system." Upper level students were required to write "themes and forensics" supervised by faculty in a range of disciplines, and "with the cooperation of instructors in nearly all departments" (Russell 54).

In 1885, the sophomore rhetoric course was moved to the freshman year and dubbed English A, Freshman English, but the upper level writing requirements in the disciplines ("Forensics") continued. In the late 1890s, writing requirements were further reduced, until Harvard dropped the forensic system altogether in 1900, substituting instead three remedial courses for students who did poorly in English A. The now-familiar twentieth-century pattern became firmly entrenched: freshman composition for all and additional remedial courses for some, augmented by research papers at the discretion of individual faculty, with no formal mechanisms for teaching, revision, or for evaluation of writing beyond the specific course (Russell 55).

Similarly, English departments at many public universities responded to the demands of other disciplines that they organize efforts to improve students' specialized writing in other disciplines. For example, Iowa State College, a Midwestern, land-grant, agricultural and mechanical college, had from its opening in 1869 required all students (in addition to a freshman course called, "Applied Rhetoric") to deliver original orations before weekly college assemblies, supervised by the professor of rhetoric as part of his regular duties.

In 1879, Iowa State began requiring seniors to write a "graduating thesis," "supervised by the Professor giving instruction in the branch of learning upon which it treats, and . . . responsible to the Faculty for its supervision and correction," and also required juniors and seniors to write four "dissertations" (brief research papers) "upon topics embraced in the studies they are pursuing, and approved by the professors and Faculties having charge of such studies." But only a year later, the dissertation requirement was quietly dropped, and English literature was required of all juniors. Thus, students were left without any college-mandated training in writing beyond the freshman year, except for a senior thesis, which also faded by 1910 (Russell 59–60).

The compartmentalized, additive structure of the modern university, with its specialized disciplinary communities separated by written discourse, had outgrown the forensic system it inherited from the oral, face-to-face community of the old college. The disciplinary/professional networks were too long and too numerous. The elective curriculum and departmental organization made a specific place for composition courses where there had been none before, and writing became one more subject among many. Thus, it ceased being a central part of all of them.

A central contradiction in the disciplining of English emerged: specialized written discourse mediated the work of all disciplines, but it was explicitly taught in only one. There was no way to purify the very messy work of written mediation in an environment where disciplines, including English, were ignoring the messy mediators in an attempt to purify their activity. Whether in the scientific positivist emphasis on "facts" and "laws," or the humanist idealist emphasis on universal truths, the writing of students and professionals in their daily work was officially ignored, and students' development as writers of specialized discourse folded, often unconsciously, into their training. The English department assumed official responsibility for improving students' writing, but messy work of writing improvement was relegated to elementary, low-status courses emphasizing correctness, because that was all English could teach about writing, given the specialization of discourse, the modern drive toward purification, and the lack of a discipline to study the differences in written rhetoric. In the new discursive economy, all professors were still responsible for assigning and grading papers, and for teaching the "material" from which those papers were "composed." They were and were not composition teachers. English professors were responsible for teaching writing, but that teaching was not integral to the object and motive of their discipline. English professors were and were not composition teachers. English submerged the contradiction—and then harnessed it—by constructing two new and largely separate activities, each with different motives, under one covering term, English, and then marginalizing one in their own work while promoting it as a service to other disciplines.

A cycle of blame for poor student writing set in, with everyone and no one responsible for it. Faculty in other disciplines could blame the English department. And as early as 1879, Hill complained that the new university professor, "absorbed in his specialty, contented himself with requiring at recitations and examinations knowledge of the subject-matter, however ill-digested and ill-expressed," and thus could not be relied on to systematically improve students' writing (46).

In the economy of the new university, composition lacked disciplinary or departmental status—and thus lacked the wherewithal to compete for resources to enact meaningful department-wide or university-wide reforms. Faculty in the disciplines (including English), complained they did not have the time or support to focus on writing development, and writing was so embedded in the professional activities of their disciplinary communities that it was largely transparent, and difficult to reconceptualize as something more than an elementary transcription skill. To faculty in all disciplines, the mediation of writing seemed to disappear as the purification of disciplinary activity became the norm. And the new English departments, purifying their own specialized teaching and research agendas, rarely had the means or the will to push successfully for college-wide writing requirements.

There was no place in the play of purified specializations for a discipline that took as its object the writing (student) in any social practice, any network of activity. Not until the emergence of the writing-across-the-curriculum movement in the late 1970s would writing and rhetoric in a wide range of social practices be constructed as an object of disciplinary inquiry, though only very marginally associated with English departments.

Boundary Work with Weaker Disciplines: Consolidating Gains, Handling Rebellions

Before the disciplinary object of a literary canon became more or less stabilized in the early 1900s, professors who wished to focus on literature established alliances with professors who wished to focus on texts of other kinds, with different motives. Many colleges and universities formed grab-bag departments of English (sometimes with other titles) to house composition courses, primarily, and literature courses, but also philology, journalism, debate, oratory, elocution, drama, creative writing, business and technical writing, English for foreign students, pedagogy, and even rhetoric, including upper level rhetoric courses (e.g., argument).

Yet in order to achieve a firm identity and status in the new institution, professors of English had to give up the study of a range of texts and the activities they mediated, and purify their own network, as the study of a literary canon. Many kinds of teaching (and potential research interests) left the English department. In the 1910s and 1920s there was a series of rebellions—sometimes quite bitter—as professors with other objects and motives seceded from English and formed their own professional organizations. Those interested in pedagogy formed the National Council of Teachers of English in 1912, which quickly focused on high school teachers and is now the largest professional organization of teachers in any discipline (though many in the NCTE were affiliated with education departments, most remained in English departments) (Stewart). Debate, oratory, and elocution formed their own departments after a dramatic break with English in 1914 to form departments of speech. Theater allied with departments of speech or fine arts, beginning in the 1920s. Journalism, first housed in English departments and taught by English professors, left English to construct its own departments and schools, with the professional association forming in 1917. Some philologists allied themselves with classics departments and joined the American Philological Association, while others allied with linguistics, which formed a professional association in 1924, and the teaching of English as a second language professionalized as applied linguistics in the 1930s. In all of these moves, English ceded, in part, teaching and research in the production and circulation of texts, the work of textual mediation, to other social practices, retaining only a purified study of reception. In the new, purified university, reading was divorced from speaking and writing, and the reading limited to the canon.

Upper level writing and rhetoric courses often remained in English departments, but were marginalized and gradually dropped (Miller). Business and technical writing, taught from the late nineteenth century, were marginalized, like composition, as "service" courses (teachers of these courses formed an association in 1910). Or they moved to business and engineering schools. In the 1930s some engineering colleges (e.g., Michigan, Washington) founded their own separate humanities departments to give their students a broader approach to texts than English departments allowed. Even the production of "creative writing" (constructed into another category than "literature") was separated from its reception. Creative writing was given a secure if marginal place in English departments in the 1940s, with the creation of MFA programs (appropriating the category from the fine arts, not the humanities) and creative writers formed a professional association in the 1960s.

Conclusion

By simultaneously devaluing rhetoric as an intellectual tradition and using it (reconstructed as composition) to obtain cultural and institutional credit, English was able to flourish—within rather narrow boundaries—in a potentially hostile environment. Without composition, English might have had to remain much smaller (as with philosophy) or justify its disciplinary existence thorough other kinds of social involvements, such as community literacy improvement (on the model of psychology [mental health] and sociology [social work]), or service to an industry or profession (on the model of journalism, engineering, and other professional schools). But the boundary work accomplished by the construction of general composition—bracketing rhetoric, performance, and pedagogy—made it possible for more and more English professors to spend more and more of their working day focused on the emerging object of their discipline's activity, the literary canon, performing their discipline's characteristic action: interpreting the canon for other members of the discipline.

In the last twenty years English as a discipline has begun to forge alliances in ways it was denied or rejected almost a century earlier. The MLA now has a pedagogical division, and has some collaborations with the NCTE. The teaching of writing now his its own division under the Teaching category. Though some 200 English departments grant Ph.D.s in rhetoric and composition, until 1998 the MLA recognized research in composition, rhetoric, and writing only in the form of a discussion group, as it did other traditionally marginalized groups (e.g., women, lecturers and adjuncts, gays and lesbians, the disabled, ethnic studies, and politics). Today specialists in rhetoric and composition have their own division, under the Language Studies category, called History and Theory of Rhetoric and Composition. And there is even an MLA technical writing subsection, and a few MLA publications devoted to that field. (There are some forty graduate programs in professional communication within English departments, though none in the old elite institutions.)

In a broader sense, much literary study now takes what might be called rhetorical approaches, concerning itself with texts of a much greater variety and the ways texts mediate culture, though usually from the point of view of reception, not production (see for example Scholes's proposal to remake English into the study of *texts*). There has also been some networking with the natural and social sciences: MLA divisions or discussion groups exist on Literature and Science, Anthropological Approaches to Literature, and Sociological Approaches to Literature (all within the "Interdisciplinary Approaches" category). Critical theory approaches important in English studies are shared by some other disciplines, at least on their margins. And there is even some small use of social science methods, especially qualitative, in literary study (e.g., Radway). Whether or not the object of the discipline will change (or has changed) is a matter of continuing, heated debate—and historical rethinkings such as those in this volume. But in the wake of the "culture wars" of the 1980s and 1990s, when its social credit was damaged, the profession clearly sees a need to extend its networks as it never has before, to give up in certain respects its hard-won purity, and English has taken some steps in the direction of mediating its work through and with other powerful social practices. Chief among these is the field of composition, which professionalized over the last thirty years while remaining primarily in English departments, and now accounts for 20 to 30 percent of new Ph.D.s from English. Dame Rhetoric finally found her way into English via the back stairs, as she found her way into the twentieth century when it rejected her as too impure.

Notes

1. The story of how composition instruction remained on the fringes of the department, without disciplinary status, has been well told by others (Berlin, Douglas, Ohmann, Applebee, Miller).

2. Large-scale professionalization is a characteristically modern phenomenon, though it has roots as early as the eighteenth century. Latour in *We Have Never Been Modern* uses the phrase "work of translation" for the activity of tool-mediated networks without gaze of modern purification, though elsewhere he uses the term *mediation*.

Works Cited

Adams, Katherine. *A History of Professional Writing Instruction in American Colleges.* Dallas: Southern Methodist UP, 1993.

Applebee, Arthur N. *Tradition and Reform in the Teaching of English: A History.* Urbana: NCTE, 1974.

Berlin, James A. *Rhetoric and Reality: Writing Instruction in American Colleges 1900–1985.* Carbondale: Southern Illinois UP, 1987.

Blair, Hugh. *Lectures on Rhetoric and Belles Lettres (1819).* Delmar, NY: Scholars Facsimiles & Reprints, 1993.

Bledstein, Burton J. *The Culture of Professionalism: The Middle Class and the Development of Higher Education in America.* New York: Norton, 1976.

Brereton, John, ed. *The Origins of Composition Studies in the American College, 1875–1925: A Documentary History.* Pittsburgh: U of Pittsburgh P, 1995.

Douglas, Wallace. "Accidental Institution: On the Origins of Modern Language Study." *Criticism in the University.* Ed. Gerald Graff and Reginald Gibbons. Evanston, IL: Northwestern UP, 1985. 41–78.

Gieryn, Thomas. "Boundary Work and the Demarcation of Science from Non-Science." *American Sociological Review* 48 (1983): 781–95.

Graff, Gerald. *Professing Literature.* Chicago: U of Chicago P, 1987.

Graff, Gerald, and Michael Warner. *The Origins of Literary Study in America: A Documentary Anthology.* New York: Routledge, 1989.

Grafton, Anthony, and Lisa Jardine. *From Humanism to the Humanities.* London: Duckworth, 1986.

Halloran, S. Michael. "Rhetoric in the American College Curriculum: The Decline of Public Discourse." *Pre/Text* 3 (1982): 245–69.

Hill, Adams Sherman. "An Answer to the Cry for More English." *The Origins of Composition Studies in the American College, 1875–1925: A Documentary History.* Ed. John Brereton. Pittsburgh: U of Pittsburgh P, 1995. 45–57.

Hill, Adams Sherman, LeBaron R. Briggs, and B. S. Hurlbut. *Twenty Years of School and College English.* Cambridge: Harvard UP, 1896.

Kaufer, David S., and Kathleen M. Carley. *Communication at a Distance: The Influence of Print on Sociocultural Organization and Change.* Hillsdale, NJ: Erlbaum, 1993.

Latour, Bruno. *We Have Never Been Modern.* Cambridge: Harvard UP, 1993.

Miller, Susan. *Rescuing the Subject: A Critical Introduction to Rhetoric and the Writer.* Carbondale, IL: Southern Illinois UP, 1989.

Ohmann, Richard. *English in America: A Radical View of the Profession.* New York: Oxford UP, 1976.

Ohmann, Richard. *The Politics of Letters.* Middletown, CT: Wesleyan UP, 1987.

Parker, William Riley. "Where Do English Departments Come From?" *College English* 28 (1967): 339–51.

Rudolph, Fredrick. *The American College and University: A History.* New York: Knopf, 1962.

Russell, David R. *Writing in the Academic Disciplines, 1870–1990: A Curricular History.* Carbondale, IL: Southern Illinois UP, 1991.

Scholes, Robert. *The Rise and Fall of English Studies: Reconstructing English as a Discipline.* New Haven: Yale UP, 1998.

Shumway, David R. *Creating American Civilization: A Genealogy of American Literature as an Academic Discipline.* Minneapolis: U of Minnesota P, 1994.

Stewart, Donald C. "The Status of Composition and Rhetoric in American Colleges, 1880–1902: An MLA Perspective." *College English* 47 (1975): 734–46.

Veysey, Laurence R. *The Emergence of the American University.* Chicago: U of Chicago P, 1965.

Warner, Michael. "Professionalization and the Rewards of Literature: 1875–1900." *Criticism* 27 (Winter 1985): 1–28.

Watts, George B. "The Teaching of French in the US." *French Review* 37 (Oct. 1963): 5–165.

Wilson, Elizabeth. A Short History of a Border War: Social Science, School Reform, and the Study of Literature." *Poetics Today* 9 (1988): 711–735. See also chapter 3 in this volume.

Wilson, Edmund. *The Triple Thinkers: Twelve Essays on Literary Subjects.* New York: McGraw, 1948.

Yates, JoAnne. *Control through Communication: The Rise of System in American Management.* Baltimore: Johns Hopkins UP, 1989.

Three

A Short History of a Border War: Social Science, School Reform, and the Study of Literature

Elizabeth A. Wilson

Despite a frequently expressed desire to improve society, literary criticism has long opposed itself to the practical work of social reform. The responsibility of critics to uphold "standards" and defend "civilization" has rarely been taken to mean concrete interventions in particular circumstances. Rather, the task of the critic has been to express the universal truths and reveal the face of an eternal "humanity." Matthew Arnold's *Culture and Anarchy,* though subtitled *An Essay in Political and Social Criticism,* argues against political agitation and practical reform as a means of social improvement, holding that a disinterested exploration of culture would be ultimately more effective. Yet Arnold was far too "interested" for later critics such as T. S. Eliot, who remarked disdainfully: "Arnold . . . went for game outside of the literary preserve altogether, much of it political game untouched and inviolable by ideas. This activity of Arnold's we must regret; it might perhaps have been carried on . . . by some disciple . . . in an editorial position on a newspaper" (xiii). Irving Babbitt insisted on the distinction between humanism and humanitarianism to mark the difference between the lofty work of the thinker, concerned with the universal truths of man, and the narrow interests of the practical reformer. The disdain for things of the world evident in criticism after Arnold suggests that modern criticism has predicated its authority on a renunciation of the mundane. Literary criticism, according to the high tradition, has moral claim precisely to the extent that it abstains from practical work.

The sociologist Pierre Bourdieu has argued that the idea of "disinterestedness" expressed in the aesthetic discourse of modern capitalist societies presupposes distance from the material need that constitutes the bourgeois experience of the world. Though the opposition "interested/disinterested" has remained structurally constant since its emergence in the late eighteenth and early nineteenth centuries, the content of the opposed terms has periodically varied. While politics remains a legitimate target for attack, aesthetic discourse in the twentieth century, especially that originating inside the academy, has divined an easier target. With a narrow focus on specific problems and a lack of appeal to higher truth and man's essential nature, the social sciences have been subject to a ritualistic flaying by literary critics. Auden spoke for a generation of artists and literary critics with the mock commandment, "Thou shalt not sit/With statisticians nor commit/A social science" (225).

The worldly success and general acceptance of the social sciences has always been particularly galling to literary critics because the social sciences are intellectual rivals for the study of human culture and behavior; the natural sciences, though also contributing to the demystification of existence, have a different object of study. The rivalry between the humanities and the social sciences explains the conflicting attitudes of literary critics toward the social sciences. Though expressing high-minded scorn and contempt for the values and practices of social science, literary critics have feared that the rise of social science would precipitate the end of literary study. Hazard Adams called literary professors interested in the cinema and in structuralist analyses of popular culture "lemmings" marching to "the great amorphous sea of social science" (66). In even more hyperbolic visions, the triumph of social science appears to threaten the free world. In 1940 Allen Tate warned direly: "Under the actuality of history our sociological knowledge is a ready-made weapon that is now being used in Europe for the control of the people, and it will doubtless soon be used here for the same purpose" (239). The fairly recent tradition in literary criticism of jeremiads against the social sciences is now so ingrained and reflexive that its origin and import have scarcely been subjected to scrutiny. Yet the interaction between academic literary criticism and the social sciences is central to the development of the professional study of literature in the twentieth century. Since each discipline is defined, at least in part, by its relation to the other disciplines, any change in the disciplinary field has consequences for the practice of an individual discipline. Given the fears and resentments of literary scholars toward social science, it is imperative to view the history of literary studies in the early and mid-twentieth century in relation to the parallel history of the social sciences.

Dewey, School Reform, and the Profession

Nineteenth-century philologists had considered themselves scientists discovering laws for the social world as natural scientists had discovered the laws for the natural world. An early president of the *American Philological Association* made sweeping claims for the discipline: "By philology we can reconstruct prehistoric man, and read the history of times before the Olympiads and Nabonassar. . . . By this science, the original unity of the human race is already nearly proved. The philologist is also in part a physiologist and an anatomist, because he must study the organs of speech. He seems to be the centre of all science" (Crosby 8). However, as the twentieth century proceeded, scholars of literature began to affiliate themselves professionally less with natural science than with the "humanities," an intellectual and academic category not widely employed before 1900. A series of events in the early part of the century established a distinction in the academic world between the humanities and the social sciences. The Rockefeller Foundation was reorganized in 1928 to include a Division of the Social Sciences separate from the Division of the Humanities (Higham 17). The American Council of Learned Societies (ACLS), founded in 1920, originally included all of the humanities, as well as the

American Historical Association (AHA), the American Economic Association, the American Political Science Association (APSA), and the American Sociological Association (ASA). But the latter three withdrew from the ACLS and joined with the American Statistical Association in 1924 to form the Social Science Research Council (SSRC). The AHA joined the SSRC a year later (Kiger 444). After a survey of the history of the humanities from 1880 to 1930, historian Laurence Veysey concludes wryly: "By implication, the definition of the humanities greatly clarified itself when several organizations seceded from the ACLS to form the Social Science Research Council (SSRC) in 1923. The humanities were what was left" (57). The union of statistics with political science, economics, and sociology was a watershed in the differentiation of the social sciences from the humanities. Humanists have long considered the use of quantitative methods—to this day abjured by literary critics—to be the distinctive feature of the social sciences.

In an essay on the history of English studies in America, Phyllis Franklin notes that presidential addresses delivered to the *Modern Language Association of America* (MLA) during the thirties were "essentially defensive" (26). She attributes this defensiveness to attacks on scholarship from literary critics located outside the academy. But a review of the *Publications of the Modern Language Association of America (PMLA)* in that period, especially presidential addresses, committee reports, and official publications, suggests that progressive education and the growth of the social sciences were equally responsible for the dismay of scholars. In his 1936 Presidential Address to the MLA, Carleton Brown spoke of an "attack on the castle," referring, however, not to a challenge from criticism but from progressive education.

Progressive education has been described by the historian Lawrence A. Cremin as the "educational phase of American Progressivism writ large" (viii). Largely inspired by John Dewey but disseminated far beyond his influence, progressive education survived as all organized movement until the fifties and has left an enduring legacy in American education. Emerging well before World War I, progressive education was in part a response to the exponential growth in secondary school and college Student populations. Realistically aware that the new population could not all enter into the educated professions, progressive educators were committed to changing educational practices to meet the challenge of universal public education. As Cremin writes, "Compulsory schooling provided both the problem and the opportunity for the progressives" (128).

There was a direct relation between progressive education and the social sciences, for the progressives directed education toward social problem solving and thus fostered attitudes in primary and secondary schools compatible with those underlying social science inquiry. The height of the progressive influence in education coincided with the consolidation of the "social sciences" as an integral field differentiated from both the natural sciences and the humanities. The conjuncture of these forces combined with the rise of structural linguistics and anthropology to create a crisis in literary scholarship that eventually issued in the New Criticism.

The numerous references to progressive education and the defensiveness of the official MLA position suggest that literary scholars took progressive education quite seriously. As early as 1917 Edwin Greenlaw warned, "[S]ince the classics are slowly but surely losing their hold in our colleges we must rely more fully upon literature in the native tongue as a bulwark against utilitarian tendencies in education" (454). When James Taft Hatfield, then president of the MLA, complained in 1934 about the "philistines" who were widening the term "literature" "to include prospectuses for oil-burning furnaces, and the folders of omnibus lines" (1283), he had progressive education in mind. Brown's 1936 address was followed by the creation of a Committee on Trends in Education Adverse to the Teaching of Modern Languages and Literatures, chaired by Howard Mumford Jones of Harvard University. At the 1937 MLA meeting, the committee delivered a report. Believing "that the drive against teaching of the modern languages and against sound conceptions of the study of English is reaching such proportions as to threaten the foundations of scholarship," the committee recommended that the MLA establish another committee "whose duty it will be to take an active part in establishing sound theories of education in these fields" (Doyle 1347). Thus was born the "Commission on Trends in Education" charged with monitoring changes in educational ideas and writing public defenses of literary study. In 1939 the chairman of the new commission, Henry Grattan Doyle, reiterated that "the general educational situation is as menacing to our subjects and to the humanities in general as ever" (1348).

The actual practices of progressive teachers varied widely but in general they were united in the belief that the "everyday life of the community must furnish the main content of education" (Cremin 293). Progressive educators might, for example, ignore grammar books and classic texts and substitute magazines and newspapers for standard classroom reading materials. Because the stimulus for education was to be found in the everyday world, traditional divisions in subject matter were undermined. Rather than learning disparate and unrelated subjects such as "math," "English," and "history," a student might focus on a specific project— building a boat or running a mock farm. Demanded from the progressive teacher were skills and breadth of knowledge few were likely to possess; this may be one reason why the tangible success of progressive education in small experimental schools proved difficult to replicate in schools at large.

A useful introduction to the main theoretical principles of progressive education may be found in two influential works by Dewey, *School and Society* (1900) and *The Child and the Curriculum* (1902). The goal of education as outlined by Dewey is to make the child's early education more concrete and connected to the child's experiences in the home and at play, in short, to reconcile the opposition between the child and the curriculum. The key term *experience* represents the goal of all enlightened education: to fashion education so the child perceives the relation between knowledge and his everyday life experiences (Dewey, *Child* 22). The teacher of the primary school child should be concerned with subject matter only insofar as it represents "*a given stage and phase of the development of experience*" (23).

Dewey saw a class prejudice in the antipathy of intellectuals toward manual labor and practical learning. He also shrewdly observed that, from the perspective of the ideal of contemplative or disinterested knowledge, even "civic or political and moral knowledge" is considered "a low and untrue type. Moral and political action is practical; that is, it implies needs and effort to satisfy them" (110). Where contemplative philosophers and literary idealists wished to distance themselves from moral and political knowledge intended to solve social problems, Dewey's reconstructed philosophy was aimed precisely at practical knowledge: "The prime function of philosophy is that of rationalizing the *possibilities* of experience, especially collective human experience" (122). According to Dewey, science has developed to an astonishing degree, producing wealth, luxury, and innovation on an unprecedented scale. The problem is that human sociality has not kept pace with these advancements: "I need only cite the late war [World War I], the problem of capital and labor, the relation of economic classes, the fact that while the new science has achieved wonders in medicine and surgery, it has also produced and spread occasions for diseases and weaknesses. These considerations indicate to us how undeveloped are our politics, how crude and primitive our education, how passive and inert our morals" (125–26).

Progressive education as conceived by Dewey was intended to repair the breach between scientific and moral development by teaching the child to apply the scientific method to social material. Briefly put, Dewey advanced a program of liberal meliorism designed to correct the defects of capitalism by realizing human potential through education. In outline, there were significant similarities between Dewey's "Democracy" and Marx's socialist state. The similarity explains the rapprochement between versions of progressive education and Marxism during the thirties. In 1934, Dewey along with educators at Teacher's College, Columbia, launched the radical journal *Social Frontier*, dedicated to the idea that educators should actively seek to reconstruct the social structure. Most progressive reform was far more conservative than that advocated by *Social Frontier* but the journal gained for the entire progressive movement a Marxist reputation it would never entirely outlive.

The acceptance of progressive ideas by the educational mainstream was signaled in 1918 with the publication of the *Cardinal Principles of Secondary Education* by the Commission on the Reorganization of Secondary Education of the National Education Association (NEA). This pamphlet announced the main goals of progressive educational theory: health, command of fundamental processes, worthy home-membership, vocation, citizenship, worthy use of leisure, and ethical character. The *Cardinal Principles* amounted to an overthrow of the principles announced twenty-four years earlier in 1894 by the NEA's "Committee of Ten," which had recommended that all secondary students, whether college-bound or not, be educated in the liberal arts and study English, foreign languages, mathe-

matics, history, and science (Ravitch 47–48). Traditionally, college entrance requirements—and thus academic subjects—had largely determined the content of
the secondary school curriculum, regardless of whether the students were college-
bound or not (Hays 70). But in the early twentieth century, secondary school
teachers began to supplement the academic curriculum with a practically oriented
alternative and to protest the influence of entrance requirements.[1] Even though
progressive education was largely aimed at primary and secondary schools, it directly influenced such colleges as Bennington, Sarah Lawrence, and the General
College of the University of Minnesota (Cremin 308–18). Changes in secondary
school curricula exerted a more diffuse but still tangible effect on other institutions. In "The Crisis in Liberal Education," published in the journal *School and
Society* (the name taken from Dewey's book), Homer Rainey observed, "Once secondary education began to assert its independence and to chart its own course in
the light of its own chosen objectives, troubles for the traditional type of higher
education began" (249). That progressive education had designs on the college curriculum was suggested by the formation in the early thirties of a "Committee on
the Relation of School and College" by the Progressive Education Association
(Graham 133–34). One frightened professor wrote: "They ask for an extension of
'progressive' high-school experimentation into the first two years of college work,
knowing full well that if they can get by with this, the whole college system, including the graduate school, will soon be at their mercy" (Wakeham 923).

It is easy to see why professors in traditional subjects were threatened by
progressive education for, in practice, it destroyed the integrity and coherence of
their subjects, when it did not declare them entirely irrelevant. The "correlation"
of subjects to one another and to "life" became the hallmark of reforms influenced
by Dewey's thought. His proposition, "[r]elate the school to life, and all studies
are of necessity correlated" (*School* 91), could function as a slogan for progressive
education.

The progressives also took direct aim at liberal education, calling it suited
only to an aristocratic leisure class. According to Dewey, "culture when isolated
tends to become a purely external polish and refinement, a mark of an invidious
class distinction" ("Culture" 239). Rather than a mark of individual refinement, he
proposed that culture could be seen as "the habit of mind which perceives and es-
timates all matters with reference to their bearing on social values and aims" (239).
Liberal humanists, such as Arnold and Goethe, were criticized by Dewey, not for
their ends, which he approved—the "improvement of society"—but for their
means, an "exclusive reliance upon literature and history as a means of reaching"
these ends. For Dewey, traditional scholars committed to knowledge for its own
sake were "socially isolated and socially irresponsible," and he identified aestheti-
cians in particular as proponents of one of philosophy's main errors, the idea that
value is inherent (*Reconstruction* 172, 170).

Though maintaining the need to join the "culture factor" ("acquaintance with the best that has been thought and said and done in the past") to the "practical factor" ("the factor of adaptation to the present need" [*Educational Situation* 84]), Dewey assigned traditional culture a compensatory value in his socio-educational program:

> Without ignoring in the least the consolation that has come to men from their literary education, I would even go so far as to say that *only the gradual replacing of a literary by a scientific education* can assure to man the progressive amelioration of his lot. Unless we master things, we shall continue to be mastered by them: the magic that words cast upon things may indeed disguise our subjection or render us less dissatisfied with it, but after all science, not words, casts the only compelling spell upon things. (Archambault 191; emphasis added)

In the philosophic and pedagogical texts, Dewey mainly regards art, religion, and poetry as means by which man idealizes reality, fulfills the wishes denied by actual circumstances, and represents the facts of industrial life (*Reconstruction* 103–104; 142). Homer's Penelope, for example, is a "classic" in literature because "the character is an adequate embodiment of a certain industrial phase of social life" (*School* 90).

Progressive education then did not simply compete with liberal education but sought explicitly to undermine it as a bastion of social privilege and undemocratic ideals. Social utility became the criterion for evaluating education, though an ambiguity existed as to whether "utility" meant the ability to *change* society or to *adjust* children to existing social norms.

Dewey himself was not an empirical social scientist nor did he advocate empiricism for its own sake. His entire project was intended to reconcile the dispersed subjects of traditional education under the mantle of the scientific method in the service of social reform. In "My Pedagogic Creed," he remarked, "it is the business of everyone interested in education to insist upon the school as the primary and most effective interest of social progress and reform. . . . [E]ducation thus conceived marks the most perfect and intimate union of science and art conceivable in human experience" (Archambault 438). But, given that the explicit metaphor for the progressive school is the laboratory, the development of the social sciences follows as a kind of corollary to the educational project. Thus, his "creed" continues, "with the growth of psychological service, giving added insight into individual structures and laws of growth; and with the growth of social science, adding to our knowledge of the right organization of individuals, all scientific resources can be utilized for the purposes of education" (438). History, rather than literature, was the privileged discipline in Dewey's curriculum but history was redefined (for the educator) in *School and Society* as "indirect sociology—a study of society which lays bare its process of becoming and its modes of organization" (155, 151).

Initial Response of the Profession

Given the relation between progressive education theory and the social sciences, it is clear why references to progressive education by literary scholars were often coupled with an attack on the social sciences. Carleton Brown, for example, traced ideas hostile to the "classical tradition" in the *Annals of the American Academy of Political and Social Science* (1935) and a book entitled *A Challenge to Secondary School Education* to a 1934 Report of the Commission on the Social Sciences of the American Historical Association (AHA). Quoting from an article in the *Annals*, Brown noted that all these documents expressed the view that:

> Our whole curriculum has too long been dominated by the idea of culture, by history for history's sake, by the classical tradition. . . . An education that is unrelated to life rests upon the leisure class idea. It is wholly out of place in a democracy where each individual must perform some useful function. (Brown 1298)

Brown goes so far as to suggest that the new "socialized" curriculum amounts to little more than a power play on the part of the social sciences to "subordinat[e] the humanities and all other fields of intellectual effort to the position of mere tributaries to the social sciences" (1303). Echoing Brown's themes, Eduard Prokosch in the next year looked back nostalgically to the turn of the century when, to his mind, language departments were regarded as "peers" by other departments (1321). Then English and modern foreign languages "were not looked down upon by Mathematics, Naturall [*sic*] Sciences, History, Philosophy, Psychology—and perhaps least of all by the social sciences" (1321). Literary scholars *perceived* a clear relation between social science and progressive education and were as antagonistic toward social science in colleges as they were toward progressive education in high schools.

A connection between progressive education and the social sciences was drawn in another public declaration. At the 1938 meeting of the MLA, a Joint Committee on Trends in Education sponsored a statement by a group of twenty-four teachers on "The Aims of Literary Study." The "Committee of Twenty-Four" pronounced that the study of literature usefully serves the citizens of a democratic state—a theme clearly prompted by the utilitarian demands of the progressives. The "Committee of Twenty-four" opened their statement by "clarify[ing] the relation of . . . the humanities to the social sciences." Referring to progressive education, the statement declared that "the movement in education for the last quarter of a century has clearly emphasized" the social sciences.

I. *The Humanities and the Social Sciences.*—Because of the current demand that literary study should primarily inculcate "social values," we begin with an attempt to clarify the relation of literature as one of the humanities to the social sciences.

The movement in education for the last quarter of a century has clearly emphasized these latter subjects. We do not question either the necessity or the desirability of this tendency, but we believe there is considerable danger that "social values" may be overstressed at the expense of those values of individual enrichment without which the democratic state cannot long endure. By the nature of their task the social sciences are required to examine men in the mass: i.e., to examine the action of social forces over large areas of the population. The implication is almost irresistible that the individual, thus submerged in the social mass, is merely a cipher, a helpless unit whose thought, feeling, and actions are determined by impersonal forces over which he has little or no control.

The democratic state, however, depends for its existence upon the life within it of the largest possible number of richly endowed and self-reliant individuals, sensitive to the individual lives of their fellow men and to their own personal potentialities. Whatever the errors of rugged individualism in the economic sphere, the concept of political democracy assumes the efficacy of rugged individualism on the plane of the spirit. (Rosenblatt 1367–68)

The "statement" adumbrates a strategy that literary scholars would repeat and refine throughout the war and the postwar years: the idea that the study of literature resists totalitarian impulses by promoting the cultivation of the individual. The logic of the "Statement of the Committee of Twenty-Four" reveals that the demands for "relevance" made by progressive education led traditional literary scholars to reconceive the role of the literary professional—and thus to accept "criticism" as a professional practice. The authors define the function of literature in three ways, as teaching aesthetic taste, conveying the great truths of past civilizations, and offering imaginative experience—"experience," we have seen, was a key word in the progressive vocabulary. That the authors stressed the value of literature in promoting social empathy is clearly a concession to the progressive demand that education further social, rather than individual, goals: "[T]hrough literature," the authors write, "[the student] may understand sympathetically the demands of others upon himself and sense the impact of his own personality upon others" (1368). Since the practice of scholarship was clearly inadequate to this purpose, the authors, with the imprimatur of the MLA, accordingly redefined the task of the literary professional. "The task of the teacher [is] not the sterile accumulation of bibliographical and biographical facts—what may be called the cold-storage of literary history—but the interpretation of literary classics" (1371).

Internal critique proliferated. In the same year, the Committee on Research Activities complained to the membership at large about the type and quality of the manuscripts submitted to it for review. Stating that "[t]he purpose of research in the modern languages and literature being the increase of humane learning," the committee encouraged the submission of manuscripts "which directly present im-

portant scholarly interpretations of subject matter" rather than "additional machinery for scholarship," bibliographies, indexes, word lists (Hamilton 1338). The
distinction between "humane learning" and "scholarship" would not have occurred in the discourse of nineteenth-century philologists convinced of the direct
relation between rigorous empirical work and *Bildung*. Such a distinction reflects
the discipline's growing awareness of what professional allegiance to "the humanities" entailed. Evident throughout this report is concern with the Association's external prestige. In a rather astonishing admission, the Committee observed:

> A very large proportion of the works published or sponsored by our Associ-
> ation are painstaking, sound, and useful contributions to learning; but it
> must be admitted that they are not of extraordinary interest, nor do they ex-
> hibit that element of "important scholarly interpretation" which the Asso-
> ciation is in principle committed to promote. (1338–39)

Complaints such as this committee report are significant in calling, from within
the MLA, for something other than *scholarly* business-as-usual. The MLA was particularly sensitive to the charge that liberal education was suitable only for an aristocracy out of place in American society. Often scholars responded by affirming
their responsibility to preserve the *true* aristocracy of spirit. This was the general
position of the New Humanists; and it was taken as well by J. S. P. Tatlock, president of the MLA in 1938: "If as the Educators tell us the high-schools must no
longer offer an aristocratic education, all the more the colleges and graduate
schools must; for an intellectual and cultural aristocracy we must have, or we shall
be left to the tender mercies of an aristocracy of mere wealth and position" (1320).
Given the general terms of the disagreement between literary scholars and progressive educators, it is not surprising that we find a scholar referring, even if ironically, to the "sans-culottism of progressive education" (Pollock 60).

As progressive education gained ground, less confrontational positions were
officially adopted. But the charge of elitism was invariably mentioned. In 1942,
the MLA's Commission on Trends in Education published a pamphlet entitled
Literature in American Education intended for wide circulation:

> It is suspected . . . that humane letters are merely the remnant of an out-
> moded "aristocratic" education, in which they were often diverted from
> their true meaning to become the badge of snobs, the toy of the rich and the
> idle. . . . There is also a growing body of educators who prefer to slight great
> books and emphasize "creative activity" and "self-expression" . . . on the part
> of their students. Letters, in the opinion of some present-day educationists,
> should be wholly or chiefly contemporary letters, books linked easily with
> "life" and our practical up-and-coming world. (Lowry et al. 979)

In this public defense, the MLA stressed the ability of literature to establish sympathy among people of different backgrounds. Reiterating many of the themes in the "Statement by the Committee of Twenty-Four," *Literature and American Education* stressed imaginative identification and suggested that the sciences are totalitarian to the extent that they sacrifice the individual to the "abstraction called 'society'" (981).[2] What is interesting about *Literature and American Education* is that the existence of the social sciences appeared to challenge literary scholars to define what was specific to their discipline: "The social sciences have no monopoly on sympathy and compassion. Strictly speaking, they have, as sciences, nothing to do with sympathy and compassion, except insofar as they borrow them from the field of the humanities" (985). This statement underscores the reversal of priorities in literary study, from a scientific accumulation of facts to the communication of human experience.

Predictably, progressive education was reviled by the New Humanists, who used it as an occasion to further their attacks on the philological establishment. The New Humanists, Irving Babbitt, Paul Elmer More, and their followers, were a minority voice in the late nineteenth and early twentieth century but, in the twenties, their work received renewed interest. The first general articulation of literature's new position in the academic field, New Humanism attempted to supplant historical scholarship with a humane interest in the universal truths of man embodied in literature (see Foerster *Humanism*; Grattan). The New Humanists took the unconventional view that progressive education and philology, like every other aspect of modernity they disliked, were two manifestations of the same historical phenomenon, naturalism. According to Babbitt, naturalism has both a scientific and a sentimental aspect, the former represented by industrialism and the latter by romanticism. "[T]he sentimental and scientific worship of nature," though apparently antithetical, converge in their respective effects on education (Babbitt 92). "The former, working up into the college from the kindergarten, and the latter, working downward from the graduate school, seem likely between them to leave very little of humanistic standards" (92). Educators from kindergarten to graduate school "in their anxiety not to thwart native aptitudes" encourage the individual "in an in-breeding of his own temperament" that culminates in "his specialty" (94).

Babbitt's younger colleague, Norman Foerster, cited the father of progressive education and the founder of the modern university as twin culprits in the "demoralizing process" undermining education (Foerster, *State University* 7). Foerster objected to the "leveling" effect that inevitably occurs when the "unfit," specifically defined as the immigrant populations of America's cities, are permitted to enter the citadels of higher education. He outlined a decline in American education accompanying the democratizing of education, largely through land-grant universities and changes in curricula brought about by progressive education. Courses that earned his special ire were "Practical Applications of Psychology," "Human Development and Personal Adjustment," "Current English Reading" (explicated by Foerster as referring to magazines and newspapers), "Appreciation of Motion Pictures" (184), all titles that can be traced to progressive education.

The implication of the New Humanist position was that the modern university was a product of the same shift in educational philosophy that produced progressive education in secondary and primary schools. This view had currency among official historians of the MLA as late as 1958. MLA Secretary George W. Stone, reflecting on the history of the MLA as a learned society, observed that

> the very spirit in American education which brought the MLA into existence threatened now to destroy it. It was this practical, revisionary spirit that discarded the classics and, for a time, at least, suffered the modern languages to fill the resultant gap in the curriculum. This same spirit, in the 1920's, began to grow critical of *all* traditional and liberal disciplines, hence of modern language study. (31)

If one compares the "New Education" of Harvard's Charles W. Eliot to progressive education, there are similarities, to be sure (Charles W. Eliot; see Elliott; Painter). But although "New Education" strove to broaden access to education beyond a narrow social segment, its main impetus occurred before the waves of immigration from southern and eastern Europe in the late nineteenth century. Progressive education took as its mission precisely the working class and immigrant masses disparaged as the "unfit" by the New Humanists. The response of the New Humanists and the majority of the academic literary establishment to the social phenomena of immigration and urbanization was to retrench behind a tradition of aristocracy. The progressives, in contrast, sought to integrate new populations into the structures of American society.

The comments of George Stone and others indicate that literary scholars were haunted by the specter of the classics. Classical study had been the heart of college education before the rise of the university but, by the twenties, it had been largely shunted aside. The teachers of the modern languages, including English, had led the attack on the classics; but when attacked themselves, they identified with the lost classicists—perhaps with a guilty sense of just retribution. "[H]istory, government, and economics . . . now threaten to take away from us the primacy of position which we took away from the classics," declared Percy Long to the MLA (2). Carleton Brown opened his 1936 address by recalling a warning issued a quarter century earlier by a Col. Elliot F. Shephard who called attention to the assaults on the classics and then declared, "But it is not for the scholars in the Modern Languages to regard this attack upon the classics with indifference or complacency. For, believe me, gentlemen, if this attack succeeds your turn will come next." Brown concurred sagely, "Seldom has more inspired prophecy been uttered, although of those who listened to his warning probably few imagined that they would live to see the fulfillment of his prediction" (1295). The extent to which scholars identified with the fallen classicists betrays a sense of despair and collective resignation about their own historical fate.

In the thirties, the professional study of literature suffered not only from a general depression resulting from the economic downturn but from a climate of opinion aggressively organized against it. The erosion of literary scholarship was more than a matter of words, however, for progressive education and the rise of the social sciences materially affected the location of the study of literature in the intellectual and educational fields.

Material Changes in the Status of the Profession

In 1949, MLA President Percy Long described relations between literary studies and the social sciences using a sequence of military metaphors:

> We may have won the war; but we did not win the peace. The phalanx of Education and the cohorts of the Social Sciences began promptly to make aggressive movements into our territory. Instruction in English deteriorated in the presence of a fifth column devoted to current events and the preparation of youth for leadership in democracy. The necessary aristocracy of real education became taboo. (7)

Progressive education, it is true, took aim at the liberal arts, yet philologists might have repulsed those verbal assaults but for the remarkable (and demoralizing) growth in the social sciences during this period. More than anything else, this growth lent substance to the progressive attack on the liberal arts.

In the period 1920–1950, at the University of Pennsylvania, for example, there was a 36 percent decline in the ratio of language and literature faculty to the total faculty in arts and sciences. At Princeton there was a 33 percent decline. But while the languages and literatures declined in relative terms, the proportion of professors in the social sciences (psychology, political science, anthropology, economics, sociology) increased—by 132 percent at the University of Pennsylvania and by 113 percent at Princeton. Even at Harvard, where faculty positions in the languages and literatures increased slightly in relative as well as absolute terms, growth in the literary disciplines was small compared to that of the social sciences, whose relative size increased by 112 percent.[3] Though one pessimistic report estimated that in 1933 completed dissertations in sociology would exceed available vacancies by a ratio of seventeen to one (Chapin 508), another published in the same volume of the *American Journal of Sociology* painted a brighter picture (E. Faris 509–12). A historian of the University of Chicago Sociology Department stated flatly that "no extended period of unemployment of trained sociologists ever occurred" (R. Faris 120). Of course many trained sociologists never took academic jobs but the mere existence of alternative employment opportunities gave the field considerable advantage over the depressed humanities.

The MLA gradually mobilized to respond to the changed circumstances of its existence. But professional and institutional inertia made a swift response impossible. Literature scholar Hayward Keniston summarized the situation:

> For while we were checking our footnotes and correcting our galley-proofs, things were happening in the world outside, and particularly in the educational world. The triumph of science was now clear; the social "studies" became social "science." And because both the natural and social sciences were so intimately and evidently related to the life of every day, they claimed, in our practical society, an ever-increasing part in the programs of our schools and colleges. The humanities, undefended by the leaders of the profession who were absorbed in their books, were gradually pushed aside, as having nothing to contribute in education. (20)

Defenders of traditional scholarship such as Eduard Prokosch often conceded that the state of the profession justified criticism but they felt the situation could be remedied by reestablishing high standards. The problem with this line of defense was that the progressives attacked the *principles* of traditional scholarship, not the failure to live up to them. Not until 1950 did the MLA take aggressive action but, by then, the damage had been done. The delay on the part of the MLA enabled challengers to the philological tradition to take the initiative in shaping the profession's response.

In 1950 the constitutional charter of the MLA was changed, signaling a change in attitude on the part of MLA leadership, a desire to make the MLA competitive, and a recognition of criticism as a legitimate professional activity. Feeling that the charter (dating from 1928) restricted the activities of the MLA to the "advancement of research," Secretary William Riley Parker and the Executive Council campaigned for a change redefining the purview of the MLA to include criticism and broadly professional activities, such as advocacy with government and private foundations. The revised charter read: "The object of the Association shall be to promote study, criticism, and research in modern languages and their literatures." The connotation in the shift from "advancement" to "promotion" signaled the Association's awareness that it would have to work harder to sell its wares in a changed educational market. Shortly after the change was secured, Parker was empowered to approach the Rockefeller Foundation for a three-year $120,000 grant to study the declining state of modern language education in universities and prescribe remedies. It is testimony to the MLA's reputation for disinterest in the practical matters of the world that the grant officers at the Rockefeller Foundation were initially skeptical about the depth of support in the general membership for this initiative. Parker was requested to prove support by asking members to engage in a letter-writing campaign. Upon receipt of numerous favorable letters, the Rockefeller Foundation was persuaded to fund the project.[4]

The MLA's late appeal to the Rockefeller Foundation points to another factor contributing to the growth of the social sciences. The funding available to research through the foundations and the federal government grew dramatically during this period. Federal support of such research had begun in 1929 with President Hoover's Research Committee on Social Trends and continued in an ad-hoc fashion throughout the New Deal (Lyons 47, 50–62). During World War II, the federal government extensively funded scientific research on military projects through a central mechanism, the Office of Scientific Research and Development (OSRD). In 1945 Vannevar Bush, the director of OSRD, proposed that the government create a separate agency to fund natural science research on a permanent basis. Until 1950, when a bill creating the National Science Foundation (NSF) was finally passed, debate raged as to whether the social sciences should participate in the new agency (Boyer 172–73). The content of this debate reveals that the prestige of the natural sciences outpaced that of the social sciences, even as the social sciences dwarfed the humanities. Social science participation in the NSF was finally made optional, not mandatory, a blow to social scientists. But the social sciences soon had new opportunities for military funding with the outbreak of the Korean War.

Even more consistent and influential than government support was the growth in private monies available for social science research (see Arnove). Funds could be donated directly to universities for designated research or could be given to one of the organizations that served as an umbrella for the related disciplines (e.g., the ACLS and the SSRC). Generally, the specific purpose of funds donated directly to universities was not noted in the annual report, so the distribution of funds over specific areas is difficult to determine. But Eduard C. Lindeman gathered data enabling such a breakdown in his pioneering 1936 study *Wealth and Culture*. According to Lindeman, in the decade, 1921–1930, foundations donated to institutions of higher learning $13,210,899 earmarked for the social sciences, plus an additional $97,500 for psychology (categorized separately by Lindeman), while the natural sciences received $1,183,705 and the "general humanities" $3,375,620 (70–75). (Of this figure, "Classics" received $399,392 and "English" only $3,915.) For the purpose of research, foundations provided $13,455,013 for the social sciences, compared to $20,272,163 for the natural sciences and $807,166 for the general humanities (78–83). These figures do not include support for associations, publications, and conferences in the various fields nor corporate sponsorship of the fine arts and museums.

Evidence suggests that corporate sponsors often echoed the language of progressive education in their remarks about the humanities in this period. A trustee of the Rockefeller Foundation complained in 1934 that the humanities were suffering from "what might be called the snobbishness of the classical tradition" (Fosdick 241). In 1937, Raymond B. Fosdick, the president of the Rockefeller Foundation, invoked an oft-repeated charge against the humanities in calling for a change in their content:

> From being aristocratic and exclusive, culture is becoming democratic and inclusive. The conquest of illiteracy, the development of school facilities, the rise of public libraries and museums, the flood of books, the invention of the radio and the moving picture, the surge of new ideas—and above all, perhaps, the extension of leisure, once the privilege of the few—are giving culture in our age a broader base than earlier generations have known. . . . New interests are in the making—an adventurous reaching out for a fuller life by thousands to whom non-utilitarian values have hitherto been inaccessible. . . . Any program in the humanities must inevitably take account of this new renaissance of the human spirit. (241–42)

In Fosdick's retrospective on the Rockefeller Foundation, he titled the chapter describing the Foundation's activities in the humanities, "Humanism as an Interpreter." Here, as in the "Statement of the Committee of Twenty-Four," the demand for contemporary relevance in scholarship led those making it to turn to "interpretation" as an alternative.

Though there was absolute growth in the size and material resources of most disciplines between 1920 and 1950, the *relative* growth of the social sciences far outpaced that of the humanities. At the same time, the social sciences were evolving new methodologies and assumptions that accentuated the gulf between the humanities and the social sciences.

History, Literature, and Quantification in the Social Sciences

By the twenties, the social sciences had begun to embrace a version of positivism deeply suspicious of any statement or generalization whose truth could not be empirically tested, either with current or currently envisioned technology. A key difference between the positivism of the nineteenth and twentieth centuries resided in the latter's embrace of operationalism in methodology, the belief that "every scientifically meaningful concept must be capable of full definition in terms of performable physical operations and that a scientific concept is nothing more than the set of operations entering into its definition" (Schlesinger 544). The desire to translate social data into units capable of mathematical manipulation constituted a distinct change over the assumption of earlier social scientific work that placed empirical information within a basically narrative framework.

The adoption of statistical methods by the social scientists, though never as complete as humanists imagined, had an important consequence for the academic balance of power in this period because it forced professional history to choose its affiliation. Was history one of the humanities—or was it a social science? To some extent, historians never fully committed to one or the other but remained divided. However, beginning in the thirties, an important tendency in modern historiography was the effort to develop quantitative methods for historical research (see Kuklick). But while history was drawn toward the social sciences, philological scholarship remained predicated on the validity of historical approaches to culture. Even though academic history had long ago ceased to be incorporated within literary studies (Hofstadter 4), the broad interests of literary philologists had ensured a continuing relationship between the two disciplines in the late nineteenth and early twentieth centuries. For example, in 1929, George Lyman Kittredge produced a general history of witches and witch trials in addition to his specialized studies on linguistics. Though renowned as a "progressive historian" for his work on American thought, Vernon Parrington was in fact a professor of English. In the twenties, he won a Pulitzer Prize in history, an act of intellectual miscegenation that offended the New Humanists. Norman Foerster complained, "[W]hen more and more books and dissertations are of such a nature that they merit more attention in historical than in literary reviews and only historians are really competent to pass judgment upon them, something is fundamentally wrong with our conception of literary scholarship" (*American Scholar* 23). By the thirties, however, professional historians were eager to distance themselves from literature and climb aboard the bandwagon of progressive education.

The American Historical Association (AHA) broadly endorsed the principles of progressive education, strove to adopt progressive rhetoric, and oversaw a massive study of social studies instruction in high school intended to bolster enrollments. In the thirties, a Commission on the Social Studies of the AHA produced several studies intended to promote the study of "social studies" in high schools and to bring social sciences education in line with the new demands of an integrated national and world economy. The commission's chairman prefaced the commission's first publication, Charles Beard's *Charter for the Social Sciences* (1932), by bestowing a kind of approval on the educational changes advocated by progressive education:

> The careful reader will find both expressed and implied in [the *Charter*] the conviction on the part of educators and social statesmen that there is need of wise readjustment in our thinking and our educational program to a world that has become urbanized, mechanized, and interlocked in its social, economic, political, and cultural interests. It is a tribute to the high sense of public responsibility held by educators and scholars in the social sciences that they were neither unconcerned about, nor indifferent to, the educational implications of these changes. (Beard iv)

The authors of the sixteen projected titles in the Commission's Report included a diverse group of professional educators (Bagley, Counts, Newlon, Horn), political scientists (Merriam), and historians (Curti, Beale, Pierce, Johnson, and Beard).

The University of Chicago and Teacher's College, Columbia University—the centers of the social sciences and progressive education, respectively—were disproportionately represented among the authors.

In 1934 the Commission on the Social Studies formulated a definition of the social sciences that included "the entire range of human history, from the earliest times down to the latest moment, and the widest reaches of contemporary society, from the life and customs of the most remote peoples to the social practices and cultural possessions of the immediate neighborhood." Counted among the social sciences were "the traditional disciplines which are concerned directly with man and society, including history, economics, politics, sociology, geography, anthropology, and psychology" (6). The absence of literature was conspicuous.

The AHA's receptivity to progressive education and the social sciences contrasted sharply with the MLA's hostility. In effect, the shift in the AHA's professional affiliation legitimated the progressive critique, isolated the MLA, and undermined the professional relation between history and literature. The shift had intellectual implications as well, for it strengthened the position of literary scholars opposed to historical approaches to literature. In a professional context where history was making overtures toward progressive education and the social sciences, the concept of a separate ontology for literature must have been reassuring. As John Crowe Ransom declared in the collection of essays *The World's Body* (1938), "If jealous science succeeds in keeping the field of history for its own exclusive use, it does not therefore annihilate the arts, for they re-appear in a field which may be called real though one degree removed from actuality. There the arts perform their function with much less interference, and at the same time with about as much fidelity to the phenomenal world as history has" (132).

Conclusion

Philology had defined itself as *Geisteswissenschaft*, the study of the cultural products of man. The growth of the social sciences disrupted the balance of academic power achieved earlier between philology and natural science. In the intellectual distribution of the late nineteenth century, the study of nature proper was accorded to the sciences but that of *human* nature and the products of human nature belonged to the philologists. The social sciences rejected philology's reliance on historical documents in favor of empirical research but addressed a similar intellectual field. Consequently, the rise of the social sciences directly cut into the philologist's share of the academic pie. Though the majority of philological work was linguistic and textual, establishing the reliability and authority of texts and tracing patterns and structures of language, philology was also concerned with general civilization. In *The Province of Literary History*, Edwin Greenlaw went so far as to declare that "nothing related to the history of civilization is beyond our province" (35). Given this scope, the rise of alternative approaches to the same subject matter, approaches without deference to—indeed, without acknowledgment of—literature itself, could only be viewed as a threat.

Thus, the circumstances for the emergence of New Criticism included a professional intellectual field dislocated by the conjuncture of a number of forces. Professional historians had begun to identify their interests with those of the social sciences, influential educators were aggressively questioning the value of liberal education, the material and institutional resources of the social sciences were rapidly expanding, and the relative size and strength of literature departments were declining. Each of these interrelated developments helped to undermine the institutional position of philological scholarship, eventually opening a space in the profession that allowed criticism to enter.

With its insistence on the specificity of literary language, New Criticism provided strong institutional protection against the social sciences, ensuring the need for at least a minimum of specialists competent in the aesthetic realm. The implicit ontology in professional discourse—the idea that the existence of a profession of literary study requires the definite object, "literature"—dates from the rise of New Criticism.[5] All this is not to attribute New Criticism's success solely to institutional politics nor to suggest that its synchronic focus was simply a professional necessity or conscious choice. New Criticism was not a mechanical adjustment of the system or a completely opportunistic position. But it shifted the ground for literary study and enabled the profession to survive in a changed environment.

Notes

1. The National Council of Teachers of English was organized in 1911. It quickly created a committee to work with the NEA on college entrance requirements.

2. With the onset of the Cold War, the enemies of progressive education helped to undermine the movement by associating it with the threat of communism. Ravitch gives an overview of this history in the chapter "Loyalty Investigations." To this project, the MLA Commission on Trends in Education lent a hand, recommending to educators, parents, and scholars V. A. McCrossen's essay "How Totalitarian Is Our Education?" which compared the educational theories of Nazi Germany and Soviet Russia to progressive education. McCrossen, a humanist, noted suggestively, "Lenin, Lunacharsky, Trotsky, Krupskaia, have all said that the certain way to make a good communist out of a pupil is to have him deny God, love sex and study the social sciences" (441).

3. Pennsylvania's long history of practical education, dating back to Benjamin Franklin's original charter, probably made Pennsylvania somewhat anomalous in its openness to the social sciences. However, Pennsylvania was by no means unique; Harvard, Columbia, and Chicago, for example, also had strong departments in the social sciences by this time.

The figures for Harvard and Princeton were obtained by dividing the total number of faculty members in all languages and literatures, including philology and classical languages, by the total number of faculty for the years 1920 and 1950, then calculating the percentage decline. Disciplines whose status as either a social science or humanity is equivocal (such as history) were not included. The figures for Penn required additional analysis because the catalogue for 1920 lists all faculty in one group, whereas the catalogue of 1950 gives separate listings to the individual schools and cross-lists many of the faculty. To correct for this, I eliminated all engineering, law, medical, and architecture faculty from the figures for 1920. I also included the Wharton school along with the College in the figures for 1950 because many social science departments were included within Wharton at that time. The figures thus arrived at are consistent with those for Harvard and Princeton. In my calculations, I did not include visiting or emeritus professors or instructors below the rank of assistant professor.

Harvard apparently exhibits an increase in the relative strength of the languages and literatures, but in another measure of departmental strength, number of graduate students, they exhibited a sharp relative decline. The proportion of students in the English department to the total number of graduate students declined by 42 percent in the period from 1920 to 1947 (data for 1950 were not available), while in classics the figure was 58 percent, etc. Decline in the traditional foreign language departments (Romance, German) was partially offset by growth in the new departments of Slavic and Far-Eastern languages.

Data were taken from the following sources: *Catalogue of Princeton University, 1920–1921* (32–58), *Princeton University Catalogue, 1950–1951* (32–58), *Harvard University Catalogue, June, 1948* (217–34), *Harvard University Catalogue of Names, 1920–21* (11–33), *Catalogue of the University of Pennsylvania for the Session of 1920–21* (21–43), *Catalogue of the University of Pennsylvania, 1950–51* (6–12).

4. Phyllis Franklin graciously let me explore a portion of the MLA archives. Information about this episode was gathered there.

5. Hazard Adams expresses this attitude when he writes, "When everything verbal or actable . . . becomes literature, literature is nothing and the tribal subject is merely more grist for the mill of the social sciences, or, as William Blake put it, '. . . a web, dark & cold, throughout all/The tormented element stretched. . . .'" (67).

But the idea that the profession depends upon the distinctive ontology of literature is found, as late as 1975, even in the work of a dissenting critic such as Richard Ohmann. *English in America* opens with a discussion of Robert Frost's poem "Design," and Ohmann's first comments about it are to demonstrate that it "*is* a piece of literature." In Ohmann's text, the ontology of the professional object is the *precondition* for a critique of the profession: "This is a poem; other things are not; we do have a subject matter" (7).

Works Cited

Adams, Hazard. *The Academic Tribes.* New York: Liveright, 1976.

Archambault, Reginald, ed. *John Dewey on Education: Selected Writings.* Chicago: U of Chicago P, 1964.

Arnold, Matthew. *Culture and Anarchy: An Essay in Political and Social Criticism.* Cambridge: Cambridge University Press, 1971.

Arnove, Robert F., ed. *Philanthropy and Cultural Imperialism: The Foundations at Home and Abroad.* Boston: G. K. Hall, 1980.

Auden, W. H. *Collected Shorter Poems, 1927–1957.* New York: Random House, 1966 [1946].

Babbitt, Irving. *Literature and the American College: Essays in Defense of the Humanities.* New York: Houghton, Mifflin and Co., 1908.

Baugh, Albert C. "Justification by Works." *PMLA* 68(1953): 3–17.

Beard, Charles A. *A Charter for the Social Sciences.* Part I: Report of the Commission on the Social Studies, AHA. New York: Charles Scribner's Sons, 1932.

Bourdieu, Pierre. *Distinction: A Social Critique of the Judgement of Taste.* Trans. Richard Nice. Cambridge: Harvard UP, 1984.

Boyer, Paul. *By the Bomb's Early Light: American Thought and Culture at the Dawn of the Atomic Age.* New York: Pantheon Books, 1985.

Brown, Carleton. "The Attack on the Castle." *PMLA* 51(1936): 1294.

Chapin, F. Stuart. "The Present State of the Profession." *American Journal of Sociology* 39(1934): 506–8.

Commission on the Social Sciences. *Conclusions and Recommendations of the Commission.* New York: Charles Scribner's Sons, 1934.

Cremin, Lawrence A. *The Transformation of the School: Progressivism in American Education 1867–1957.* New York: Alfred A. Knopf, 1962.

Crosby, Howard. "President's Address." *Proceedings of the American Philological Association* 2(1871): 8.

Dewey, John. *The Educational Situation: Contributions to Education 3.* Chicago: U of Chicago P, 1902.

———. *Reconstruction in Philosophy.* New York: Henry Holt and Company, 1902.

———. "Culture." *A Cyclopedia of Education.* Ed. Paul Monroe, 4 volumes. New York: The Macmillan Company, 1911.

———. "My Pedagogical Creed." Archambault 1964, 427–39.

———. "Science as Subject Matter and as Method." Archambault 1964. 182–92.

———. *School and Society.* Chicago: U of Chicago P, 1971 [1900].

———. *Child and Curriculum.* Chicago: U of Chicago P, 1971 [1902].

Doyle, Henry Grattan. "Some Fundamental Problems for the Modern Languages and Literatures (A Preliminary Statement for the Commission on Trends in Education)." *PMLA* 54(1939): 1346–55.

Eliot, Charles W. "The New Education." *Atlantic Monthly* 23(1869): 203–20, 358–67.

Eliot, T. S. *The Sacred Wood: Essays on Poetry and Criticism.* London: Methuen & Co., Ltd., 1920.

Elliott, A. Marshall. "The Real Gymnasium Question." *PMLA* 1(1884–85): 227–46.

Faris, Ellsworth. "Too Many Ph.D.'s?" *American Journal of Sociology* 39(1934): 509–12.

Faris, Robert E. L. *Chicago Sociology: 1920–1932.* Chicago: U of Chicago P, 1967.

Foerster, Norman. *The American Scholar: A Study in Litterae Inhumaniores.* Chapel Hill: U of North Carolina P, 1929.

———. *Humanism and America: Essays on the Outlook of Modern Civilisation.* New York: Farrar and Rinehart, Inc., 1930.

———. *The American State University: Its Relation to Democracy.* Chapel Hill: U of North Carolina P, 1937.

Fosdick, Raymond B. *The Story of the Rockefeller Foundation.* New York: Harper & Brothers, 1952.

Franklin, Phyllis. "English Studies in America: Reflections on the Development of a Discipline." *American Quarterly* 30(1978): 21–38.

Graham, Patricia Albjerg. *Progressive Education: From Arcady to Academe. A History of the Progressive Education Association.* New York: Teachers College Press, 1967.

Grattan, Clinton Hartley. *A Critique of Humanism: A Symposium.* New York: Brewer and Warren, Inc., 1930.

Greenlaw, Edwin. "English in Modern Education: Aim and Method." *School and Society* 5(1917): 451–59.

———. *The Province of Literary History.* Baltimore: Johns Hopkins Press, 1931.

Hamilton, George L. "Committee on Research Activities. (Information Concerning its Activities)." *PMLA* 53(1938): 1338–39.

Hatfield, James Taft. "Standards." *PMLA* 49(1934): 1283–94.

Hays, Edna. *College Entrance Requirements in English: Their Effects on the Curriculum in High Schools; an Historical Survey.* Contributions to Education No. 675. New York: Bureau of Publications, Teachers College, Columbia University, 1936.

Higham, John. *Writing American History: Essays on Modern Scholarship.* Bloomington: Indiana UP, 1970.

Hofstadter, Richard. *The Progressive Historians: Turner, Beard, Parrington.* New York: Alfred A. Knopf, 1968.

Keniston, Hayward. "We Accept Our Professional Responsibility." *PMLA* 68(1953): 18–24.

Kiger, Joseph C., ed. "Social Science Research Council (SSRC)." *Research Institutions and Learned Societies,* vol. 5, *The Greenwood Encyclopedia of American Institutions.* Westport, CT: Greenwood Press, 1982.

Kuklick, Bruce. "History and the Social Sciences: The Response of American Historiography." Published in Italian as "Storia e Scienze Sociali: Un Secolo di Storiographia Americana." *Il Mondo Contemporaneo. Gli Strumenti Della Ricerca 2,X Questioni di Melodo.* La Nuova Italia, 1983.

Lindeman, Eduard C. *Wealth and Culture.* New York: Harcourt, Brace and Company, 1936.

Long, Percy. "The Association in Review." *PMLA* 64(1949): 1–36.

Lowry, Howard F., et al. "Literature in American Education." *PMLA* 65(1950): 977–97.

Lyons, Gene M. *The Uneasy Partnership: Social Science and the Federal Government in the Twentieth Century.* New York: Russell Sage Foundation, 1969.

McCrossen, V. A. "How Totalitarian is Our Education." *Association of American Colleges Bulletin* 28(1942): 432–49.

Ohmann, Richard. *English in America: A Radical View of the Profession.* New York: Oxford UP, 1976.

Painter, F. V. N. "Recent Educational Movements in their Relation to Language Study." *PMLA* 2(1884–85): 83–91.

Pollock, Thomas Clark. "Report of the Commission on Trends in Education." *PMLA* 68(1953): 59–62.

Prokosch, Eduard. "Treason Within the Castle." *PMLA* 52(1937): 1320–27.

Rainey, Homer. "The Crisis in Liberal Education." *School and Society* 28(1928): 249–55.

Ransom, John Crowe. *The World's Body.* Baton Rouge: Louisiana State UP, 1965 [1938].

Ravitch, Diane. *The Troubled Crusade: American Education, 1945–1980.* New York: Basic Books, Inc., 1983.

Rosenblatt, Louise, Howard Mumford Jones, and Oscar James Campbell. "Statement of the Committee of Twenty-Four: The Aims of Literary Study." *PMLA* 53(1938): 1367–71.

Schlesinger, G. "Operationalism." *The Encyclopedia of Philosophy.* Ed. Paul Edwards. New York: Macmillan Publishing Co. and The Free Press, 1972.

Stone, George W. "The Beginning, Development, and Impact of the MLA as a Learned Society, 1883–1958." *PMLA* 73(1958): 23–44.

Tate, Allen. "The Present Function of Criticism." *Southern Review* 6(1940–41): 236–46.

Tatlock, J. S. P. "Nostra Maxima Culpa." *PMLA* 53(1938): 1313–20.

Veysey, Lawrence. "The Plural Organized Worlds of the Humanities." *The Organization of Knowledge in Modern America, 1860–1920.* Ed. Alexandra Oleson and John Voss. Baltimore: Johns Hopkins UP, 1979.

Wakeham, Glenn R. "A Scientist Analyzes a New Mode of Attack on the Colleges, 1931." Vol. 2 of *American Higher Education: A Documentary History.* Ed. Richard Hofstadter and Wilson Smith. Chicago: U of Chicago P, 1961 [1931].

Four

Period Making and the Discipline: A Genealogy of the Idea of the Renaissance in *ELH*

Craig Dionne

More than any other historical period in English literary studies, the Renaissance has been redefined, refashioned, and rediscovered. Though its popular usage as a term to mean "the birth of individualism" is typically indebted to Jacob Burkhardt's monumental *The Civilization of the Renaissance in Italy* (1860), the argument that art and literature in the fourteenth and fifteenth centuries—and later in northern Europe—utilized classical learning differently to express a more secular view of human nature emerged in nineteenth-century French and German scholarship.[1] Seroux d'Agincourt is often noted for first embellishing in print this modern usage of "la renaissance" in his *Historie de l'art par les momumens*.[2] The debates about when the ideas associated with the rebirth of classical learning and its effect on literary history—the question first asked by Eduard Kollof in 1840, "Where do the Middle Ages end and where does the Renaissance begin?"—shapes much of the work of twentieth-century Renaissance literary criticism.[3]

By far the strongest model of the period was Burkhardt's narrative of the Renaissance as a time when "man became a spiritual individual and recognize[d] himself as such." Many of the period concepts that followed did not emphasize with the same zeal the belief in autonomy, but they did reiterate the theme that Renaissance writing is removed from the intellectual systems that characterized earlier literatures. Even E. M. Tillyard's idea of a world picture—of a divinely ordered cosmos—implied that writers utilized the medieval tropes of hierarchy and degree in an implicitly "Elizabethan" manner; similarly, Douglas Bush's idea of Christian spiritualism mediating humanist learning suggested that writers integrated secular perspectives from a distinct vantage point in the Renaissance. Many different critical terms were used to project a continuity in and through the literary texts in question, to produce what can be called epochal cognates, regardless of their proximity in time and place. "In the first half of this century," Margreta de Grazia observes, "world picture was used with an array of psychologizing terms to designate the distinctive feature of an era—spirit, character, mind-set, temperament, mentalité" (8). What makes current literary theory cautious of such terms, perhaps, is the postmodern belief in the polyvalent text, that any historical category as such silences the contradictory voices in the text (and by implication the interpretive freedom of the reader). As de Grazia observes, "[T]he days of uniform, coherent and comprehensive historical pictures seem to be over" (8), as we begin to rearrange the periods we teach by proposing different frames of reference.

It is not so much the dates one uses to distinguish the period, but the texts themselves that determine the way the Renaissance was—and still is—invested with significance. One can, for example, arrange the period around new discursive groupings to configure a startlingly new and different Renaissance—colonial travel literature instead of lyric poetry, commonplace books instead of secular drama, handbooks and laws instead of religious verse. Such a move dispenses with the modern formal categories of generic literary types and places the emphasis on specifically cultural themes: representations of femininity rather than Tudor drama, the rogue as other instead of sixteenth-century pastoral poetry. Along these same lines, one can just as easily frame this period around the cabalistic and hermetic traditions, rather than the neo-Platonic and secular influences we typically observe. Such groupings test the aesthetic logic at work behind the traditional periodization of the Renaissance because they expose how one's frame of reference determines the epoch one chooses to write. While it appears natural, for example, to emphasize Bruno's or Calvin's influence on the period of writing (but now we begin to see how even this term *period* is contingent upon many preconceived ideas about European history), it would not be impossible to imagine a Renaissance period whose geist is captured in those anonymous social scripts of holiday custom and civic ceremony.

Such contexts obviously assume quite a different idea of English studies, but it cannot be argued that such groupings provide an incomplete or inadequate picture when compared to a traditional mapping of Renaissance writing, especially when one considers that many of these hypothetical arrangements mentioned above already shape the focus of the new early modern cultural studies. This is to suggest that the cultural object that we choose to interpret—the Renaissance—does not contain an immanent value or character that we immediately recognize in the texts we teach and study. As William Kerrigan and Gordon Braden explain in their *The Idea of the Renaissance,* "The utility of period concepts does not derive from their isolated generality. . . . They do their most important work in narratives, where they mingle with act and coincidence to help us plot stories of traditions" (xi). The act of reading history, then, is not a neutral parsing of value-free facts but a process of self-confirmation. "We probably tend to discard period concepts," Kerrigan and Braden continue, "when the narratives they have mainly served, the traditions they have highlighted, no longer seem crucial to us" (xi). As de Grazia suggests, "[A] world picture or period concept or ideology may be less a methodological convenience than an epistemological necessity" (8). "Without such an act of enframing," she explains, "the past would appear either as a massive monolith or as myriad details . . . blur[ring] into the present" (8).

In the following essay I am interested in uncovering the story of when and why period concepts became popular ways of framing the historical moment we call the Renaissance. Ironically, many of the intellectual studies of Renaissance scholarship tend to reproduce a history-of-ideas model by only looking at the individual critics in dialogue with one another: so it seems that Douglas Bush's idea that Christian humanism responds to Burkhardt's emphasis on paganism, making Bush's idea free of any institutional motivations (likewise, Cassirer's interest in Renaissance philosophy is read as a subtle additive to Burkhardt leaving philosophy out of the mix; or Stephen Greenblatt's vaguely existential decentered Renaissance self is read as a response to Tillyard's fixed cosmological order, etc.). As such, the intellectual histories of the Renaissance as a period concept tend to subtly reconstitute their own birth narratives around the great critics who painted our most compelling portraits of the Renaissance. What I am interested in are the institutional mechanisms involved in this process of period making: how the idea of period difference evolved in the setting of educational institutions at a time when research in the nineteenth century was becoming the goal of academic pursuit. De Grazia has argued that it was Hegel's narrative of progress—his idea of the dialectical step-by-step evolution of period-geists supplanting and evolving through one another—that popularized the idea that entire epochs can have cohesive pictures of themselves. "After Hegel, hundred-year spans start to look like superannuated life spans; centuries start to develop anthropomorphic traits, not only character and feeling but also consciousness" (12). But even this birth narrative ignores how the idea of period concepts took hold in specific institutional settings. It is this process of bracketing and anthropomorphizing a period that I want to look at by asking how the organization of the academy as a research institution may have necessitated a self-projection onto the past of a series of periods that were the focus of the newly invented specialist's interpretive skills. The goal of any genealogy is to demystify the natural object of discourse, to examine how our neutral acts of reading are grounded in the institutional affiliations that authorize our encounters with the text. In this case, I want to examine how the idea of the Renaissance period is invested in the process of boundary making that some historians of the discipline have recognized as the key feature of English as a discipline.[4] As Michel Foucault explains, "[A] history, guided by genealogy, is not to discover the roots of our identity, but to commit itself to its dissipation. It does not seek to define our unique threshold of emergence; it seeks to make visible all those discontinuities that cross it" ("Nietzsche" 95). By disclosing the variety of ideological determinants of the discourse of English literature, genealogy dissipates the naturally given and metaphysically ordained sovereignty of our positions as subjects within the discipline by locating our identities—as students, teachers, and critics—within specific formations of cultural production. One important site of the cultural production of these local identities is the academic journal, where one can observe how the boundaries that shape the periods we read as natural markers of our textual experiences are discursively inscribed. What follows is a case study of one moment in the larger narrative of the formation of English as a profession. For the purposes of my study, I will focus on *ELH* and how it played a powerful role in the period making of the Renaissance in the American academic context. I will explore how the discourse of the Renaissance idealism—the view that English sixteenth and seventeenth-century literature expressed an original idea of spiritual autonomy and textual artifice—emerged at a crucial time in the formation of the discipline when literature was moving from the club culture of Literary Societies to the halls of academia, and how this transition gave shape to the professional ethos of that new breed of man, the "Renaissance specialist," whose affinities for literature and culture were mediated by a distinctly romanticized narrative about the loss of self, a professional identity that continues to this day.

Research and Discipline

I want to begin by situating the idea of research in the context of a crisis in authority felt in graduate institutions such as Johns Hopkins University, one of the first American schools to adopt the German model of research. In "Original Research" (1903), Ira Remsen, the president of Johns Hopkins University, speaks of the inadequacies of the newly spawned graduate programs:[5]

> At first, we thought it would be sufficient simply to let the students come together and select their courses. They were advanced—they were college graduates—they would do whatever was right, and the results would be satisfactory. We found very soon . . . that something was needed to keep them in line. There was a good deal of indefinite browsing. They would fly from one thing to another. They would find something peculiar about one teacher, and something they did not like about another teacher. There was a good deal of what I might call puttering. And those of us who were charged with the management of affairs concluded that we must take advantage of the degree. We must offer something in order to keep these students in line. The Ph.D. degree was the next thing after the A.B. degree, and we recognized that we must offer this in order to keep the body of workers in line, and that, in order to secure the results we wanted, it was also necessary to require a piece of research as a requisite for that degree. That is the machinery we used. We thought, at first, that we might avoid it, but we found that we must adopt it. (quoted in Veysey 313–14)

Nearly forty years after Remsen's letter, *ELH*, A Journal of English Literary History (1940), published a special edition of articles in commemoration of an English professor at Hopkins, Raymond Dexter Havens, editor of *ELH* (1945–1948) and *Modern Language Notes* (1925–1948). The journal was a salute to Havens's sixtieth birthday and his "ceaseless intellectual curiosity" in "the 18th and 19th Centuries" (iii–iv). "His course in 18th Century Romanticisms, which has assumed the character of legend, he has developed into a comprehensive, vital, and provocative analysis of this significant period of English life and letters" (iv). The facing page displays an austere photograph of Havens, his face emotionless, a pair of spectacles in his right hand. Following the summary of his "professed faith" in English literature, there is a complete bibliography of his works: one book, *The Influence on Milton of English Poetry* (1922), and another in press, *The Mind of a Poet, a Study of Wordsworth's Thought with Particular Reference to 'The Prelude,'* thirty-five articles (201 pages of material), and sixteen book reviews.

The brief synopsis of Havens's career marks the completion of Remsen's project. The photograph, synopsis, and bibliography express how Havens is to be measured within the institution. His value to the discipline is based much more on his research than it is on his teaching. Remsen's estimation of his students as "workers" and the Ph.D. programs as "machinery" clearly demonstrates that research, at its inception, was to work primarily as a disciplinary system to manage the time and energies of students. "Research" became the established form of evaluation within the profession, a tactic employed to stratify and disperse the interests of the "body of workers" and to solidify the boundaries of the discipline. As demonstrated in the letter, Remsen sets in motion this system of obedience and evaluation to reinforce individual labor and reconstitute what Michel Foucault might call the "internal mechanisms of power" of the institution. Foucault's work lets us situate Remson and Havens in a larger narrative about the dispersal of a distinct form of self-monitoring and self-evaluation that comes to characterize the institutional setting. Many have tried to universalize Foucault's history of the prison house to rewrite the story of modernity into a tale about the ever-tightening social constraints and more powerful mechanisms of control that visited the "body" in Western civilization, a narrative that stresses the transition from the centralized power of the absolute monarch to the diffuse but efficient power of the panopticon as paradigmatic to modern experience generally. When considering the way academic life is rendered in Remsen's memorable tale of "how it all began," it is interesting to rethink the utility of Foucault's master narrative, since in this context the university is literally imagined as a kind of work house—its classrooms, examinations, study halls, publishing houses, the treadmill in which knowledge will be produced, emerge as a necessary tool for maintaining localized power relations. I am most interested in the discursive and ideological aspects of Havens's "faith" in "English literary history" as a professional pursuit. During the crisis of authority in the graduate halls of English literature, knowledge was being divided into taxonomies of historical periods in order to administrate efficiently students on an individual level (Remsen's quotation speaks volumes about research as a kind of panacea). It is this context that "writes" the history of period making as a discursive mode.

Disciplinary Affiliations

The first two years of *ELH* were privately funded by a couple of the members of the Tudor and Stuart Literary Club of Johns Hopkins University in 1934. *ELH* was originally published with the subtitle, *Journal of English Literary History.* The editorial control after the first few privately published volumes remained in the hands of the Tudor and Stuart Club through 1954. The history behind this club and its affiliations with Hopkins reflects the general texture of the journal. John C. French, Librarian Emeritus of Hopkins and member of the club's "Committee on Publications" for several years (as was Havens), provides an account of the club's origins in his *A History of the University Founded by Johns Hopkins.* One of the doctors of Johns Hopkins, Sir William Osler, a man "much interested in literature for its own sake," donated the money for the creation of the club in 1919 in memory of his son, Edward Revere Osler, who died in World War 1.[6] In a letter to President Goodnow, Osler states the general purpose of the club: "to the encouragement of the study of English Literature in the Tudor and Stuart periods." The letter names those honorary members who are to be included in the club's organization.[7] As noted, Osler had a great interest in literature; enough of an interest to believe that the "promotion of fellowship and love of literature" was indispensable at Johns Hopkins. Within this club the Renaissance eventually took on a space—a room built to reflect Tudor architecture was constructed and dedicated to Osler's son; afternoon tea-times were arranged so that students could sit in the hyperreal surroundings of the Renaissance and discuss literary matters. Here we have a basic contradiction: a club whose purpose is to promote fellowship, but fellowship in the limitied sense of a club culture. All members were either close friends of Osler—from the upper-class social elite of Toronto, Boston, New York, or Washington—or students at Johns Hopkins. In fact, most members were taught to think of "literary history" in terms that might preclude any broad or inclusive form of fellowship or community.

Most members of the Tudor and Stuart Club were students and alumni of an English program that was, by and large, representative of a great philological tradition of scholarship. The university was beginning to establish itself in the 1880s as one of the first research universities. Most of this was due to the school's president, Daniel Coit Gilman, whose push for research predated the trend that most institutions took toward constructing specialized fields of knowledge. As we saw with Remsen, research was being rationalized as a means to focus the energies of wayward students. There were 399 graduate students in America in 1875, which grew to eight thousand by 1908. Libraries during this time were forced to expand to meet these new demands. Gerald Graff quotes Remsen, who explains how professors had to oversee different levels of knowledge production in this critical phase of development: "'Only after 1875 was the buying of books . . . put on a methodological basis, by men who have known exactly what was best in their particular fields. A college library was likely to be a sorry accumulation, open a hour or two a week," and, Graff goes on, "some librarians became legendary for their resistance either to purchasing books or to letting anyone borrow them'" (26).

The Tudor and Stuart Club was created after this expansion, but in many ways it signaled a bygone era. Its relation to the journal tells the important narrative of literature's transition from the parlors of polite society to the corridors of academe, the object of aesthetic taste as defined by middle-class club taste to the domain of professional discernment and licensed expertise. As the foundation of the first *ELH* publications, the club served as the institutional home of its earliest editors. Its history also reminds us of how the discipline of English emerged in the rich context of coterie culture that would eventually shape the aesthetic discourse of its predecessors and determine in "actually existing" material ways the resources and substances with which it could define itself. The Tudor and Stuart Club inherited in the form of moveable goods its first collection of books from a former club member. The "Revere Osler Collection" reached Baltimore in 1922, three years after Dr. Osler's death. It contained special editions and works from Osler's private Oxford library: "a good run of works of Thomas Fuller, a few important Milton items, a number of valuable Shelleys including a copy of *Queen Mab* inscribed by the author as a gift to Fanny Godwin, and a notable though small collection of Walt Whitman" (French 320).

The club took its "several thousand dollars accrued income" and concentrated on finding and purchasing more Renaissance texts, the works of Edmund Spenser. One might think that since the club was organized around the Tudor and Stuart epochs, it would only make sense to focus on the purchasing of Spenser's works. Yet it appears that in part the decision to buy Spenser's works and "an adequate apparatus for research and editorial work" (French 320) was to attract Edwin Greenlaw, a professor of English from the University of North Carolina, "to accept the chairmanship of the Department of English" at Hopkins in 1925, "for research in Spenser was Dr. Greenlaw's chief scholarly interest" (French 321). After he took the chair, the faculty encouraged the Johns Hopkins Press to publish a ten volume variorum edition of Spenser, "to be edited by a group of American scholars with Edwin Greenlaw as editor-in-chief" (French 321). The department evidently used the money from Osler's donation to lure the likes of Greenlaw to a department that was no doubt feeling the pressure to generate an image compatible with the university's name in research.

The newly spawned graduate programs with their increasing numbers of students tested the boundaries of the individual disciplines. At Johns Hopkins the concern with research wasn't entirely unrelated to this growth in enrollment. When President Gilman constructed a university based on scientific forms of knowledge, he "reversed traditional priorities, taking the sciences as the central model of knowledge and letting humanistic subjects adapt themselves as best they could" (Graff 65). Gilman established at Hopkins a pioneering institution in research.[8] Laurence Veysey tells of the diversified spirit of the research in those early days: "[T]he early Hopkins men prided themselves on absence of form, ritual, or ceremony; they boasted of their liberty to pour forth their energies uninterruptedly into the substance of whatever study engrossed them. Yet simultaneously the pressure toward hard work was intense, for it was enforced by a constant, close-range comparison with one's peers. Everyone longed continually to 'prove' himself" (164). This simple observation could be said to underscore the dialectical context of *ELH*'s emergence, since it contrasts the two opposing sources of literary appreciation respectively, that of an "uninterrupted" and free-ranging spirit of self-motivated interest in whatever study engrossed the individual student, and an enforced system of evaluation that would become the hallmark of academic research. The unbounded and sometimes unfocused studies of the "early Hopkins men" were supported by Gilman's own broad humanistic standards (161). But as disciplines strove to standardize and regulate the methods and procedures of study, this eclecticism met with institutional restraints. As we saw, Remsen's letter intends to provide a remedy for the apparent slipshod research that characterized the "indefinite browsing" and "absence of form, ritual, or ceremony" exhibited by students before the Ph.D. is introduced.

The student members of the Stuart and Tudor Club went through Remsen's newly standardized curriculum with its stringent emphasis on research. *ELH* is perfect for a case study, not only because it was developed at a school devoted so strongly to the pioneering spirit in research (Graff 65), but because its original editors were all trained in the same courses, and all belonged to the Tudor and Stuart Club.[9] Arthur Dubois, Ray Heffner, Edward Hooker, Clifford Lyons, and Edward Norris all received their Ph.D.s in English at Hopkins between 1928 and 1932. The way they were trained, and the resources they shared through the Tudor and Stuart Club, fostered a unified perspective of the English Renaissance. As such, *ELH* grew out of Johns Hopkins's affiliation with the residual emphasis on the positivistic tradition of investigating a language as a cultural history of a people, a model of philological endeavor made famous by H. A. Taine's *History of English Literature* (1863). Translated from the French, Taine's study set a standard for historical inquiry in early modern language departments throughout America. Taine's own account of his method is perhaps closest to the type of history reproduced throughout the early pages of the *ELH*. For Taine, philological inquiry meant finding an essential "master idea" in and around which the characteristic features of the national culture of the literature flourished. According to Graff, "Taine conceived the object of historical science to be not a mere accumulation of disconnected data, but a search for the underlying unity that draws together the disparate aspects of a culture" (70). In Taine's own words: "[W]hen the work is rich, and people know how to interpret it, we find there the psychology of a soul, frequently of an age, now and then of a race" (Graff 70).

The essentializing we see in this earlier historical method worked to hierarchize knowledge and make space for a new period-coverage system. The epochal cognates we recognize today as "Renaissance"—the birth of individualism, the celebration of "man's" mastery of nature through the stylized forms of courtly poetry and art—were indeed part of the landscape of historical thought before *ELH* developed into the dominant journal in literary studies. The idealization of the Renaissance became a deeply held ideology of order that allowed for the homogenization of the various and often contradictory ideologies of early modern literature to voice this code of aesthetics. This idealization is what distinguished the Renaissance from other periods generally. It became the lost garden of all subsequent epochs. In this fashion the discourse of literary study could indeed demarcate, in Ira Remsen's words, the institutional "lines," or "fields," of research in English, implying nonetheless that those periods that followed the Renaissance never quite reach the zenith of literary merit or artistry. In "Shakespeare's Old Men" (1940), an article written by L. Wardlaw Miles, a professor at Hopkins and one-time president of the Tudor and Stuart Club, we read how this idealized view of the Renaissance serves to tell an important story about Western history:

> In the pauses of song and speech is heard the faint splash of a fountain, whose irregular cadence weaves a charming contrapuntal pattern with the more formal music. And up and down the symmetrical gravel walks, between grotesque and formalized clipped yews, move the young people of a Renaissance but recently escaped from that castle in the background which we call Mediaevalism. (288)

Miles sums up the singular age that shapes the Shakespeare he reads, and what directly follows is a lament about feeling separated from this age:

> It is not likely that fate will ever give us another Shakespeare; it is equally unlikely that it will present another world of Renaissance Youth for another Shakespeare to picture—a world where passion, wit, artifice, and harmony can be synchronized, untroubled alike by our modern vices and virtues. Behind these Italian gardens stands the castle of Mediaevalism, in front of it today's factory, polling booth, and laboratory. (288)

In this moment the past is carved out in opposition to the industrial cityscape. Almost in the mode of a confessional, Miles exposes how his fascination for the period is predicated on a historical narrative that writes the Renaissance as a respite from the horrors of some impressionistically sketched "Mediaevalism" (what's taking place in the castle?) and the cold comforts of the Enlightenment. The Renaissance Youth walk down a path surrounded by clipped yews and the irregular cadence of splashing fountains, leaving behind an unspeakable confinement. In this simple equation, the Renaissance comes after the barbarism of an imagined dark ages and before capitalism's (enforced) democracy, here pictured as a drab and inauthentic form of freedom in a mass-experienced political process, the "polling booth." The Renaissance is viewed as island of tranquility—like the Club furnishings themselves, perhaps—an escape of the highest order with "wit, artifice, and harmony." But it also helped to rationalize the contradiction felt at the heart of the discipline that was undergoing a radical shift in its larger goals. As research became more and more a norm in the institution, the older ideals of liberal culture lost ground and became less important. "It was the mentalistic universalism of the idealistic view," Laurence Veysey explains—with its moral "Absolutes" and categories such as that of the universal mind—that "clashed[ed] with the whole conception of laboratory science" (192). As a vehicle of "research," the essays published in *ELH* in these early issues express an internalization of the residual ideology of liberal culture as the discipline sought to provide form to a new age of utilitarian diligence that displaced anxieties about research by depicting the Renaissance as a kind of textual wish-fulfillment, a hold out of a bygone era of coterie culture. It may be the work of our profession that alienates us, but it is our object of study—the art of literature of the English Renaissance—that best expresses our latent potentials.

Recent work in literary historiography, particularly in the Renaissance, has done much to disclose the theoretical underpinnings of this idealized "World Picture," a model used to emphasize almost to the exclusion of all else how texts produced in and around the early modern period reflect the simple ideas of order and harmony, a period that was characterized by Don Cameron Allen—one-time editor of *ELH*—as a moment in time where "we come on man universally merry for the last time in the modern world" (167). Here we may see the ideological import of *ELH,* a journal developed within a club that fetishized Renaissance literature. This idealism, I want to suggest, can be read as a response to the pressures that were being felt in the discipline at the time to standardize and regulate the very methodologies that Hopkins conjured into being in its push to establish itself as the model research institution (Veysey 158–64). The confessions we find in the earlier essays of *ELH* about the wonders of Renaissance aesthetics function as a local ideology that not only helps to legitimate the demarcation of the "field" of Renaissance period-study, but also to ameliorate the uneasy tensions that evolved due to literature being "disciplined" and moved from the club to the university. In this context, it is not hard to read Miles's image of the Renaissance Youth walking blindly into the future "laboratories" as its own unconscious expression of alienation—an attempt to cling to the fellowship fostered by the club—an image made more stirring if we imagine the passage being presented as an oratory to other members lounging in the reified surroundings of Tudor furnishings as they meditate on ironies of their institutional condition. So along with the expropriation of Anglo culture comes the necessity to identify with the ideals of an outmoded aesthetic idealism, "tradition" and "harmony" are rationalized as the rewards of this particular kind of professional work. The fellowship fostered in the club developed in reaction to the central values of the democracy of professionalism touted as a general cultural ideal (at least the professionalism developed at Gilman's Hopkins), with its liberty to compete in the marketplace of knowledge production. This idealization of the Renaissance emerged as an ideology to critique the complexities of what Miles sees as the modern condition, with its mass production, laboratories (the birth of "objectivism" and science), and polling booths.

So while the discourse of Renaissance criticism emerged in the discipline of English as one discursive "field" among others, it worked ideologically to smooth over particular social contradictions at the heart of the machinery that produced it. (How does one promote the code of liberal culture and its ideal of the urbane gentleman in a new competitive era of research?) As Graff points out, the field-coverage system is designed to work in a similarly ideological fashion, as it tends to rationalize precisely these questions of motive and intent. "The presence of an array of fully staffed fields [makes] it unnecessary for anybody to have a theoretical idea of the department's goals in order for it to get on with its work" (8). The field-coverage model is a distinctly modern phenomenon of the institution of English literature; the fetishizing of the Renaissance may have given the modern mind an opportunity to visualize a time when literary practice was not tainted by such objective boundary making. During the emergence of *ELH* the choice to invest in the Renaissance answered to a desire to retreat from the very setup that ensured its place in Hopkins's new research model. The bygone days of the Renaissance are represented in contrast to an age that conflates the naturally "synchronized" human traits of passion, wit, and harmony, traits that are now, the Tudor and Stuart Club members might agree, wiped away by modernity.

Don Cameron Allen, in a prose style he acquired as a Fulbright at Oxford, reminds us of the pessimism inherent in this perspective: "It seems that man was, for a moment, putting aside the ancient doubts, that he was becoming more certain of himself, and that a bright new world was seemingly parading before him.... Then suddenly it is all over. There was no noise, no tumult; it was an apocalyptic end. One day they were listening to the lutanist and the next day they were struck with infinite despair" (167). The "modern" moment is characterized more completely by Moody Prior. Though he contradicts in many ways the idea that the Renaissance is the age of merriment, in "The Thought of Hamlet and the Modern Temper" (1948), Prior still provides a similar ideological representation of a modern aporia by arguing that Hamlet exhibits "modern symptoms of uncertainty and melancholy." "A reader of our century," he tells us, "might with some justice come to regard Hamlet as the first great imaginative work of the post-medieval world in which may be discovered in clear outline these characteristic features of thought and sensibility which have come to be identified as the modern temper" (284). The modern world—which now this Renaissance play anticipates—is still seen to be a world of doubt and insecurity. Prior's is not so much a radical rewriting of a historical period as it is a reaffirmation: we can now read texts of this period to identify with the angst of the prescient Elizabethan artist.

In these idealizations of the Renaissance, the modern is ushered in as its own particular time period, complete with imagistic pictures of imposing urban space and secular uncertainty. We hear the familiar tone of disaffection that characterizes much of what John Fekete has termed the "post-romantic" phase of critical theory, where "Culture" is defined as "unalterably permanent" and "attains exaggerated prominence as a superior reality" in the face of an incomplete or somehow defunct social life. Following Arnold's definition of culture as a refuge from a civilization hostile to the potentials of the human imagination, postromantic criticism envisions an aesthetic process that is wholly autonomous from social activities outside the mind: "[O]nce its formal integrity is ensured," Fekete explains, "an independent culture can be posited as the truth of life, its source of authority, or its governing principle, and can press the claims of its superior reality on the life of society" (9). In the Tudor and Stuart Club interpretations of the Renaissance, we sense that this aesthetic space has been given a very real habitation and a name, a fully dimensional world whose textures and depths speak to a newly realized human potential. "The function of education," Fekete explains, "in this conception is to teach us to live so 'exclusively' in the ideal that 'the mere drift or debris of our days comes to be as though it were not.' The highest goal, then, is to live in a constructed imaginative vision of the ideal. This is a position of full flight; the ideal is refuge, not stimulus" (14).

When compared to the early *ELH* criticism one wonders if the now familiar identity of the Renaissance specialist turned "new historicist" is not speaking in a rather recognizable professional idiom. Although it is counterintuitive to read the recent New Historicism as promoting this idealized view of the Renaissance, one wonders if its master narratives about alienation, power, and self-display do not predicate the unspoken assumptions about aesthetic escape. Stephen Greenblatt's depiction of the early modern period intends to write a Renaissance that is the Escher-like mirror-image of Allen's postromantic history, an age when modes of self-erasure emerge among the interstices of early modern absolutism and colonization. To live the history of Renaissance English literature today, for Greenblatt, means to feel "that the culture to which we are as profoundly attached as our face is to our skull is nonetheless a construct, a thing made, as temporary, time-conditioned, and contingent as those vast European empires from whose power Freud drew his image of repression" (174). No fleeting escape from the horrors of modernity, the Renaissance is now discursively produced within an existential framework as a sounding board for intellectuals who fear a loss of individual power, a virtual erasure of will "in the midst of anxieties and contradictions attendant upon the threatened collapse of this phase of our civilization" (174). Unlike the discourse that produced human subjects that perceived Renaissance literary history as an escape into a more thoroughly integrated realm of self-understanding, the new historical discourses produce subjects who gaze into the *Unheimliche* of the strangely familiar Renaissance Absolutism and see how the culture and art they hold so deeply and passionately are ideological appendages to colonial institutions. But at times it appears that the professional identity of the classic Renaissance critic dies a slow death when we read that the aesthetic playfulness of the early modern literatures provide evidence of the possibility of escape from such repression. Greenblatt's curious asides profess an affinity to the traditional post romantic faith: "The literary text remains the central object of my attention in part because . . . great art is an extraordinary sensitive register of the complex struggles and harmonies of culture and in part because, by inclination and training, whatever powers I possess are released by the resonances of literature" (5).

We see in the outset of this literary discourse, at least in *ELH,* that the romantic visions of the Renaissance grew in reaction to the genuinely felt tensions of making English fit into a disciplinary performance of professional expertise and competitive research relations. For the members of the Tudor and Stuart Club, the Renaissance was constructed as an imaginary landscape that contrasted starkly with the smokestacks, warehouses, and office buildings on the dim Baltimore horizon. Ideologically, the Renaissance seemed to offer something of a never-never land for the lover of Renaissance poetics to advance among the ranks of a slowly developing institutional hierarchy, with its growing disciplinary procedures, while at the same time dream of fountains and clipped yews. In this peculiar process of reification the Renaissance takes on all of its qualities in relation to the very real feelings of the contemporary critic. It is out of the present that the past becomes defined: what is modern is not Renaissance. More importantly, what is modern can only be defined in terms of what has been lost. The ideological superstructure that is constructed around the master narrative of "Renaissance order-Modern disorder" is one that produces subjects who see history as a series of man's failures to transcend the present. Someone got it wrong along the way, so the best we can do in the world today is retrieve and celebrate what it is we lost from this distantly abstract and spiritual life and set it into play. As such the Renaissance literary specialist sees himself the minister of Western Culture's lost youth, and his research is visualized in the face of contemporary social reality as a green shade of repose where we can be universally happy maybe one more time.

Notes

1. See Wallace Ferguson. *The Renaissance in Historical Thought; Five Centuries of Interpretation,* especially chapter 6, "Conflicting Trends and the Beginning of a Periodic Concept," 133–78.

2. See Barrie Bullen, "The Source and Devlopment of the Idea of the Renaissance in Early Nineteenth-Century French Criticism."

3. Kollof noted in Ferguson 150. For a summary of the twentieth-century period debates see William Kerrigan and Gordon Bradan's *The Idea of the Renaissance.*

4. Gieryn has argued that disciplines regularly engage in "boundary-work," the production of arguments and strategies to justify, maintain, and construct the divisions of knowledge. See also Graff's argument about the "period coverage system" as it applies to the profession of English Literature.

5. Noted in Veysey as: Remsen, "Original Research," *Association of Collegiate Alumnae, Publications,* ser. 3, 1903, 24–25.

6. Osler gave to Johns Hopkins "securities, realizing between $1500 and $2000 a year" (French 316).

7. A brief history of the foundation of the Tudor and Stuart Club can be found at: http://musicbox.mse.jhu.edu:8000/inv/rg15-100.txt:

8. Gilman's "novel experiment" in a research university exemplifies the manner in which distinct forms of knowledge production were isolated. In a letter to G. J. Brush (1875), Gilman explains that the usual "college machinery of classes, commencements etc may be dispensed with: that each head of a great department, with his associates in that department—say of mathematics, or of Language or of Chemistry or of History, etc. shall be as far as possible from the interference of other heads of departments, & shall determine what scholars he will receive & how he will teach them" (Veysey 160). While delegating the authority over each discipline to respective departments, Gilman also made sure that a moral idealism drove each student within the different fields to individual projects: "[T]here will be no fetters," he said in an address to the Society of Friends (1877), "placed upon those who are seeking truth" (Veysey 163).

9. Four of them were fellow classmates in graduate school at Hopkins (DuBois, Hooker, Lyons, and Norris). Norris is a key figure, because he is the only member of the editorial board who received entire schooling at Hopkins (A.B. 1921, and Ph.D. 1932). He became the managing editor of the journal. Two co-founders of *ELH,* Dubois and Hooker, went through school together: both were undergraduates at Union College, both received A.M. at Syracuse, where they were instructors between 1924–1928. All of the original editors were born between 1899 and 1904 (which means they would have been between twelve to seventeen years old at the outset of World War I).

Works Cited

Allen, Don Cameron. "Style and Certitude." *ELH* 15:3 (1948): 167–75.

Bledstein, Burton. *The Culture of Professionalism: The Middle Class and the Development of Higher Education in America.* New York: Norton, 1978.

Bullen, Barrie. "The Source and Development of the Idea of the Renaissance in Early Nineteenth-Century French Criticism." *Modern Language Review* 76 (1981): 311–22.

Burckhardt, Jacob. *The Civilization of the Renaissance in Italy.* Trans. S.G.C. Middlemore. New York: Harper and Row, 1929.

de Grazia, Margreta. "World Pictures, Modern Periods, and the Early Stage." *A New History of Early English Drama.* Ed. John D. Cox and David Scott Kaston. New York: Columbia UP, 1997.

ELH. Baltimore: Johns Hopkins Press, 1934–1987.

Fekete, John. *The Critical Twilight : Explorations in the Ideology of Anglo American Literary Theory from Eliot to McLuhan.* Boston: Routledge, 1977.

Ferguson, Wallace. *The Renaissance in Historical Thought; Five Centuries of Interpretation.* Boston: Houghton Mifflin, 1948

Foucault, Michel. *Discipline and Punish: The Birth of the Prison.* New York: Vintage, 1979.

———. "Nietzsche, Genealogy, History." *The Foucault Reader.* Ed. Paul Rabinow. New York: Pantheon, 1984.

French, John C. *A History of the University Founded by Johns Hopkins.* Baltimore: Johns Hopkins Press, 1946.

Gieryn, Thomas F. "Boundary-Work and the Demarcation of Science from Non-Science: Strains and Interests in Professional Ideologies of Scientists." *American Sociological Review* 48: 8 (1983): 781–95.

Graff, Gerald. *Professing Literature: An Institutional History.* Chicago: U of Chicago P, 1987.

Greenblatt, Stephen. *Renaissance Self-Fashioning.* Berkeley: U of California P, 1979.

Kerrigan, William, and Gordon Braden. *The Idea of the Renaissance.* Baltimore: Johns Hopkins UP, 1989.

Miles, L. Wardlaw. "Shakespeare's Old Men." *ELH* 7:4 (1940): 286–99.

Prior, Moody. "The Thought of Hamlet and the Modern Temper." *ELH* 15:4 (1948): 261–85.

Tudor and Stuart Club Archives. http://musicbox.mse.jhu.edu:8000/inv/rg15–100.txt nv/rg15–100.txt

Veysey, Laurence. *The Emergence of the American University.* Chicago: U of Chicago P, 1970.

Five

Emerson and the Shape of American Literature

David R. Shumway

Emerson's influence, from his day until ours, had helped to account for what I would call the American difference in literature, not only in our poetry and criticism, but even in our novels and stories.
—Harold Bloom, "Mr. America"

It may be that the canon wars are largely a thing of the past.[1] The canon is, of course, always under revision, but it was only in the 1970s and later that the idea of the canon came under attack, while at the same time women and minorities were for the first time taken seriously as candidates for canonization. As a result, the canon has changed significantly. It now includes authors whom it previously excluded, and we don't think of those included with quite the same reverence as we once did. The discussion of the canon, however, has remained mainly an issue of who is included and who is excluded. Canons, or traditions as they were uncritically named in previous times, are not just lists of books and authors. They are, rather, imaginary spaces that have been mapped. They have centers and peripheries, peaks and valleys, heavily defended boundaries and contested frontiers, and other features that might seem to belong not to literature but to geography. This essay concerns the shape of American literature as the discipline constructed it around a central figure, Ralph Waldo Emerson. My argument is that Emerson's centrality is not a historical claim about the cultural context of nineteenth-century American literature, but rather a post hoc aesthetic judgment offered for reasons that have to do with both the politics of the discipline and the politics of twentieth-century America.

There can be no question of decanonizing Emerson. In the 1920s when Lucy Lockwood Hazard was writing, it was still possible to imagine an American literature in which Emerson might be regarded in the same light as we now regard his New England contemporaries, the schoolroom poets, among whose number he was sometimes previously included. One could argue with Hazard that Emerson's writing is weak and his ideas pernicious, but that argument would only contribute to a discussion that keeps Emerson in the pages of scholarly journals and on the spines of monographs. The truth is that authors drop from the canon because scholars become bored and stop discussing them, and not because of arguments against the authors' work. Were the latter effective, surely Ernest Hemingway would have been driven out by now, and yet he remains only slightly diminished after years of persuasive aesthetic and political critique. There is no sign that Americanists are bored with Emerson, and this paper, though it does not mainly concern Emerson's own writing, will contribute in some small way to his perpetuation.[2] My task is not to displace Emerson, but to understand better what his place has been.

Why did Emerson become the Central Man of American literature? The most obvious answer, actual historical influence, will not do, although Emerson was without a doubt influential. Several other canonical figures are linked to Emerson by personal contact. Clearly Thoreau, whom Emerson supported financially as well as intellectually, must be regarded as his most important disciple; the others are not given much attention these days. Moving away from Concord, all Americanists know that Whitman was "simmering, simmering, simmering" until "Emerson brought me to a boil" (quoted in Trowbridge 367). These two figures are Emerson's contemporaries who clearly *read* what Emerson had written; it is not surprising that the leading American lecturer of his day had some impact beyond his immediate circle. But not all of Emerson's important contemporaries are clearly his literary progeny. Emily Dickinson may be hard to imagine without Emerson's break with Christianity behind her, but according to Cynthia Griffin Wolff, Emerson's influence was limited and late (141–142).[3] And while many since F. O. Matthiessen made the case in *American Renaissance* have interpreted the work of Melville and Hawthorne as a reaction to Emerson, the biographical evidence for this is weak. Emerson probably had some impact on both, yet neither begins with Emerson or against him, but in another place altogether. As fiction writers, they had rather little truck with Emerson.

Bloom and others like him go far beyond Hawthorne and Melville, however, in their assertions of Emerson's influence, and thus claim more than can be sustained by any historical investigation. For them, Emerson seems to exist like a spirit eternally pervading American literature and culture. Bloom claims that Emerson in the last twenty years has returned from a period of obscurity, and Richard Poirier is arguing much the same thing when he describes Emersonianism as being suppressed by an Anglo-American modernism that was "largely, almost exclusively, Eliot's personal triumph" (*Renewal* 22). Poirier's citation of *The Cambridge History of American Literature* as his representation of Emerson's stature earlier in the century reveals the limitation of the point of view he and Bloom share. Both ignore the academic study of American literature, which became a subdiscipline of English in the late 1920s. Here Emerson's centrality in American literature has been a general point of agreement almost as old as the field itself. As Leo Marx puts it, "Emerson, the historical figure whose importance is measured largely by the influence he exerted upon other writers and artists, cannot be said to have 'returned,' for he never departed—never was displaced from the anthologies or university courses" (36). Yet, Marx's characterization of academic study of American literature as historical in this limited sense was no longer accurate even in the

1950s. By then, Matthiessen's conception of the field was dominant, and literary interpreters such as R. W. B. Lewis and Marx himself were defining Emerson's importance. The discipline of American literature has since been rife with theories that go far beyond simple influence, and the assumption of Emerson's centrality has been one of most tenacious, no doubt in part because it has not been recognized as a theory.[4]

Those who attacked Emerson, T. S. Eliot and Allen Tate, for example, though they both influenced the discipline of English, were not part of it. New Critical tastes such as those of Eliot and Tate disapproved of American literature and of Romantic literature, and, as a result, both of these fields were out of fashion for a period during the New Critical ascendancy. But being out of fashion did not keep them from being studied by academics. Literary criticism during the middle of this century found itself divided between academics and intellectuals. While most intellectuals were teaching at universities by the 1950s, many had first made a living as writers and journalists. These literary intellectuals understood themselves as political and social critics. The academics, on the other hand, inherited from philology the values of scholarly disinterest. As a result, they were less openly political. The academics that concern us here are the Americanists who inhabited the English Departments of Southern and Midwestern universities or programs in American Studies; the two major groups of intellectuals are those centered in Nashville and New York. A major point of division is their attitude toward American culture; Americanists embraced it, while the intellectuals rejected it and embraced modernism. Each group developed its own realm of cultural hegemony. The intellectuals dominated the more visible organs of taste, but the Americanists prevailed in the university curriculum, where courses in American literature proliferated during the 1950s.

Between 1945 and 1965, when Bloom claims that Emerson was buried, he was consistently treated as a major figure in American literary history, and by some as the central figure. During this period, changes in American literature textbooks reflect an increasingly narrowed canon. Jane Tompkins points out that anthologies of the late fifties and early sixties reduced the number of authors to as few as eight, and Emerson was included in this one as well as all of the others (188). The MLA published its first review of research and criticism in American literature, *Eight American Authors,* in 1956, and Emerson was among them. The *Literary History of the United States,* edited by Robert Spiller, first appeared in 1948 and it devotes thirty pages to Emerson, more than to any other author except Melville who got thirty-one. The *History* does not advance any explicit theory, but it does claim, in a chapter Spiller himself wrote, that "Emerson emerged as the delegated intellect" of his era and was "spokesman for his time and country" (358). In another place, Spiller calls Emerson, the "recorder of the American mind" and "its poet and its prophet" (*Cycle* 53). The traditionally historical Spiller treats Emerson as central to his own era.

There were much stronger claims made on Emerson's behalf, however. Hyatt Waggoner, in one of the two major studies of the American tradition in poetry, argued that "Emerson is the central figure in American poetry"(xii).[5] Waggoner traces everything of importance back to Emerson, and, following the odd logic of literary tradition making, he even traces the poetry of Puritan Edward Taylor forward to Emerson (16–24). This move is explicitly borrowed from Leslie Fiedler, who argued that "without understanding Emerson" one cannot "appreciate the true meaning of Edward Taylor" (209). Perry Miller's essay "From Edwards to Emerson" has been a more influential exercise of this kind. Miller admits that "there is no organic evolution of ideas from Edwards to Emerson," but he goes on to assert that "certain basic continuities persist in a culture" (184–85). Now the project of defining culture in terms of continuities that exist over vast stretches of time and in spite of significant social change is always risky, but not illegitimate.[6] To be fair to Miller, he is attempting a kind of historical study of influence within a loosely knit but clearly identifiable institution, the New England church in which Emerson trained and briefly served as a minister. But there is also nothing to prevent us from making the usual assumption that New England and America are identical for literary purposes, at least until Mark Twain. Secondly, Emerson is used by Miller as a synecdoche for an entire cultural era. He is, more than a representative man, more than "the Central Man," the man who takes the place of all of his contemporaries.

Paradoxically, the claims for Emerson, if anything, grow stronger in the 1970s and 1980s. Bloom not only credits Emerson with accounting for the American difference in literature, he asserts that "the mind of America perhaps was Emersonian even before Emerson" (178). Besides Bloom, we have Larzer Ziff, who in *Literary Democracy* (18) calls Emerson's "The American Scholar" a declaration of intellectual independence, Irving Howe, who titled his last book, *The American Newness: Culture and Politics in the Age of Emerson*, and Alfred Kazin who in *An American Procession* argues that Emerson founded a national literature. Poirier is more modest in crediting Emerson with beginning one line of American poets including Frost and Stevens, but this modesty does not prevent Poirier from making the bizarre assertion that Emerson is "the father of American pragmatism" (*Renewal* 17).

In asking why Emerson has become the St. Peter of American literary history, the rock upon which all else is built, I am suggesting that the answer cannot be found in literary history or in literary texts themselves. Material historical influence I have already discounted, but Emerson's texts themselves might yield an answer. If, for example, it could be shown that Emerson's ideas were taken up and expressed repeatedly in American culture, then he could serve as an accurate representative whether he was an influence or not. The problem here, however, is that Emerson was not a little mind and was apparently never troubled by consistencies, foolish or otherwise. Thus, the usual problems of agreeing on what an author meant are compounded by the fact that Emerson so often says explicitly contradictory things. Although we are likely to agree that individualism, for example, is important to American culture, and that Emerson at least discusses individualism, we are not likely to agree on what Emerson says about it. Furthermore, Emerson's importance to American culture changes radically if we agree that his individualism is typical, but that individualism itself is pernicious.

Given that Emerson's prominent position in the canon cannot be explained either on the basis of historical influence or on the more general grounds of his having articulated positions that important American writers have shared without Emerson's influence, other explanations are needed. The ones I will offer will fall into three categories. The first is that Emerson fills a place required by the discourse of literary study itself. Secondly, Emerson has been read in such a way that he is taken to represent an ideology, humanism, that has currency in the larger culture as well as literary studies. Finally, claims for Emerson's centrality are in part a function of a struggle for dominance within literary studies and by the discipline within the culture. The creation of a national literary tradition by members of an academic discipline reflects demands from three sources: the discipline's own discourse, the ideologies it shares with the larger culture, and intradisciplinary and extradisciplinary struggles for influence and legitimacy. Although one could say that if Emerson had not existed, the discipline of American literature would have invented him, the more exact account is that it invented him anyway.

Statements that ascribe to Emerson a preeminent position in the American tradition usually use one of three metaphors. Two of them are allusions to Emerson's own work, "representation" and "centrality." Although these metaphors are by no means identical, both imply Eliot's conception of a literary tradition as an organic whole. Claims for Emerson's centrality or representativeness are not characteristic of histories such as Parrington's which do not seek to establish a single tradition, but picture literary history in terms of conflict. Parrington's model was influential, but it was never dominant within the discipline. Matthiessen's became dominant because the shape it gave to the American literary tradition was already familiar, having been borrowed from the discipline of English. American literature scholars needed to constitute a tradition like the one the British had constituted so that they could prove the value of their subject. Their mission was precisely to displace *The Cambridge History of American Literature,* which depicted American writing as a hodgepodge lacking in major figures, with a history that would look like English literary history. The discourse of the new discipline demanded the constitution of a tradition with a center, a literature, rather than a history of an assortment of writings.

Matthiessen's model fit the bill. It is no coincidence that Matthiessen grouped Emerson, Thoreau, Hawthorne, Melville, and Whitman into a "renaissance," since the Renaissance was the peak of English literature. American literature needed to have its geniuses, the equivalents of Chaucer, Spenser, Shakespeare, and Milton, but it also needed to understand them not as mere historical figures, but as transcendent ones. Thus, Matthiessen borrowed Eliot's conception of a literary tradition as an ideal order of eternal objects. Actual historical connections took a back seat to broad cultural tendencies and patterns that Emerson and the other "major figures" were said to embody.

Disciplinary discourse also prescribed the other metaphor by which Emerson is described, "fatherhood." This metaphor in no way contradicts the other two, since fathers in our culture are typically taken to be representative of and central to their families, but it does suggest several other dimensions of the discursive regularity of literary studies. The first should today be obvious to everyone: the founder could not be a mother. The tradition needed to be patrilineal. The odd daughter might be included, but a woman could not be the founder. For example, no history of American poetry traces its founding to Emily Dickinson even though her writing has far more in common with most twentieth-century American poetry than does that of either Emerson or Whitman.[7] Secondly, the metaphor of fatherhood suggests the need for an authority that would justify the aesthetics of American literature. Here I do not mean the authority of Emerson's aesthetic arguments, although the fact that he offered such arguments doubtless made him an impressive candidate. The father of a tradition serves the same function as the father of a child: his name confers legitimacy. Without a father, American literature is the bastard of British literature. It is derivative rather than original. Emerson makes "the American difference in literature" in a way he might have appreciated: merely by giving it his name.

The disciplinary discourse of English is not identical with the ideology of humanism, but they are also not unrelated. The discipline probably presupposes humanism, but the need for a center and a father are broader, or perhaps, deeper than the particular ideology. Nevertheless, their existence as discursive spaces within literary studies is congenial to humanism, by which I mean a conservative cultural politics that covertly endorses the social and political status quo. This humanism, which was the explicit doctrine of the New Humanists, but which was also the position of the New Critics, became the ideology of the tradition of American literature itself. Humanism is the positive side of an ideology that excluded from the canon works by women, blacks, and other minorities. It defined the human on the model of the white and the masculine. Aesthetic success meant writing like a white male aristocrat or burgher (Lauter; Tompkins 123). Humanism is more than an affirmation of race, gender, and class privilege, however; it also affirms the inevitability of hierarchy, the elimination of conflict, and the belief in the higher reality of spiritual values. In short, it affirms that it is better not to seek or demand power, in the process putting the privileges of the powerful beyond challenge (Foucault). The ideology of humanism is expressed both through the narrative by which the tradition is constructed and in its very structure as a canon.

It probably is no surprise these days to hear that the American literary canon embodies an ideology, but if my argument is correct, then we will have to revise

our account of that ideology. Humanism is usually said to have been rejected in favor of formalism by the New Critics. Richard Ruland's influential study, *The Rediscovery of American Literature,* treats humanism as a force that was already spent
by the time Norman Foerster published his symposium, *Humanism and America,*
in 1930 (184). While Ruland admits that humanism's influence persists, he treats
it as marginal. This is true if one regards humanism as an explicit doctrine deriv-
ing from Babbitt and More. But humanism as an ideology is a broader phenomenon.[8] It describes a way of conceiving literature and culture that derives from
Matthew Arnold and which Eliot and other New Critics shared even as they rejected the New Humanist movement because it was moralistic and antireligious.
Thus, the opposition of the New Humanism and the New Criticism was epiphe-
nomenal. The New Criticism "won" but humanism survived, not as a movement,
but as an ideology expressed in the way the narrative of American literary history
was written. That narrative, as told by many and varied voices, usually revolves
around the figure of Emerson and the ideas of transcendentalism, and the readings
given Emerson typically constitute him as a humanist. In reading Emerson as a humanist and building the American tradition on his shoulders, American literary
scholarship continued to be governed by humanism, even as it has accepted as
canonical works that might be read as directly opposed to humanism.

Norman Foerster was one of those who helped to begin the academic field
of American literature. He edited *The Reinterpretation of American Literature* under the auspices of the newly formed American Literature Section of MLA—of
which Foerster was one of the founders—a self-described manifesto advocating the
study of American literature. Foerster's own essay in the volume describes the now
familiar categories in terms of which American literary history has come to be written: Puritanism, the Frontier spirit, Romanticism, and Realism ("Factors"). But
Foerster was also a member of the second generation of New Humanists, and he
provides us with an explicit reading of Emerson as a humanist.

Foerster's account of the basic principles of humanism, articulated in the last
chapter of *American Criticism,* shows us humanism for what it is, an elaborate apol-
ogy for the social and intellectual status quo (235–52). Platonism, according to
Foerster, is the foundation of humanism. It cannot do without the belief in eternal, extrascientific truth, and nature is its central concept, completely displacing
the alternative concept, custom or convention. Humanist metaphysics are based
on a dualism of spirit and nature resulting in a denial of the significance of conflicts
of all kinds. For unlike Hegelian dialectics, the humanist dualism assumes that
spirit and its opposite are locked in an eternal struggle; progress and synthesis are
not possible. The goal of knowledge is harmony; knowledge of eternal truths serves
to allow acceptance of the universe, as Margaret Fuller is praised for finally coming round to. Such knowledge is, humanism acknowledges, not for everyone. It is
intended for the *aristoi,* the natural aristocrats who ideally should be those with
power. Humanism is antidemocratic; the ideal of equality violates human nature.

"Democracy is only a means to an end—the good life. But what is the good life? Democracy, whether Jeffersonian or Jacksonian, has never given this question a firmly spiritual answer" (*University* 28–29). Only the tradition can help us arrive at such an answer.

In works devoted both to American literature and to humanism, Foerster invokes Emerson explicitly as a humanist writer. Of course, Foerster acknowledges that Emerson's thought is not pure, that he is sometimes a romantic, sometimes seeming too much the monist. Nevertheless, in *Nature in American Literature*, Foerster concludes that Emerson was a "true descendant of the Puritans" who was assured of "'the eternal distinction between the soul and the world' and the ineluctable authority of moral sentiment" (68). Emerson is read explicitly as a dualist and as a moralist, a keeper of standards. In *American Criticism*, Emerson is approvingly called a "traditional critic," and Foerster claims that the New Humanism displays a critical attitude toward contemporary culture that can be traced back to Emerson and Lowell. Elsewhere, Foerster includes Emerson with people such as Arnold and Babbitt whom he regards as "critics of the foundations of the whole of our culture" ("Esthetic Judgment" 66). Emerson, then, is the father of what Foerster most values in American literature. The value placed on Emerson and transcendentalism stems from its controlling, pacifying influence, its affirmation of hierarchy, and its preservation of the tradition. While often presented as a rebellious movement, transcendentalism according to Foerster's interpretation is conservative. Its central role in American literary history can in light of this be understood as having filled a need for a native, cultural elite, but one that presented itself in the rhetoric of radical individualism and democracy.

I am not claiming that Foerster is responsible for the canon, or for Emerson's central place in it. Foerster is of interest because his own aesthetics did not prevent him from articulating positions others shared, but did not explicitly state. He is willing to say he likes Emerson because he agrees with him, where other critics refrain from commenting on Emerson's beliefs. Furthermore, Foerster's own carving up of American literary history, presented in "Factors in Literary History," remained standard through most of the twentieth century. In this essay, he asserts that American romantic writers "virtually created American literature" ("Factors" 32). This myth of origins—which clearly did not itself originate with Foerster—has continued to hold sway, and the writer most often singled out for fatherhood remains Emerson.

It might be argued that although a humanist such as Foerster will understand Emerson in light of his beliefs, what may be less clear is that these principles are present ideologically in American literary scholarship and the humanities disciplines in general. It is true that not everyone who places Emerson in a dominant role within the American tradition would accept Foerster's readings let alone his explicit doctrine. In fact, most would not. But that is just the point. Emerson carries the burden of humanism even when the tradition is constructed from the perspectives of other systems of belief.

Matthiessen's treatment of Emerson illustrates this point. Hardly one to subscribe explicitly to views as antidemocratic as Foerster's, Matthiessen reads Emerson quite differently, emphasizing the formal strengths of Emerson's work and presenting his ideas in the light of twentieth-century thought.[9] Although Matthiessen treats Emerson as the least of five artists the book examines, his title names the period he discusses after Emerson who is its presiding figure. By placing Emerson in this position, Matthiessen assures the presence of humanism in spite of his own beliefs. The way in which Matthiessen deals with Emerson's individualism illustrates this point. Instead of engaging it as a theory that might have social implications, Matthiessen treats it merely as a personal problem. He quotes Emerson as saying that "[t]he individual is the world" and that "[n]othing is sacred but the integrity of your own mind" (Matthiessen 8). Matthiessen was a socialist, and so it is not surprising that he perceives the potential for a destructive individualism here, and that he quotes John MacMurray's *The Philosophy of Communism* to support that perception: "[t]he 'last effort to preserve one's precious self' can lead only to the loss 'of everything that gives selfhood positive significance'" (Matthiessen 8). But Matthiessen goes on to argue that Emerson was saved from this position by his belief that "'the highest revelation is that God is in every man.'" "What stirred [Emerson] most deeply," Matthiessen claims, "was not man's separateness from man, but his capacity to share directly in the divine superabundance" (8). This seems to me to be the quintessential humanist move. The individual is primary, but all individuals are valued. What gets lost here is the reality of conflict made unnecessary by divine superabundance. Matthiessen's treatment of Emerson reflects his treatment of American literature. It reconciles the differences among American writers so as to produce a precisely Emersonian vision of "each and all."[10]

The fact that Emerson is frequently acknowledged to be a rebel might seem to compromise my assertion that he is consistently made to represent humanism. But again, just the opposite can be argued. For Emerson's story is seldom told as that of a successful revolutionary, which within Unitarianism he certainly was, although he had long since left that religion. In the literary histories, however, Emerson is described accurately enough as a rebel who leaves the institution to strike out on his own. His rebellion is not an attempt to gain power, but a renunciation of power. As a rebel, he is pictured as rejecting established forms without seeking to establish his own. Instead, his is a poetics "open to experience. . . . The poet is the student, the receiver of wisdom; not the teacher" (Spiller, *Cycle* 53–54). Thus, Emerson the rebel becomes a humanist model of conduct in that he rejects whatever is crass or materialistic in his age, and goes off on his own to seek eternal truths.

To understand the Emerson "revival" that began in the 1980s, we need to consider in addition to literary discursive practice and humanist ideology, the pol-

itics of academic and cultural influence. In this light, the Emerson "revival" is perhaps better described as the return of the intellectuals to claim their grounds from
the natives. As we will see, it sometimes may also be described as the repressed returning to claim the intellectuals. Howe in his autobiography, *A Margin of Hope,*
describes his own return to Emerson. He and other New York intellectuals in the
Partisan Review circle of the 1940s and 1950s were "indifferent to and ignorant of
Perry Miller's version of American literary history" and had "abandoned Emerson
even before encountering him" (142, 143). But Howe renounces his youthful errors and gives witness to his conversion, his return to the American fold. Where
once Emersonianism seemed pale, now Howe "knows better," and "recognizes
that, except for Edith Wharton, every major American writer bears the stamp of
Emerson. To evade Emerson was to evade both America and its literature. . . .
[A]lways, the spirit of Emerson kept looming over our culture" (*Margin* 143). Actually, Howe's return represents the homecoming of a second group of intellectuals, many New Critics having already arrived. For example, Cleanth Brooks and
Robert Penn Warren demonstrated their affiliation to the national literature in the
enormous, lavishly introduced anthology they edited with R. W. B. Lewis, *American Literature: The Makers and the Making,* published in 1973. The return of the
intellectuals needs to be understood, not as a change in their aesthetics, but as an
attempt to extend those aesthetics into new fields. But, nevertheless, their taking
up of the American tradition does change them. This does not need to be explained
in terms of anything intrinsic to American literature—it has been read otherwise—
but because the American literature they come to is the university's American literature, and because the intellectuals themselves have become the university's.[11]

Thus, in *The American Newness,* Emerson plays the same humanist role as
he did in the earlier histories where his centrality was invoked. Howe, a lifelong
socialist and the editor of *Dissent,* capitulates to Emerson's individualism even as
he shows an awareness of its inadequacy. As Leo Marx had pointed out, to ask as
Howe does, "Is there not something unsatisfying in that view of human experience
which proposes an all-but-absolute self-sufficiency of each individual and makes
self-reliance the primary value?" is to concede the point, to make judgment of this
issue dangerously subjective (Marx, "A Visit" 36–37, quoting Howe, *American
Newness*). More importantly perhaps, Howe treats Emerson as achieving an almost
Christ-like success in his failure. To have lost power is to have gained it. Howe is
far more moderate in his claims for Emerson, however, than another New York intellectual, Alfred Kazin. Kazin, of course, had always written about American literature and had always been less political than Howe, so his treatment of Emerson
is less surprising. We are also less surprised that Kazin's *An American Procession* is
more typically humanist given the powerfully meliorative humanism of *A Walker
in the City.* In *An American Procession,* we get another version of the now familiar
formulation that Emerson "founded a national literature" (xiii). Kazin's procession—19 men, 1 woman, and 0 minorities—is suffused with humanist ideology,

and Emerson's role is clearly indicated when Kazin asserts that it was Emerson's project to overcome all skepticism (41). It is the skepticism of science that humanism cannot tolerate.

Given this understanding of humanism, it would seem Harold Bloom's reading of Emerson should escape its grasp: Bloom reads Emerson's work as Gnosis, that is, as a kind of skepticism. This is of a piece with a yet more stunning move wherein Bloom announces that "deconstructing any discourse by Ralph Waldo Emerson would be a hopeless enterprise" all the while he has been performing just such an operation (*Agon* 156). Thus in *Nature*, "everything is a cheerful error" (*Agon* 157). Bloom seems to forget, here, that deconstruction claims that texts are always already deconstructed, and this slip allows Bloom to celebrate Emerson as a grand exception and to locate the source of his reading *in* the text and not in the will to power of the interpreter, as Bloom's own theory demands. This bit of legerdemain comes from one who claims to treat Emerson as a Nietzschean. Quoting Bartlett Giammatti to the effect that Emerson gave us a theory of power freed from all moral limitations, Bloom attributes to Emerson Nietzschean genealogy. But there is nothing in Bloom's Emerson that looks like such a genealogy. In typical humanist fashion, he takes all of the teeth out of amoral power: "The will to power in Emerson as afterward in Nietzsche is reactive rather than active, receptive rather than rapacious, which is to say that it is the will to interpretation" ("Mr. America" 22). Emerson finally teaches us nothing except to be individual *readers.* Thus, Bloom laments that what he perceives as the decline of this species: "[S]o now we get academic covens akin to what Emerson himself called 'philanthropic meetings and holy hurrahs,' for which read now Marxist literary groups and Lacanian theory circles" ("Mr. America" 23). Agon is apparently only interesting if it involves a good old duking it out in the ring with one's peer, team sports being distinctly lower class. Bloom's humanism is more strongly elitist and less meliorative than that of most Americanists. For example, he offers this contribution to the theory of human nature: "*[C]ontra* Foucault the human mind cannot conceive of interpretive power without the king" ("Mr. America" 23). Thus, Bloom responds to the elitist Emerson where Matthiessen responded to the democratic Emerson, but both Emersons serve humanist ends.

Bloom's return to Emerson has a different genealogy than that of the New York or Nashville intellectuals. Bloom and Poirier are not intellectuals; they have never had a base outside of the academy and are not openly political.[12] But they have identified themselves with the intellectuals' internationalism and their construction of a modernist, rather than nationalist, canon. Bloom and Poirier mirror Howe and Kazin almost perfectly here, since Poirier has consistently written about American literature, where Bloom has come to it more recently. In moving to take American literature away from Americanists, Bloom is much more self-consciously imperialistic than Howe. But he has also already been depoliticized by the humanism of the academy. Bloom and Poirier, whatever their stated differences with Eliot, retain his elitism. Thus, when they move into the new territory, they bring with them a humanism that finds itself immediately at home.[13] However, their rhetoric is unfamiliar, and that inhibits our recognition of the same old stuff. If Bloom's invasion has not resulted in much overt conflict, it may be in part because Americanists no longer saw it as a fight worth joining. Feminist Americanists and others have begun to change the entire field. These feminists are the most important species in a rapidly evolving new family, the university intellectuals, which also includes Afro-Americanists as well as Marxists and other radical theorists.[14] In general, this group has forced literature back into its specific history and material conditions, a reflection of their growing political engagement. It is into the vacuum created by this shift within American literature as a field that we find Bloom rushing to—or being sucked into—proclaim the old news of Emerson's centrality and the lack of history in America.

One question yet needs to be addressed: why Emerson? Couldn't other figures have served his function just as well? Most have in fact been read as humanists; the blackness of Hawthorne and Melville, for example has been treated as spiritual malady and not as critique. Although I have tried to remain neutral here with regard to whether Emerson's thinking is being correctly read as humanist, it is probably obvious that I think much of him can be. On the other hand, I am not convinced that he is necessarily the best fit. Foerster thought Thoreau was, and Paul Elmer More found much to dislike in Emerson (Foerster, *Nature* 119–42; More). Nina Baym, in direct opposition to Spiller's remark that Emerson was "not the teacher," believes that the academic field of American literature chose Emerson as its central man because he was a "teacher. . . . When American literature became an academic field, it was constituted as an assemblage of works to be taught . . . that themselves comprise teachings . . . with moral import. Many if not most literature teachers are clerical in mentality if not in actuality. . . . Emerson ideally represents such a group." Baym is clearly correct in this judgment, which supports the notion that Emerson was put to humanist uses, but she fails to recognize that it is a judgment Americanists would have found difficult to acknowledge. There is, I would argue, a more important reason for Emerson's prominence: Emerson besides being a moral inspirer, a poet, and an essayist was the leader of a literary and intellectual circle. Howe regards this last role as significant, and he gives Emerson credit for several more firsts: "[He was] the first American man of letters. Emerson surrounded himself with intellectuals—free-lance writers, stray and erratic thinkers, heterodox ministers—who created a fragile avant-garde, probably the first this country has ever had" (*American Newness* 15). Baym is right to point out that there were earlier avant-gardes, and other literary circles, but this is irrelevant. The point is not that Howe's vision of Emerson is historically correct, but that it was a widely shared vision. Those who built the field of American literature undoubtedly thought of themselves as teachers, but they often preferred to think of themselves in other terms. They saw themselves first as scholars who produced new knowledge, and later as critics, or men of letters. As Spiller's picture of Emerson as a student reveals, their aesthetics often led them to deny the teaching function of literature, just as their desire for academic legitimacy led them to play down their own roles as teachers. Emerson as a culturally influential man of letters could easily become important to literary academics seeking to establish themselves in a culture that looked on both art and intellectualism with suspicion. By elevating Emerson to cultural preeminence, literary academics were also elevating themselves in a more powerful way than if they had chosen to single out a mere poet or novelist. In fact, one might argue that Emerson's failure as a poet made him all the more suitable for the part. This kind of maneuvering continues today in the form of claims such as Poirier's for Emerson's paternity in American philosophy.

Of course, all intellectual positions serve both ideological and genealogical ends. But it is not clear what other ends are served by talking about literature as if it were an organized body with a center or a family with a progenitor. This is not to say that we will ever be without a canon. Some books will always be read more than others. But we do not need to conceive of American literature as a whole, the product of a single, unified culture. Rather, we would do well to conceive of American literature as a field traversed by many different figures and groups, some of which converge and many of which conflict. It is naive to assume that the name "American" will cease to be a site of struggle as long as the nation survives. But it is not necessary for literary scholars and critics to choose to engage in that struggle. Instead of arguing about what is most American, a more productive discussion might consider the ideological, political, and economic work various literary texts perform as aesthetic and didactic objects. Such a discussion would not impose nor seek a single narrative of American literary history, but welcome partial and competing narratives that tell different stories and different versions. An American literature with many shapes—a shape shifter—would be all the richer.

Notes

I want to thank Nina Baym for her useful commentary on this essay when it was first presented at the American Studies Association, and for kindly providing me with a copy of her remarks. Several short bits of this essay are taken from my book, *Creating American Civilization*.

1. I take John Guillory's rehabilitation of the canon to mark the beginning of this truce.

2. For recent work on Emerson, see Levin, Mitchell, Newfield, Poirier, *Poetry*, and Rowe. Some of this work is critical of Emerson in various degrees, but as a body it testifies to his continued centrality.

3. The assumption of Emerson as a major influence on Dickinson is widely held in spite of scanty evidence to support it. Spiller, *Cycle* 131, illustrates the kind of logic that is often at root of this assumption but not usually revealed when he says apropos of Dick-

inson's retirement from society: "[T]here was more Yankee than Calvinist in her move. Perhaps she had been reading Emerson's recent essay on 'Self-Reliance.' Certainly the faith to which she retired had the skepticism of the Transcendentalist rather than the submission to God's will of the Calvinist."

4. For an account of them as theories, see Reising.

5. For the other, see Pearce, who places Whitman at the center of American poetry.

6. Thus, I would not tar Leo Marx, Henry Nash Smith, or R. W. B. Lewis with the same brush as those who have built the canon around Emerson. For one thing, their work is often explicitly critical of the cultural patterns they describe. In fact, the exposure and analysis of cultural myths is at least a necessary prerequisite for a critique of American ideology. Secondly, these critics connect the work of canonical figures to their noncanonical contemporaries.

7. Since Dickinson's poetry was largely suppressed until the twentieth century, she could not have been an actual historical influence on the poets of the early part of this century. But if claims for actual historical influence help support Emerson's paternity, the importance of such devices as "the Emersonian spirit," which can preexist the man himself, show that arguments for Dickinson as founder could have been offered.

8. The humanist ideology I discuss here is not identical with what the religious right calls "secular humanism," although it is obviously related to this older and broader set of assumptions.

9. Yet Matthiessen may have agreed more with Foerster's humanism than the former's politics suggest would be possible. Matthiessen cites Foerster's treatment of Emerson's theory of expression in *American Criticism* as "a thorough summary" (5, n. 1).

10. Arac and Pease agree that *American Renaissance* "reconciles" (Arac) and devises a "national consensus" (Pease) thereby suppressing conflict. But both connect Matthiessen's position too closely to the events surrounding World War II, and not enough to the humanism that was central to his discipline. Pease credits Emersonian individualism with a far bigger role than it actually has in *American Renaissance*.

11. See Jacoby, who convincingly demonstrates this point, despite his romanticized view of earlier generations of independent intellectuals.

12. Cf. Reising, who in discussing Poirier's *A World Elsewhere* asserts that "No other recent theorist of American literature (since, perhaps Hicks and Parrington) has defined that literature in such political and ethically progressive terms" (189). But Reising goes on to acknowledge that Poirier "devalue[s] social being" (198). I consider Poirier apolitical because his work lacks engagement in the social issues one finds in the *Fugitive* critics on the right, Hicks and Parrington on the left, or even middle-of-the-roaders such as Trilling.

13. We might even say that Bloom follows Poirier into the American field defined by Emersonianism, since Emerson was a major—not to say central—figure in *A World Elsewhere*.

14. It would be impossible to list all of the scholars and works that have contributed to the creation of a new conception of American literature. See Shumway 345–59, for a still too brief overview.

Works Cited

Arac, Jonathan. "F. O. Matthiessen: Authorizing the American Renaissance." *The American Renaissance Reconsidered.* Selected Papers of the English Institute, 1982–83, New Series, no. 9. Ed. Walter Benn Michaels and Donald E. Pease. Baltimore: Johns Hopkins UP, 1985. 90–112.

Baym, Nina. "Creating Academic Literary Culture in America." Comment delivered at the American Studies Association Convention. New York, November 24, 1987.

Bloom, Harold. *Agon: Towards a Theory of Revisionism.* New York: Oxford UP, 1982.

———. "Mr. America." *The New York Review of Books* (November 22, 1984): 23.

Fiedler, Leslie. *Waiting for the End.* New York: Stein, 1964.

Foerster, Norman. *The American State University: Its Relation to Democracy.* Chapel Hill: U of North Carolina P, 1937.

———. "The Esthetic Judgment and the Ethical Judgment." *The Intent of the Critic.* Edmund Wilson et al. Princeton: Princeton UP, 1941.

———. *Nature in American Literature: Studies in the Modern View of Nature.* New York: Russell, 1958. Rpt. of 1923 edition.

———. "Factors in American Literary History." *The Reinterpretation of American Literature.* Ed. Foerster. New York: Russell, 1959. Rpt. of 1929 edition.

———. *American Criticism: A Study of Literary Theory from Poe to the Present.* New York: Russell, 1962. Rpt. of 1928 edition.

Foucault, Michel. "Revolutionary Action: 'Until Now.'" *Language, Counter-Memory, Practice.* Ed. Donald F. Bouchard. Trans. Bouchard and Sherry Simon. Ithaca: Cornell UP, 1977.

Guillory, John. *Cultural Capital: The Problem of Literary Canon Formation.* Chicago: U of Chicago P, 1993.

Hazard, Lucy Lockwood. *The Frontier in American Literature.* New York: Crowell, 1927.

Howe, Irving. *A Margin of Hope.* New York: Harcourt, 1982.

———. *The American Newness: Culture and Politics in the Age of Emerson.* Cambridge: Harvard UP, 1986.

Jacoby, Russell. *The Last Intellectuals: American Culture in the Age of Academe.* New York: Basic, 1987.

Kazin, Alfred. *An American Procession.* New York: Knopf, 1984.

Lauter, Paul. "Race and Gender in the Shaping of the American Literary Canon: A Case Study from the Twenties." *Feminist Studies* 9 (Fall 1983): 435–63.

Levin, Jonathan. *The Poetics of Transition: Emerson, Pragmatism, and American Literary Modernism.* Durham: Duke UP, 1999.

Lewis, R. W. B. *The American Adam.* Chicago: U of Chicago P, 1955.

Marx, Leo. *The Machine in the Garden.* New York: Oxford UP, 1964.

———. "A Visit to Mr. America." *The New York Review of Books* (March 12, 1987): 36.

Matthiessen, F. O. *American Renaissance: Art and Expression in the Age of Emerson and Whitman.* New York: Oxford UP, 1941.

Miller, Perry. *Errand into the Wilderness.* Cambridge: Harvard UP, 1956.

Mitchell, Charles E. *Individualism and Its Discontents: Appropriations of Emerson, 1880–1950.* Amherst: U of Massachusetts P, 1997.

More, Paul Elmer. "Emerson." *The Cambridge History of American Literature,* Vol. 1. Ed. William Peterfield Trent et al. New York: Putnam, 1917. 348–62.

Newfield, Christopher. *The Emerson Effect: Individualism and Submission in America.* Chicago: U of Chicago P, 1996.

Parrington, Vernon Louis. *Main Currents in American Thought.* 3 Vols. New York: Harcourt, 1927–1930.

Pearce, Roy Harvey. *The Continuity of American Poetry.* Princeton: Princeton UP, 1961.

Pease, Donald E. "*Moby Dick* and the Cold War." *The American Renaissance Reconsidered,* 113–55.

Poirier, Richard. *A World Elsewhere: The Place of Style in American Literature.* New York: Oxford UP, 1966.

———. *The Renewal of Literature: Emersonian Reflections.* New York: Random, 1987.

———. *Poetry and Pragmatism.* Cambridge: Harvard UP, 1992.

Rowe, John Carlos. *At Emerson's Tomb: The Politics of Classic American Literature.* New York: Columbia UP, 1997.

Reising, Russell. *The Unusable Past: Theory and the Study of American Literature.* New York: Methuen, 1986.

Ruland, Richard. *The Rediscovery of American Literature: The Premises of Critical Taste, 1900–1940.* Cambridge: Harvard UP, 1967.

Shumway, David R. *Creating American Civilization: A Genealogy of American Literature as an Academic Discipline.* Minneapolis: U of Minnesota P, 1994.

Smith, Henry Nash. *Virgin Land: The American West as Symbol and Myth.* Cambridge: Harvard UP, 1950.

Spiller, Robert E. *The Cycle of American Literature.* New York: Signet, 1955.

Spiller, Robert E., et al., eds. *Literary History of the United States,* Vol. 1. New York: Macmillan, 1948.

Stoval, Floyd, ed. *Eight American Authors: A Review of Research and Criticism.* New York: MLA, 1956.

Tompkins, Jane. *Sensational Designs: The Cultural Work of American Fiction 1790–1860.* New York: Oxford UP, 1985.

Trowbridge, J. T. *My Own Story: With Recollections of Noted Persons.* Boston: Houghton Mifflin, 1903.

Waggoner, Hyatt. *American Poets: From the Puritans to the Present.* Boston: Houghton, 1968.

Wolff, Cynthia Griffin. *Emily Dickinson.* New York: Knopf, 1986.

Ziff, Larzer. *Literary Democracy: The Declaration of Cultural Independence in America.* New York: Viking, 1981.

Six

The Posttheory Generation

Jeffrey Williams

My Ge-Ge-Generation

We're in a strange place. We—that is, those in the post-sixties but pre–Gen X generation, and who work in the profession of literature—find ourselves facing a confused and ambivalent scene of literary studies, defined for the most part by two looming factors: first, what seems to be the dispersion or breakdown of the paradigm of Theory;[1] and second, a drastically reconfigured job market, pinched in the vise of a restructured and downsizing university.[2] It is the interrelation of these two factors that distinctively marks what I'll call the "Posttheory Generation," the generation of intellectual workers who have entered the literary field and attained professional positions in the late 1980s and through the '90s.[3]

I would normally relish this kind of manifesto for my generation, but, while heady, it taps into a series of stock tropes and clichés that do not quite accurately represent our situation. It carries with it associations of adolescent rebellion (à la James Dean or Jerry Rubin), providing a cheap shot of Oedipal displacement, clearing space to announce oneself and one's own place in the field. However, this change is not something that we have announced or precipitated, but that has befallen us. Further, it invokes tropes of natural biological cycles that have questionable application to the institutional structures of intellectual work. And it also takes a glib note from advertising, promoting the new-and-improved way of doing things, the latest product on the shelf of literary study.

I use "generation" in an alternate sense, beyond simply an age label or product advertisement, and beyond staging a faux-rebellion I'm fixed to win. I take it as an institutional demarcation, recording and diagnosing our institutional formation. Academic intellectuals are formed by similar, historically specific institutional circumstances and thus exhibit similar traits, which generate distinctive groupings that one might call "generations." Those circumstances encode professional modes, manners, discourses, concerns, and protocols as decisively as DNA. A generation might be fixed by general coordinates such as the extant critical conversation and time period, the state of the professional field, and the state of the university, as well as local coordinates such as institutional affiliation, professional connections, and mentors and teachers. Local generational markers—bluntly, who went where, when, and worked with whom—are usually consigned to trivial or peripheral status, circulated by gossip, gleaned in book acknowledgments or blurbs or picked up in anecdotes ("I played basketball with Stanley Fish, and he said . . ."), but in fact very literally distinguish those academics and have distinctive force in constructing and disseminating specific methods and practices and in maintaining hierarchical relations.[4]

They mark those coming into the profession with a set of family resemblances and a particular lineage. More general contextual factors such as the constitution of the professional field and the social function and value of the university also distinguish particular academic generations, defining the role of academic intellectuals—as teachers as opposed to researchers, as bespectacled bookworms as opposed to "public intellectuals," or as men of letters as opposed to new age, techno-cultural theorists. As Regis Debray points out, the role of the intellectual has shifted significantly through the course of this century, from teacher to writer to celebrity. Transposing Debray's formulation to the present American lit crit scene, one might say that the model of the literary intellectual has migrated from teacher and scholar to master critic or theorist to culture critic and intellectual celebrity—for instance, from R. S. Crane to Paul de Man to Andrew Ross or bell hooks.[5] To put this another way, the apex of an academic-intellectual career has shifted from teacher to researcher to star.

In some ways, this sense of generation spins off Bourdieu's seminal concept, the *habitus,* which he defines as "a system of dispositions common to all products of the same conditionings" ("Structures" 59). What you learn in graduate school, perhaps more formatively than purported texts or canons of knowledge, is precisely this system of dispositions, this code of appropriate professional behavior, expectation, and evaluation. One might summarize it under the rubric of tenure—that is, the protocols and professional assumptions that circulate around the spectral image of tenure, that enforce a certain standard of behavior, mode and choice of work, and mindset for those employed in academic departments.[6]

However, within the generative structure of the professional habitus, there occurs a range of differentiation of professional position and purview. For instance, senior colleagues entering literature departments post-World War II encountered and were formed by entirely different professional pressures, expectations, and goals than those entering c. 1990. While that historically particular grouping—for the most part those schooled under the G.I. Bill and landing jobs during the mushrooming of state universities—shares the same habitus and professional field as more recent generations, their professional expectations and horizon differ precipitously from those who entered the profession through the sixties and seventies, and farther still from those who have entered the profession through the late eighties and nineties. Given the exponential increase in research requirements, in the sheer number of publications to get tenure or even to land a job, it hardly seems as if that earlier generation is in the same profession from the standpoint of members of the Posttheory Generation.

I use the slightly ungainly term *posttheory* to define this generation to indicate both its position in the history of critical practices—its seeming lateness on the scene, coming after the monumental successes and ensuing establishment of the great Theories—and its position in the contemporary university, coming after the post-Fordist reconfiguration of the university and in the midst of a job-traumatized field.[7] Thus "posttheory" indicates the institutional position and prospect of this generation, both as a by-now established practice and institutional form, and as a shorthand for the historical coordinates of the late-twentieth-century profession of literature. Theory is not only a mode of discourse or the philosophical tenets of critical commentary, but designates what happened in and to the institution of literature roughly between 1970 and 1990. By extension, I suppose one could depict the sixties generation that came to the academy—so-called "tenured radicals"—as "The Theory Generation," since that generation marks the absorption of theory into the academy and the complex of changes signaled by the advent of Theory.[8]

The Way It Was

Once upon a time, in the halcyon days after World War II, it was a comfortable— one imagines pipe-smoking, tweed-wearing, sherry-drinking—profession. A beneficiary of the post–World War II welfare state, the profession stood witness to the PMC (the professional-managerial class) dream, an updated version of the good old American Dream. One could get a decent, federally subsidized education, bank a bit of cultural capital, and then be granted a genteel, manicured-lawn, middle-class life. Jobs were plentiful, and one only needed to be a live (white, male) body, with basic motor functions, to get an academic position through the '50s and '60s. Lest this seem too much of an exaggeration, George Levine recalls of his generation: "We were less troubled in the fifties at the very moment when English and higher education were experiencing their most rapid and rich expansions ever. When I got my degree from the University of Minnesota, *almost all my colleagues, no matter how dumb they were, got at least three job offers*" (43; my italics). The university was a booming business, both ideologically and materially, fueling the Fordist dream as a subsidiary venture of the military-industrial complex.

Wayne Booth, in a reminiscence of his several decades in the profession featured in *PMLA*, gives another revealing view of what it was like to work in that halcyon once-upon-a-time. He tells a remarkable story about his job search, which prompted him to move from an untenured job at Haverford to a tenured one at Earlham:

> When I talked with the president of Earlham about becoming head of the English department [after three years at Haverford], I said, "I assume this will include tenure?"
> "Of course," he replied, and the subject left my mind for several years . . . . Would that all young teachers could have the gift of those "several years"—I honestly cannot remember how many—to settle in, relax, think,

plan without pressure, and then, if and only if they really want to, produce a repeatedly revised and rethought book, as I released *The Rhetoric of Fiction* at age forty. I *chose* to write that book, taking seven years to make all the choices it entailed—not counting the years that went into the dissertation, fragments of which survived in the book. (946)

In light of the current job crisis and the meaner-leaner years of the retraction of the welfare state, this story now seems vaguely fantastical, but it succinctly characterizes the experience of the earlier generation. Due to the expansion of universities—state universities, such as the SUNY or California system, as well as private universities, which also benefited greatly during this period—through the massive infusion of research and development money in the wake of wartime industrial expansion and the carryover into Cold War growth, there was an extraordinarily high demand for new Ph.D.s, and there was a disproportionately high number of jobs for prospective candidates. Booth, to his credit, tells this story not as a nostalgic reminiscence but as an occasion to launch a series of proposals to remedy the fallout from present academic speed-up and the draconian pressure to publish.

Beyond what it tells about the job market, what is also revealing about this story is the effect it had on his research, or rather the model of research that is promulgated by the institutional conditions he describes. First, there is no dire necessity to publish; Booth's project is not regulated by the timeline of tenure, but the result of leisurely reflection. In other words, it is relatively disinterested since it is detached from the exigencies of employment—in blunt terms, from fear of losing a job. Further, the kind of big book that Booth wrote—that was a large-scale, comprehensive statement on novels, holding a certain provenance over the field and staying in print for nearly thirty years—is hardly feasible or practicable under current professional conditions, particularly not for junior faculty. The elite model in literary research was this kind of big book, which made a comprehensive statement on a genre, or on a literary period, or on a literary problem, and which assumed an encyclopedic range of literary reference and a definitive span of investigation. Think of the various influential critical books of the period—M. H. Abrams's *The Mirror and the Lamp,* Angus Fletcher's *Allegory,* D. W. Robertson's *Preface to Chaucer,* and so on—which stood as standardbearers for decades.

Under current conditions of productivity, it goes almost without saying that someone from the Posttheory Generation could never take ten or fifteen years to finish a book, particularly a first book, and expect to keep his or her job. Rather, the commonplace rule of the game is that one needs at least one book (and frequently a second on the way) to get tenure, as well as articles, conference presentations, and other recognizable if token markers of professional accreditation. My point here is that the exigencies of the job market influence if not determine the nature of legitimate and appropriate research (to more obviously sexy, which is to say marketable, topics, such as crossdressing, rather than Chaucer's sources) and the scope and depth of a research project (now the typical book is usually a compendium of essays, rather than a monograph on, say, Herbert). This accelerated cycle of production ups the ante on publications and reputation, again particularly for the untenured but also applying to those with it, since you need to maintain a certain level of "visibility"—one's name frequently and prominently attached to articles and books—to maintain standing.

Further, given the current cycle of intense competition and by extension overproduction of scholarship, there is a parallel speed-up of reception and effect—of intellectual shelf-life and durability. Contemporary literary scholarship hardly exists for the ages but is extraordinarily transitory and impermanent, with an average life expectancy or relevance of only a few years. This in turn influences the cycling of critical approaches and theoretical models, which move through the scene within a few years (for instance, whatever happened to reader response? and even now, one hears of "post-Butler" work). In a certain determinative sense, these changes are linked to the increasing capitalization of academic publishing; as financially pinched universities cut subsidies and other forms of support (such as office space), university presses are under a great deal more pressure to publish profit-making titles in place of the traditional scholarly staple, the (subsidized) monograph. They take their model from commercial presses, emulating the early nineties zenith of Routledge with its array of sexily jacketed, trendsetting, and profit-making books in theory and cultural studies, books that might not stay in print for more than three or four years, after their returns fall below margin. Disposability has become the rule rather than the exception, spurred by structural changes in publishing, such as recent changes in tax depreciation laws, so that presses rarely keep books in print longer than a few years, if that.[9]

The Descent of Theory

The Posttheory Generation is paradoxically positioned, intensely theoretical and versed in theoretical concerns, while at the same time comprising the generation *after* theory, that is, after the theoretical debates and wars of the 1970s among deconstructive, Marxist, feminist, reader-response, psychoanalytic, and structuralist camps that dominated the field and transformed normal practice in literary studies. They pitted themselves against the bogeyman of the New Criticism and more staid "traditional" scholarly methods and approaches. To construct a sort of genealogy, the teachers of those in the Posttheory Generation most likely served in the Theory Wars, so for the Posttheory Generation that war loomed in the background like pictures in a scrapbook, bespeaking excitement and passion but no longer carrying a sense of immediate action or danger.

Those in the Posttheory Generation might have been students of the Theory Gods and Gurus, of the major figures of the advent of the epoch of Theory—people such as Stanley Fish, Hillis Miller, Paul de Man, Edward Said, Elaine Showalter, or Fredric Jameson, all of whom have taught a number of identifiable students—or students of their students—say, of Eve Sedgwick or many other less established figures who had bitten the theory bullet[10]—or finally students of those who simply recognized the professional dominance and exigent force of theory, cynically or conscientiously, so that it became a tacit requirement for a dissertation or an article that it take a theoretical label, naming its theory in the first chapter. In short, the Posttheory Generation was taught to *take theory*—not traditional scholarly methods, not normal practical criticism—*for granted,* and theory in turn provided a threshold stamp of professional value.[11]

In part because of the institutional position and relative symbolic capital of those who espoused the turn to theory, and because of the institutional needs that theory fulfilled, within a number of years theory and its terms, discourses, moves, and mannerisms became established and part of the expected terrain of graduate school training. You learned to talk the theoretical talk to walk the professional walk. By the late eighties, theory was readily dispensed, if not on street corners, in the spate of theory anthologies, primers, book series, ad infinitum (see Williams, "Packaging"). Theory went from rags to riches, from scratching at the window to owner of the mansion; it went from being a technical pursuit, such as bibliographical theory, that only a few people did to attaining canonical status as a graduate school litmus test and as a minimum stamp of acceptability for publication. In short, it became the measure for professional accreditation.

Until about 1940 the dominant professional justification of the field was scholarship—literary history, the residual effects of philology, and so on.[12] The programmatic turn represented by the New Critics and the Chicago Critics occurred precisely in the face of the methods and concerns of the then-normal method—in the sense that Thomas Kuhn uses when he speaks of "normal science"—of historical scholarship. The twin documents, R. S. Crane's polemic for the importance of criticism, "History vs. Criticism in the Study of Literature," and John Crowe Ransom's manifesto for the professional priority of criticism, "Criticism, Inc.," argue explicitly to displace scholarship and announce the epoch of criticism and the practice of close reading. Criticism, in this moment, was envalued as the prestige and "natural" practice of literary studies—rather than history, textual scholarship, literary history, biography, or appreciation.

Following on this, one way to see Paul de Man's more programmatic statements on theory are not as arguments about theoretical issues such as interpretation, allegory, or literariness, but as polemics competing for prestige in and provenance over the literary field. For instance, "The Resistance to Theory" not only argues for the inherent inconsistencies of theoretical practices but rhetorically casts the entrenchment of theory as inevitable and competing pursuits as neurotic symptoms. Its polemic is directed at displacing the previously established practice of close reading for the sake of theory, as well as to elevate deconstruction among the menu of choices of extant theories, particularly history. The early texts of the Theory years—by Derrida, Cixous, Fish, Kolodny, Jameson, and so on—frequently invoke this polemic for the new moment and project of Theory, as well as their particular versions of theory, announcing the grand sweep of their revisions of Western metaphysics, patriarchy, interpretation, the sexist canon, class, and so on. To borrow a term from science referring to largescale projects such as the Supercollider as "Big Science" (see Weinberg), I would call this the moment of "Big Theory," to connote not only the ambitousness of its conceptual sweep, but also the prominence of its institutional placement.

To invoke another sense of generation—analogous to computer generations, to stages of product development rather than biological supercession—the Posttheory Generation registers a shift in mainstream lit crit, from the armature of dense theoretical machinery and formulations to more flexible and streamlined second and third generation theoretical elaborations. More recently, the aggregate practices of cultural studies, lesbigay studies, race studies, and so forth mark a new moment for the critical field, a shift in normal scholarly or critical work to the various and microspecified configurations of "studies" areas, in general from Big Theory to little theories.

Typically, the history of theory is drawn on the lines of the history of philosophy or of ideas, as a grand and usually victorious parade of ideas and discoveries transacted somewhere in the metaphysical ether and concretized in anthologies, primers, and introductory histories as a disembodied series of texts and arguments. However, this other sense of theory underscores its shifting professional-institutional uses and functions. Institutionally, the move to "criticism" and the methods of close reading offered a transferrable technique for the newly expanded, post–World War II university, a technique that was far more amenable and adaptable pedagogically than the older, more cumbersome memory and fact-based model of historical scholarship and philology. Gerald Graff explains in his account of the institution, *Professing Literature:* "As the university increased in size, the need arose for a simplified pedagogy, encouraging the detachment of 'close reading' from . . . cultural purposes . . . [placing] a premium on methods that . . . could easily be replicated" (145). Formalism provided a model of technological efficiency and fulfilled a new institutional need. Its success and entrenchment, in other words, derived from its socioinstitutional situation.

From the late 1960s through the 1970s, in the era of fattened research dollars, Theory provided literature departments with a high-tech research agenda (see Guillory). Rather than the pedagogical need spurred by the massive infusion of new students into the post–World War II university, Theory responded to the research needs of what Clark Kerr called the Multiversity. In the contest of the faculties within the university, a contest not only over the philosophical bases of disciplines but over funding, Theory issued a revamped rationale for the humanities beyond the appreciative and essentially belletristic rationales of previous modes.

(Whatever its technical mastery, the New Criticism was based finally on the apostrophic appreciation of poetry.) In the heyday of structuralism, it reconfigured the humanities as part of the "human sciences" (to recall a common phrase of the time that we don't hear anymore), and thus reassured the intra-institutional prestige of literature departments, particularly in the face of the growing predominance of the social sciences, which adopted largely quantitative and quasi-scientific methods.[13] Literature departments took the position that philosophy historically held as a master discipline, spearheading the "human sciences" in the United States and exporting methods and knowledges to other disciplines.

To bring the Theory story up to date, the recent turn from high theory to cultural criticism, and from characterizing ourselves as theorists to public intellectuals, indicates not so much the "exhaustion" of theory or a revival of social conscience; rather, it responds to a shift in the role of the university, to the defunding of welfare state entitlements such as education, and to imperatives for "accountability" of public institutions. Supplanting the internal rationale that theory provided when the university's public position was relatively assured, cultural criticism projects a more public rationale, putatively shedding the obscurity and internecine interest of Theory. The stakes of this shift are the topic of the last section.

The foregoing narrative of the contemporary critical field is admittedly schematic; to be accurate, different modes of critical practice are ongoing at the same time, some scholars still doing traditional historical research, some bibliographies, some close readings of literary texts, some high theory, and some have been doing "public" criticism all along. Still, the dominance of one particular model over others registers our professional position and its institutional warrants. As Bruce Robbins puts it, "Criticism is our work and its history is in a sense our collective professional autobiography" (780). The dominant image of inquiry and practice offers a self-justifying rationale for the profession and discipline, for its existence and value, and legitimates preferred research agendas—like preferred stock—that fulfill its institutional mandate. Philology now yields low residuals, but cultural criticism and its claims for public relevance yields high.

Trickle-Down Theory

Theory sometimes gets a bad rap, as obfuscating, hyperspecialized, and elitist. In this view, it overwhelms if not ruins literary studies with an obscure, jargon-ridden langauge that hardly anyone can understand. It is taken as a fall away from public accessibility or relevance, not to say from sheer communicability. Ironically, however, there is a different way to see theory: in a certain sense, through the 1970s and 1980s it served as the *lingua franca* of literature programs. Its establishment provided a common language, a common component of education, and a common filter through which to frame discussions in literary studies, so that people divided by the fences of their particular fields of specialization could communicate, particularly in the expanded university that fostered the splitting off and compartmentalization of subfields.[14] One became a hyper-specialized medievalist or Romanticist, most likely dealing with a few figures and from a particular angle (women in Old English poems or the new historical background of Wordsworth poems), rather than a generalist. Theory provided a kind of new generalism, supplanting what had once been the literature curriculum (see Guillory), a bridge over which specialists could communicate across fields. No doubt this common language is a decidedly professional one that functions as a threshold or credentializing device for legitimate critical work—you cannot publish a critical essay without cognizance of theory and the extant "critical conversation," as it is called—but, within its institutional precincts, theory comprised a common channel of communication that hip scholars tuned in to.

Around 1970 or thereabouts, Theory carried a revolutionary vista, to retool the previous mode and manner of criticial practice, to recast the canon, to reconfigure literature programs and university structures, and more generally to transform the retrograde institution of what had been known as Western civilization. As I mentioned earlier, its stated aims, depending on the theoretical camp one joined, were to subvert Western metaphysics, as Derrida rather grandly put it, and its attendant ideologies, such as Enlightenment rationalism, capitalism, and patriarchy. The Big Theory projects of those years—the litany again, deconstruction, feminism, Marxism, reader-response, etc.—were polemical nodal points, aligning those in literary studies in various camps with loyalty to specific theoretical critiques—of epistemology, of sexist oppression, of class oppression, of interpretation, etc. As Terry Eagleton puts it, "I think that back in the seventies we used to suffer from a certain fetishism of method; we used to think that we have to get a certain kind of systematic method right, and this would be *the* way of proceeding" (*Significance of Theory* 76).

If Big Theory functioned as manifesto and declaration of theoretical commitment and a vehicle of contest, as an oppositional device for the Theory Generation to displace previous modes of criticism, the clichéd tenets of philosophy, and the humanistic rationale of the university, for the Posttheory Generation it serves a different purpose, more as an already accepted background, a language that has been assimilated and imbricated in not only the discourse but the possibilities and ways issues are framed in literary studies. The broad commitments entailed by particular theoretical camps and affiliations (say, to the redistribution of wealth or the overthrow of patriarchy) have dispersed to provisional, localized, pragamatic interventions, rather than building to or drawing from a systematic critique. Posttheory, as represented in the broad range of cultural studies and organized by various modalities of identity, and as represented in the array of what Mas'ud Zavarzadeh calls "post-alities," such as post-Marxism or postfeminism, represents the balkanization of the prospects of Theory.

Recent critical work recombines and reworks older theoretical positions, developing less exclusionary, more eclectic and flexible hybrids. For instance, the deconstructive critique of center and margin underwrites the general project of postcolonialism—impossible to think of without the conceptual mediation of the "Other"—at the same time that it also draws on the Marxist critique of power and imperialism. And postcolonial studies are frequently rooted in specific historical instances and places, in local situations rather than global ones. Or the feminist distinction of sex and gender combined with the poststructural battle cry of anti-essentialism has morphed to gender studies and underwrites lesbigay studies. Rather than being unified by a single-minded front and a common cause, the project of feminism, as some senior feminists have lamented, has fractured to multiple feminisms.[15]

In a sense, to paraphrase a Rortian phrase, the current moment registers the breakdown of the "dream of Theory," that theory form a consistent system through which to describe the world. And there is a way in which these current modes of critical practice mark the end or "death" of Theory, as has been proclaimed in a number of places.[16] However, more subtly and deeply, the moves and gestures of theory nonetheless permeate and spectrally inform practice. As Derrida himself puts it in a recent interview, to say deconstruction is dead is akin to saying that Freudian psychoanalysis is dead. As Derrida explains, there is a way in which deconstruction, as an academic fashion, has waned, but "psychoanalysis has taught that the dead—a dead parent, for example—can be more alive for us, more powerful . . . than the living" (qtd. in Stephens 23–24).

Rather than being based on the paradigm of an overruling concept or structure of thought (sex, class, epistemology, and so on), posttheory takes a more adaptive and less contestatory tenor, borrowing from various theoretical camps in a way that previously would have been inconceivable. On the one hand, it is conceptually less dogmatic, but on the other hand, more amorphous than Big Theory. For instance, it seems to have trickled down to the loosely allied foci of study affiliated with or defined by identity politics, the prolific and active individual critical practices of what I'll call identity studies. I would provisionally characterize identity studies along the lines of three axes: (1) sex, those researches defined by sex, by sexual orientation or gender, which encompasses women's studies, gay and lesbian studies, the new and seemingly reactive men's or masculine studies, the more neutral gender studies, transsexual studies and work on cross-dressing (sometimes called genderfuck), pornography studies, and so on, as well as versions of feminism; (2) race, those researches defined by race or ethnicity, such as African American studies, Asian American studies, Chicano studies, Native American studies, the more general ethnic studies, Jewish studies (and attendant sub-study areas, such as Holocaust studies), of late whiteness studies or what is sometimes called "the new abolitionism," and so on; and (3) place, those researches determined by location or national affiliation, such as Caribbean studies, New Zealand studies,

Canadian studies, Pacific Rim studies, and old standbys such as American studies, as well as the more generic postcolonial or subaltern studies.

In this sorting to the various subfields of identity studies, the project of posttheory seems to have shifted to localized units of production, similar to microbreweries, away from large-scale, totalizing concepts such as class, or race or sex for that matter. This shift might be located within the context of larger historical forces (say, the end of communism, claimed by some to consign Marxism to the ash heap) and parallels the rise of contemporary identity politics, which seems to have balkanized the Left and any sort of large scale Left project. However, for the most part the move to posttheory and microspecified uses of theory bespeaks hyperspecialization and differentiation, which mirrors contemporary corporate employment alignments that are "flat" or horizontal rather than vertical. In the way that the workplace has been further cellularized and winnowed out, theory has been flattened and diffused along these axes rather than clustered around an organizing focus. Each interest takes a microtheory of its own, rather than feeding to a larger totality.

There is also an alternative sense in which theory has trickled down or been diffused: because of the intense overproduction of Ph.D.s, those highly trained in elite graduate programs have gotten jobs at places such as East Podunk University or West Jesus State College and therefore carry their professional formation and makeup to schools formerly without significant access to elite professional operations. Academic institutions are organized on a kind of stepladder hierarchy that might be divided into five stages: high elite institutions (Harvard and the rest of the Ivies, Stanford, Chicago, Duke, etc.); elite (eminent programs not quite up to the first rank, such as Emory, or distinguished state universities, such as University of Wisconsin or Rutgers); semi-elite (somewhat distinguished state universities such as SUNY-Binghamton); common (most likely state universities such as Northern Illinois University, as opposed to Illinois proper); and refugee (the Podunk schools).[17] Most often, hiring is done on a kind of status formula, whereby the candidate would most likely be hired at a level lower than where s/he was trained. In other words, someone from Yale might get a job at Michigan, but it almost never works the other way around. In the current job market, those in the Posttheory Generation have frequently placed several levels lower in the hierarchy, if they have managed to land a full-time job at all. On the one hand, this has destabilized the system of institutional status and reward, belying its tacit premise of merit. On the other hand, it has intensified the system of institutional status—a kind of dustbowl effect—putting a premium on any sort of institutional purchase. The fallout from this has the strange side effect of professionalizing the provinces, those places that otherwise would have never seen the likes of hotshots from Duke nor heard much about the posttheoretical baggage they carry with them in the previous job market. This has not only served to spread theory throughout the land, but it also serves paradoxically to level the class function of theory as a hieratic language. It has reconfigured theory from being an elite professional marker to becoming commonplace, an expected horizon and mode of discourse in the canon of the literature department.

Public Makeover

The institutional purpose that theory once served, to legitimate the field of literary studies largely within the post-Sputnik, boomer university and upgrade its professional status, is no longer as necessary or urgent as it had once been. That is, theory delivers different goods in the present socioinstitutional milieu. As mentioned earlier, Big Theory provided a hyper-professionalist rationale for the importance of literary studies or, more exactly, literature _departments_, shoring their relative position within the context of the university; now, however, the advertised preferred stock of cultural criticism and particularly public criticism—underwritten by the developments of theory but broached in more accessible terms and geared to a more general, educated if not belletristic audience—answers a demand for an overt public rationale, as a channel to justify literature departments to a public at large in a time of budget cuts, questions of accountability, and doubts about the relevance, cost effectiveness, and value of higher education. The PC debates of the early 1990s registered a crisis of legitimacy for the university and its social role, and especially for the humanities, a crisis that public, cultural criticism answers in a way that Theory couldn't.[18]

The work of Michael Bérubé stands as a prominent example of the public turn in criticism in the 1990s, in both his persistent call for more public accessibility for criticism in the essays collected in the aptly named _Public Access,_ and the example of his various pieces in wide-circulation journals such as _The New Yorker, Village Voice, Harper's,_ and the like.[19] It's no accident that Bérubé first made his name with his essays on the PC controversy rather than, say, his more scholarly work on reception theory; Bérubé's semijournalistic, hip-toned, and theoretically informed writing filled a particular space, as an academic crossover, to represent narrowly academic disourses in official channels of PMC culture, such as _The New Yorker._

The model that Bérubé proposes to counter threats to the humanities is "bite-sizing" theory, making our research more popular, easier to digest, and more marketable to a broader audience (161–78). Bérubé exhorts those of us in the humanities: "The PC wars should have taught us one lesson—namely, that if we don't popularize academic work it will be popularized for us" (163). Thus, we should restate and summarize extant work for a general audience (167). Bérubé's prescription carries a kind of Henry Ford no-nonsense sensibility that is hard to argue with; it would no doubt be a good thing if our writing were better, and if we got the word out about what we do, especially to dispel what seem caricatured misunderstandings of our work.

However, in a different sense, Bérubé's argument also works as a professionalist jeremiad (its last line is "Profession, revise thyself"), disabusing the excesses of previous practice (the obscurity of Theory), not to disband the project but to reaffirm the faith of the professional congregation through its call for a new mode of criticism. Thus, it stands in the line of Ransom's "Criticism, Inc." and de Man's "Resistance to Theory" to recast the function of criticism in response to an institutional need. In other words, while beckoning to a larger world, it also presents a hyperprofessionalist rationale (it addresses those in the profession, not outside) and reasserts the status of the profession. This projection of a larger world relevance, at the same time reassuring the status and autonomy of the profession, is a contradiction typical of professionalism, as Bruce Robbins shows in *Secular Vocations*. In this sense, rather than being revolutionary, Bérubé's call is paradoxically conservative, in that it leaves the profession essentially intact; we need to revise our self-presentation, our advertising and public image, rather than, say, our politics.[20]

Even on its own terms, the prescription for public access is not necessarily as salutary as it might seem. For one thing, people such as Frederick Crews, Harold Bloom, Roger Shattuck, and Camille Paglia already fit the bill for "public access," speaking to large public audiences, although I doubt Bérubé, who espouses a Left politics, has these folks in mind to represent the values and virtues of our work. Public access per se is thus an empty category, or finally a marketing category, applying to anyone who appears in public rather than strictly academic media. For another thing, as I've mentioned, public access largely applies to mainstream, PMC venues, such as *The New Yorker* or *Harper's*. While these certainly reach larger audiences than standard academic fare, they are still limited to a narrow slice of the public sphere and don't speak to the large mass of people who do most of the work in this country. Public access, then, must be linked with a concept of the public good; it requires a politics to be worth it, otherwise it merely yields a *public relations* for the humanities, to justify what we're doing in literature departments, rather than a political vision of what literary and critical education should do or a theoretical argument about the sociocultural function of the humanities.

Bérubé is not by any means the only one to push toward a more popular zone of writing, from the formerly insulated zone of academia to a more general (educated, largely white, middle-class) audience. The past several years have witnessed a great deal of such academic crossover work in the humanities, most prominently perhaps in the recent work of former theory gurus, such as Jane Tompkins's *West of Everything,* Henry Louis Gates Jr.'s *Loose Canons,* and Cornel West's *Race Matters,* as well as in the turn from elite criticism to personal criticism and autobiography, exemplified by Alice Kaplan's *French Lessons,* Frank Lentricchia's *The Edge of Night,* Gates's *Colored People,* and Tompkins's *A Life in School,* among many others. This turn, I believe, indicates not simply the exhaustion of Theory but speaks to a renewed rationale for literature departments; the return to literature and to belletristic modes represents a retrenchment of our presumed disciplinary object, to justify our discipline in the face of public questions of accountability. Our old standby, Literature, projects a more comprehensible public justification than undoing binaries or subverting Western institutions.

While the call for public relevance holds out a salutary vista, the biting reality is that it occurs at precisely the same time that the workforce becomes less democratic, more ruthlessly pared down, and less open to those from non-prestige positions, as state universities close down or become prohibitively expensive and less accessible to a broad social spectrum of people. In this, despite its altruism, public access might perversely serve an anti-public function by solidifying the position of those privileged enough and institutionally empowered to speak to the public, presumably for the rest of the humanities. It celebrates those who might write for the glossy mags, presenting them as the exemplars of professional success, in other words evacuating a less glamorous scholarly model for the model of the entrepeneurial crossover, the journalistic, media consultant professor. By the same token, it also carries a convenient and blatantly ideological rationale for hideous employment practices that in effect blames the victims of university downsizing: it's our fault, we haven't been out there selling our wares to a popular audience, so we deserve what we get if we don't get with the program.

A possible consequence of public access—while *material* access to the university and to the professional field becomes more and more rarefied—is to promulgate a model of academic celebrity, hypostasizing the model of intellectual star, with broad public appeal and name recognition, as an ideological carrot—a kind of intellectual Horatio Alger story—for those struggling with the blunt exigencies of employment, for those unemployed and "underemployed" to dream and strive for, at the same time that socioinstitutional conditions make that dream more and more fantastical. This negative vista of public access goes a long way to explaining the recent proclivity for academic-intellectual autobiography, to augment the star function of what James Sosnoski calls Master Critics, presenting details of the life to the paparazzi.[21] In its worst light, public access carries a careerist logic and desire, that the profession of literature might be recast in terms of media success stories, putting a more glamorous face on the otherwise disintegrating situation of public access to education.[22]

The crucial question that must precede the call for a better public image and spin on the humanities is that of the institutional conditions and channels that permit or deny access—in other words, public access not for *us,* but for those wishing to take their entitlement to a public education. It is not quite true that Left intellectuals have buried their heads in the sand and escehewed public visibility; however, actual access to the accredited institutions of media, of publishing, and of the academy are far from open and at best only allow limited forays from those outside the circuit of institutional privilege. The question of access, then, is a question of reforming and opening those institutional channels rather than simply recalibrating writing style. The pressing task of criticism in the current moment—

indeed, the obligation of critics—is to reinvent the institution of literature in ways that truly permit public access, reconfiguring the jobs and employment conditions of those who work in that institution more equitably and humanely, and restructuring the university as a place of education and opportunity for all rather than as a Darwinist finishing school for the nascent professional-managerial and ruling classes.

Notes

1. Or what Quentin Skinner, taking a note from C. Wright Mills, calls "Grand Theory," which he defines as systematic, "abstract and normative theories of human nature and conduct" (3). See his introduction to *The Return of Grand Theory in the Human Sciences,* which gathers a series of essays on major figures of the moment of Theory, including Derrida, Foucault, Habermas, Althusser, and Lévi-Strauss.

2. For the interrelation of larger historical factors and what has happened to universities—the downsizing and the evisceration of the labor force—see Ohmann. For the general characteristics of post-Fordism in which the restructured university participates, see Harvey. For more detail about the winnowing of jobs, see note 7 below.

3. See Huber's series of MLA reports on the job market in literature and languages. There was a notable upswing in the number of jobs advertised, beginning around 1986, peaking in 1987, 1988, and 1989, slipping a little in 1990, down to the trough of the present, when fewer than nine hundred jobs were advertised. These statistics give an indication of some of the causes of the formation of the present academic (sub)generation, since the years 1986–1990 represented a brief hiring peak, with more than nine thousand job positions advertised. In short, this infusion served to fix the generation by simple arithmetic.

4. Pierre Bourdieu, in his influential sociological work, deciphers how social distinctions operate in French culture. For my purposes, I draw on Bourdieu's concept of distinction to examine the construction of academic hierarchies and social relations particular to literary studies on the American scene. Despite our powerful theoretical tools, we have largely left unexamined our own system of social distinction.

5. On "master critics," see Sosnoski. Debray deals specifically with the French intellectual scene, but his basic point—that the social role and influence of intellectuals has shifted through the century, or, put another way, the role of intellectuals is socially defined—carries over to the American scene. In Debray's scheme, intellectuals have been defined as or derived their influence from being teachers roughly in the time period before World War II, from being writers in the postwar years up through the sixties (Sartre is a central example), and from being media celebrities thence (figures such as Foucault and Lacan drew hundreds to public lectures and appeared on TV, in gossip columns, etc.). For the current apotheosis of the academic as public celebrity, see the *New York Magazine* feature on Andrew Ross, "Yo, Professor" (Mead), as well as the spate of articles announcing the new public intellectuals, such as Cornel West, Henry Louis Gates Jr., or Camille Paglia.

6. See my "The Life of the Mind and the Academic Situation" on the disciplinary rather than altruistic dimension of tenure.

7. As Richard Ohmann points out, "in the mid-1960s over 90 percent of new humanities Ph.D.s had full-time tenure-track appointments; in recent years the figure has hovered around 40 percent" (231). It is hard to express the real effect, in human terms, of this shift from stable and ready employment to constant and pervasive job *in*security. Not that the immediately previous generation had it easy; as Orr indicates, the contemporary job crisis began about 1970. But, as Brodie notes, jobs are still fewer in real terms than was the case in 1975 (15).

8. For a post hoc declaration of the Theory Generation and its difference from older formalists, see Sprinker. As he puts it, "Let them have *PMLA*, if they want it. We've got *Cultural Critique, Signs, Feminist Studies . . . diacritics, boundary 2 . . . Critical Inquiry . . .*" (127). Note that almost all of these journals were founded around 1970, and definitively mark that generation. To the Posttheory Generation, most of these journals represent closed shops; rather, from our standpoint, we have a new bloc of journals, such as *Postmodern Culture, minnesota review, Journal X, differences, symplokē*, the revived *College Literature*, and so on.

As it is frequently depicted, the turn to theory in the sixties represented "politics by other means." Contrary to this usual view, though, Terry Eagleton points out that many of the figures affiliated with the advent of Theory—Fish, Gadamer, Kristeva, Bloom, Iser, and so on—were hardly revolutionaries, or for that matter on the Left. And as Eagleton also points out, there can be a way of seeing the refuge in the academy as a *displacement* of politics, to "signifiers and sexuality" (3). My point here is that the situation is no doubt complicated and the ascription of Theory as a sixties or boomer phenomenon is only qualifiedly true, though I would maintain its *absorption* occurred under the auspices of the coming to age of the boomer generation.

9. For a report on recent changes in publishing, particularly on how quickly even academic books are remaindered and go out of print, see Allen.

10. Hillis Miller was Sedgwick's dissertation director. This is Miller's list of those whom he dubs promising younger scholars engaged in the project of theory, particularly in the negotiation of the chasm between language and history, in his 1986 MLA Presidential address:

> Among those engaged in this work from one position or another, perhaps in the end from wholly incompatible positions, from one side of the canyon or down in its depths (but the more points of entry to this question the better), I name, in no particular order, not only [Andrew] Parker and [Gregory] Jay but also Michael Sprinker, Deborah Esch, Thomas Keenan, Cynthia Chase, John Rowe, Jonathan Arac, Michael Ryan, Ned Lukacher, Gayatri Spivak, Andrzej Warminski, David Carroll, Suzanne Gearhart, Jean-Luc Nancy, and Philippe Lacoue-Labarthe. (291)

One could of course construct a number of other lists and theoretical family trees.

11. See John Guillory's arguments for the use of theory to provide a research program for the humanities, in effect replacing the function of the literature canon, in *Cultural Capital*.

12. To cast farther back, see Warner for his discussion of the way in which the professional object of the field was re-formed at the turn of the century, largely from Germanic philology to literary appreciation and interpretation.

13. There's a commonplace view that the humanities competed with the fattened role of the sciences in the post–World War II university. However, Elizabeth Wilson shows that Literature competed more directly with the social sciences rather than the sciences in their mutual tasks of studying the social world rather than the natural world.

14. See Graff on the "field-coverage principle" (207–08). Relevant to this positive redescription of theory, Richard Rorty depicts theory as a new mode of writing somewhere between philosophy, literature, and scholarship, rather than simply a derivative or "service" language to literature proper (66).

15. In "The Feminism Which Is Not One," Devoney Looser discusses the present shifting moment of feminism to a third or fourth generation and the question of loyalty to an earlier, singularly minded feminism. See also Eve Sedgwick's comments on the relation of gay studies to feminism in "Sedgwick Unplugged" (60–61).

16. Barbara Johnson deals with this death trope in *The Wake of Deconstruction*. A number of recent titles testify to the tenuous position of (poststructural) theory at present, such as *After Poststructuralism* (Easterlin and Riebling) or the early polemic for cultural studies, "After Theory," a special issue of *Dalhousie Review* (Smith). These reports, which might bespeak a *desire* of the field as much as the reality of it, are not unique. For a fuller discussion of these projections of a rupture in theory, see also my "The Death of Deconstruction, the End of Theory, and Other Rumors."

17. See Terry Caesar's "On Teaching at a Second-Rate University" for a relevant discussion of academic hierarchies. I differ here from Caesar, who sorts universities on a single axis, elite and nonelite, first and second rate.

18. See Lauter for a particularly cogent analysis of the PC wars, explicitly making this connection between the scaling down of the university and PC baiting.

19. It's worth noting that Bérubé locates himself explicitly as a member of the posttheory generation, recounting the story of his coming to theory during graduate school in "Discipline and Theory" (43–58).

20. To be fair, Bérubé has consistently advocated a liberal-left politics, and has been especially active on behalf of graduate student unions and to reform the academic job market. My point is to examine the professional-institutional uses to which criticism (theory, public, etc.) is put, frequently in spite of our prescriptions and what we say we are doing.

21. See David Shumway's discussion of the star system and speculation about the recent preponderance of autobiographies of well-known theorists.

22. There is a certain way in which one can read Bérubé's text as this kind of celebratory success story. See particularly his account of his publishing in places such as the *VLS* in "Bite-Size Theory" (171). This is not to single out Bérubé unduly; rather, I take his case

as exemplary of a current trend. However, it is to register adamant reservations about this kind of prescription in light of the present job crisis, making me fear that such a celebratory prescription is like fiddling while universities and educational enfranchisement for the mass of people in this country burn.

Works Cited

Allen, Charlotte. "Indecent Disposal: Where Academic Books Go When They Die." *Lingua Franca* (May 1995): 44–53.

Bérubé, Michael. *Public Access: Literary Theory and American Cultural Politics.* New York: Verso, 1994.

Booth, Wayne. "Where Have I Been, and Where Are 'We' Now, in This Profession?" *PMLA* 109 (1994): 941–50.

Bourdieu, Pierre. *Distinction: A Social Critique of the Judgement of Taste.* Trans. Richard Nice. London: Routledge, 1989.

———. "Structures, *Habitus,* Practices." *The Logic of Practice.* Trans. Richard Nice. Stanford: Stanford UP, 1990. 52–65.

Brodie, James Michael. "Whatever Happened to the Job Boom?" *Academe* (Jan./Feb. 1995): 12–15.

Caesar, Terry. "On Teaching at a Second-Rate University." *Conspiring with Forms: Life in Academic Texts.* Athens: U of Georgia P, 1992. 145–65.

Crane, R. S. "History vs. Criticism in the Study of Literature." *The Idea of the Humanities and Other Essays Critical and Historical.* Vol. 2 Chicago: U of Chicago P, 1967. 3–31.

Debray, Regis. *Teachers, Writers, Celebrities: The Intellectuals of Modern France.* Trans. David Macey. London: New Left Books, 1981.

de Man, Paul. "The Resistance to Theory." *The Resistance to Theory.* Minneapolis: U of Minnesota P, 1986. 3–20.

Eagleton, Terry. "Discourse and Discos: Theory in the Space between Culture and Capitalism." *TLS* (15 July 1994): 3–4.

———. *The Significance of Theory.* Oxford: Blackwell, 1990.

Easterlin, Nancy, and Barbara Riebling, eds. *After Poststructuralism: Interdisciplinarity and Literary Theory.* Evanston: Northwestern UP, 1993.

Giroux, Henry, David Shumway, Paul Smith, and James Sosnoski. "The Need for Cultural Studies." Smith 472–86.

Graff, Gerald. *Professing Literature: An Institutional History.* Chicago: U of Chicago P, 1987.

Guillory, John. *Cultural Capital: The Problem of Literary Canon Formation.* Chicago: U of Chicago P, 1993.

Harvey, David. *The Condition of Postmodernity: An Inquiry into the Origins of Cultural Change.* Oxford: Basil Blackwell, 1989.

Huber, Bettina J. "The Changing Job Market." *Profession* 92 (1992): 59–73.

———. "Recent Trends in the Modern Language Job Market." *Profession 94* (1994): 87–105.

Johnson, Barbara. *The Wake of Deconstruction.* Cambridge, MA: Blackwell, 1994.

Lauter, Paul. "'Political Correctness' and the Attack on American Colleges." *Higher Education Under Fire: Politics, Economics, and the Crisis of the Humanities.* Ed. Michael Bérubé and Cary Nelson. New York: Routledge, 1995. 73–90.

Levine, George. "The Real Trouble." *Profession 93* (1993): 43–45.

Looser, Devoney. "This Feminism Which Is Not One: Women, Generations, Institutions." *minnesota review* n.s. 41–2 (1994): 108–17.

Mead, Rebecca. "Yo, Professor." *New York Magazine* 14 Nov. 1994: 48–53.

Miller, J. Hillis. "The Triumph of Theory, the Resistance to Reading, and the Question of the Material Base." *PMLA* 102 (1987): 981–91.

Ohmann, Richard. "English After the USSR." *After Political Correctness: The Humanities and Society in the 1990s.* Ed. Christopher Newfield and Ronald Strickland. Boulder: Westview, 1995. 226–37.

Orr, David. "The Job Market in English and Foreign Languages." *PMLA* 85 (1970): 1185–98.

Ransom, John Crowe. "Criticism, Inc." *The World's Body.* Baton Rouge: Louisiana State UP, 1968 [1938]. 327–50.

Robbins, Bruce. "The History of Literary Theory: Starting Over." *Poetics Today* 9 (1988): 767–81.

———. *Secular Vocations: Intellectuals, Professionalism, Culture.* New York: Verso, 1993.

Rorty, Richard. "Professionalized Philosophy and Transcendentalist Culture." *Consequences of Pragmatism (Essays: 1972–1980).* Minneapolis: U of Minnesota P, 1982. 60–71.

Sedgwick, Eve Kosofsky. "Sedgwick Unplugged (An Interview with Eve Kosofsky Sedgwick)." With Jeffrey Williams. *minnesota review* n.s. 40 (1993): 52–64.

Shumway, David R. "The Star System in Literary Studies." *PMLA* 112.1 (1997): 85–100.

Skinner, Quentin, ed. *The Return of Grand Theory in the Human Sciences.* Cambridge: Cambridge UP, 1985.

Smith, Paul, ed. "After Theory." Special issue, *Dalhousie Review* 64.2 (1984).

Sosnoski, James. *Token Professionals and Master Critics: A Critique of Orthodoxy in Literary Studies.* Albany: State U New York P, 1994.

Sprinker, Michael. "Commentary: 'You've Got a Lot of Nerve.'" *Shakespeare Left and Right.* Ed. Ivo Kamps. New York: Routledge, 1991. 115–28.

Stephens, Mitchell. "Jacques Derrida." *New York Times Magazine* 23 Jan. 1994: 22–25.

Warner, Michael. "Professionalization and the Rewards of Literature: 1875–1900." *Criticism* 27 (1985): 1–28.

Weinberg, Alvin M. "Impact of Large-Scale Science on the United States." *Science* July 1961: 161–64.

Williams, Jeffrey. "The Death of Deconstruction, the End of Theory, and Other Rumors." *Narrative* 4.1 (1996): 17–35.

———. "The Life of the Mind and the Academic Situation." *College Literature* 23.3 (1996): 128–46.

———. "Packaging Theory." *College English* 56 (1994): 280–99.

Wilson, Elizabeth. "A Short History of a Border War: Social Science, School Reform, and the Study of Literature." *Poetics Today* 9 (1988): 711–35.

Zavarzadeh, Mas'ud. "Post-Ality: The (Dis)Simulations of Cybercapitalism." *Transformation* 1.1 (1995): 1–75.

PART II

THE CURRENT ARRANGEMENTS

Seven

Composing Literary Studies
in Graduate Courses

John Schilb

*Literary theorists, critics and teachers . . . are not so much purveyors of
doctrine as custodians of a discourse. Their task is to preserve this discourse,
extend and elaborate it as necessary, defend it from other forms of discourse,
initiate newcomers into it and determine whether or not they have mastered
it. The discourse has no definite signified, which is not to say that it embodies
no assumptions: it is rather a network of signifiers able to envelop a whole
field of meanings, objects and practices.*

—Terry Eagleton, *Literary Theory*

By now, Terry Eagleton's observation has become a commonplace of English studies. Even back in 1983, when Eagleton made it at the climax of his book *Literary
Theory*, numerous readers took him to be expressing a familiar sentiment. There
had already been much theorizing about knowledge as a social construction, especially in the wake of Michel Foucault. Among other things, he and his followers
had been tracing how disciplinarity functions as a regulative ideal (see, e.g., *Discipline*). That is, they studied the ways in which an academic field's characteristic
"meanings, objects, and practices" are defined and shaped by its particular institutional agenda, which includes the field's effort to prove that its research is not
only valuable but methodologically distinct.

Inevitably, the Foucauldian analysis of disciplinarity was concerned with academic discourse. Much attention was paid to the ways in which a field constitutes
its particular area of inquiry through certain uses of language specific to the field.
These uses include conventions of writing and speaking that members of the field
feel pressured to follow. In fact, just prior to the publication of Eagleton's book,
many composition specialists in English departments began intensively studying
and teaching field-specific writing practices, as if to atone for previously treating
composing as one universally applicable routine. In literary studies, the work of
Foucault, Eagleton, and others has by now led many faculty to acknowledge that
they indeed act like "custodians of a discourse." True, plenty of their colleagues in
literature have rejected this idea, or at least disputed Eagleton's suggestion that the
field is *merely* "a network of signifiers." Still, nowadays most literature faculty are
apt to regard his emphasis on the field's discursive nature as old news.

Eagleton concluded *Literary Theory* by proposing certain programmatic moves based on his insight. Above all, he proposed that literary studies turn back to "rhetoric" as a rubric. To him, this turn would mean considering the practical effects of particular texts and critical methods; furthermore, it would involve helping students to engage in various forms of cultural production. As a specialist in rhetoric myself, I am quite sympathetic to Eagleton's proposal. But at the moment, I simply want to emphasize that few English departments have come close to implementing it. Yes, many literature faculty now accept as a truism that their field is constituted by distinct forms of discourse. I would argue, though, that this idea has stirred only some English departments to change their institutional practices. It has barely affected how most actually teach literature.

As my title suggests, in this essay I am especially concerned with lack of change on the graduate level. A few years ago, I became quite aware that many graduate students in English continue to be mystified by the discourse of literary studies. A particular moment of epiphany for me occurred during a doctoral seminar I was teaching on contemporary controversies in composition studies. Specifically, this moment involved the students' reaction to the following passage. It is from David Bartholomae's 1985 essay "Inventing the University," now considered a landmark piece of composition scholarship. In his essay, Bartholomae proposes a pedagogy for Basic Writing programs, whose students have great difficulty producing standard academic prose:

> What our beginning students need to learn is to extend themselves, by successive approximations, into the commonplaces, set phrases, rituals and gestures, habits of mind, tricks of persuasion, obligatory conclusions and necessary connections that determine the "what might be said" and constitute knowledge within the various branches of our academic community. (146)

Several of the students in my doctoral course were taking it because they planned to become or remain teachers of writing. Yet others were committed to literary studies, and even the would-be composition specialists expected to teach literature at times. Moreover, given the requirements of our department's program, everyone in the class had already taken some graduate courses in literature. I had assumed the class would analyze Bartholomae's ideas as a framework for Basic Writing, or as a philosophy for undergraduate composition courses in general. Instead, his essay led the students to remember with anguish their first graduate courses in literature. Back then, they recalled, they found themselves laboring to master a whole new set of "commonplaces, set phrases, rituals and gestures, habits of mind, tricks of persuasion, obligatory conclusions and necessary connections." For many of these students, graduate school was the first time they had to confront and manipulate the scholarly conventions of literary studies. As undergraduates, most of them had come to love literature, and they had arrived in graduate school expecting that their new program would let them revel in it. Instead, they wound up struggling to discern and deploy rhetorics unfamiliar to them. Furthermore, even though they were now well along in their graduate studies, this difficulty hadn't eased all that much. They were still unsure whether they had correctly perceived, let alone learned to wield, literary studies' favorite discursive strategies.

Our department, like many others, had required these students to take introductory courses in bibliographical methods and literary theory. But during their whole graduate career, faculty had avoided giving them formal, explicit, and sustained instruction in how to *write* as a professional scholar of literature. Nor had they found much tutelage in books and articles. While there do exist several writing-about-literature textbooks, these are geared to introductory undergraduate courses, so their advice is elementary at best. True, as I noted earlier, several theorists have emphasized the rhetorical dimension of literary criticism. Also, certain discursive moves in the field have been widely noted and keenly interrogated: for example, the New Historicists' use of anecdotes, as well as feminist critics' turn to autobiography. But there haven't been many detailed anatomies of the prose styles found in, say, *PMLA*. Note, too, that the few diagnosticians of this rhetoric tend to mock it. They want to change, not teach, the manner of writing they find characteristic of literary studies now.[1]

Presumably a major aim of graduate programs in literature is to help students become actual contributors to the field's scholarship. In our discussion of Bartholomae's essay, my students noted that many of our department's graduate literature courses explicitly required them to produce a publishable article. Furthermore, these students knew that they had to get their work into professional journals if they were to succeed in the tight market for academic jobs. Admittedly, some of them were uncomfortable with seeing themselves as just "custodians of a discourse." But all of them wanted to know more about ways of excelling at that discourse, especially so they could make their vitae strong.

Why do graduate literature programs offer little or no formal writing instruction? I can think of several reasons. One involves curricular overcrowding. Although a burgeoning number of people claim that the age of High Theory has passed, designers of graduate English curricula act otherwise. As usual, they want students to become familiar with literary periods and methods of research. But now they also want them to master assorted schools of thought, by reading selected manifestoes in anthologies and casebooks. The result is an agenda with less room than ever for discussions of how to write.

The next few reasons for this paucity of writing instruction strike me as interrelated. One is that graduate literature faculty hope students will come to them already articulate. Another is that many of these faculty, perhaps unconsciously, believe that writing ability is a natural gift rather than a teachable art. Yet another reason is literary studies' basic assumption that published texts are ultimately far more important than students' unpublished, in-process writing. What ties these three reasons together is that they all reflect the average English department's enduring failure to make composition studies truly integral to its mission. Most English departments continue to regard composition as merely a set of "service" courses: that is, as an obligation to their school as a whole. If graduate English faculty are even hazily aware of composition, that's usually because several of their students are teaching assistants in first-year writing courses. Greater acquaintance with the field would mean seriously considering its present assumptions: for instance, that writers at any level have much to learn; that rhetorical prowess can indeed be taught; and that students' production of new texts is just as important as their ability to interpret existing ones.

[A graduate literature course would be more apt to examine the field's discourse in detail if the teacher and students already had common terms for analyzing nonfiction.] Unfortunately, few students in English graduate programs were taught as undergraduates to identify strategies used in genres other than fiction, poetry, and drama. Most teachers of literature haven't had this education either. Again, the problem is related to the marginality of composition in English departments. Today, many composition specialists know terms of rhetoric and use them to discuss various kinds of texts, including works of literary criticism and theory. Yet such terms remain unfamiliar to their literature colleagues. I hasten to add that discourse might be analyzed with all sorts of tools, not just those of rhetoric. As Ellen Messer-Davidow, David Shumway, and David Sylvan point out, "the practice of studying disciplinarity draws from various disciplines a diverse set of terms and a large methodological repertoire" (3). Nevertheless, rhetoric is a strikingly untapped resource in undergraduate as well as graduate teaching of literature.

Perhaps graduate literature courses also neglect writing instruction because doing so helps the field maintain a disciplinary aura. If its conventions were explicitly identified and exhaustively detailed, professional scholars of literature could have trouble distinguishing themselves from amateurs, dilettantes, and newly arrived M.A. candidates. A strategy of mystification can, of course, alienate too many of the field's would-be members, thereby depriving it of new blood. Yet English graduate faculty may increasingly dismiss that risk, given their inability to guarantee their students jobs. I, for one, observe more and more of my literature colleagues becoming social Darwinists, ready to give up on graduate students whose writing doesn't immediately dazzle.

To be fair, most English graduate faculty offer at least some ad hoc writing instruction. Once they have assigned a paper, they confer with individual students about how to develop it. Once they receive final drafts, they provide feedback through written comments. Furthermore, in many a graduate seminar, students read their work-in-progress aloud to classmates and get reactions from them. Probably quite a few people would argue that writing instruction on the graduate level actually works best when it takes a case-by-case approach. After all, it lets students get advice on specific projects. On the other hand, their writing may or may not be improved by class discussion of their field's larger rhetorical repertoire.

Yet the ad hoc approach ultimately seems dysfunctional. In my experience, it leaves many graduate students feeling they have gained only a few insights into the discourse of literary studies. Besides, more elaborate discussion of this discourse can serve as a springboard for examining disciplinarity. More precisely, it enables students to consider how a discipline defines itself *as* a discipline through the writing practices it favors. Historically, treatises on literary education in the academy have tended to focus on the undergraduate level. Graduate courses, however, seem an especially good site for considering how literary studies is constituted as a discipline through discourse. As writing researcher Paul Prior notes,

> In graduate education, students' production of texts and professor and peer response to those texts are activities central to disciplinary enculturation. These activities provide an opportunity space for socialization into discursive practices, represent a social medium for the display of disciplinarity, and mediate the reproduction of disciplinary social structures as students achieve relative levels of "success" and "visibility." Situated examination of the way texts are produced and read within the activity structures of graduate programs is, thus, a key nexus for understanding disciplinarity. (489)

Prior uses this observation to introduce research he did on an advanced doctoral seminar in sociology.[2] Specifically, he examined how a particular student in the seminar developed a dissertation prospectus by presenting drafts of it to the other class members and getting their reaction. In applying Prior's observation to literary studies, I am suggesting that the implications of his statement be explored *within* a graduate class, as a key part of its agenda. Students would consider the ways in which their own writing matches or departs from their discipline's main rhetoric. They might also consider how that rhetoric compares with the writing practices they themselves have taught. Graduate students with assistantships often teach first-year writing while they study the likes of Milton, Dickinson, and Rushdie. Others may teach writing in grade school, high school, or a community college while they pursue their graduate degrees. Why not give them the chance to discuss what they are learning about writers, writing practices, and the teaching of writing as a result of their pedagogical experiences?

To identify characteristic strategies of literary criticism and theory, graduate classes might look at particular examples of these genres. One good source is the theory casebook, now a staple of English departments' introductory graduate courses. I have in mind books such as Bedford's Case Studies in Contemporary Criticism, each volume of which includes a literary work and essays illustrating various theoretical approaches to it. My sense is that most instructors who adopt one of these Bedford volumes are mainly using it to teach principles of deconstruction, feminist criticism, psychoanalytic criticism, reader response theory, and the like. But the essays in these volumes can also be examined for their rhetoric. Look, for instance, at the first two paragraphs of Hilary Schor's essay on *Great Expectations,* which is included in the volume on that novel to illustrate feminist criticism:

> Of all Dickens's fantastic accounts of boys' lives, each part fairy tale and part horror story, none more insistently plays with the story of the fairy princess, or more insistently rewrites its darker side, than does *Great Expectations.* Pip casts his own story as a romance, with Estella as at once the beautiful, cold, distant "light" of his existence and the reward for his trials; as he carefully positions her (the star by which he can navigate), so she must remain, in order for his story to have coherence. We, too, mark our positions by her distance: to the extent that we are ironic readers of the novel, we will focus on her unsuitability and Pip's obsession; if we choose to value Dickensian sentiment, we will emphasize her changed heart and her altered form, and we will, with Pip, look for no "shadow" of a further parting. The Estella who has been "bent and broken" will in either case monitor *our* progress and wisdom and our assessment of Pip's growth.
>
> But one of the persistent problematics of *Great Expectations*—the real shadow that haunts its ending—is not whether Pip ever marries Estella but whether Pip ever *sees* Estella: Does he ever free her from her fixed place as the guiding light of his existence? This question matters as an emblem not only of Pip's maturity but of Dickens's relation to his hero—his narrator—throughout the novel. Pip, as everyone knows, is an insufferable young man, but fewer readers have commented on the ways in which he remains insufferable to the end of the novel. No character points out his shallowness throughout more effectively than Estella, questioning and teasing him, mocking his efforts to be his own hero. But more to the purpose here, no character so writes her own novel, escaping Pip's monomaniacal obsession, than Estella, who throughout is wiser, sadder, and funnier than Pip—and who is the character most entirely "bent and broken" by the novel into another form. (541)

Much can be said about the strategies Schor employs. In a graduate class, I would emphasize how she uses rhetoric typical of literary studies to signal what rhetoricians would call her *exigence:* that is, her purpose for writing, the contribution she will make to scholarship.

Schor's chief attempt at establishing exigence comes in the second paragraph. Four times there, for instance, she uses "but," fully exploiting that little word's capacity to suggest that the critic is moving beyond familiar truths or easy insights into deeper levels of analysis. Furthermore, her opening sentence makes use of a classical rhetorical technique, which Chaim Perelman and Lucie Olbrechts-Tyteca refer to in their book *The New Rhetoric* as the appearance/reality disjunction. Whereas most readers of *Great Expectations* have pondered Pip and Estella's marriage prospects, Schor will go beyond surface issues and deal with "the real shadow."[3]

Creating exigence often involves, too, stressing the *significance* of one's concerns. Schor insinuates that her question about Pip and Estella is hardly trivial. She describes it as "one of the persistent problematics" of the novel, and by using the conveniently vague word "emblem," she connects it to the presumably larger question of how Dickens views his protagonist. Schor also indicates significance by resorting to the vocabulary of "more" and "less," a stratagem discussed by rhetoricians as far back as Aristotle. She verges on a language of ultimate concerns when she resorts to such phrases as "more insistently plays," "more insistently rewrites," "more effectively," "more to the purpose," "no character so writes her own novel," and "most entirely." On a related note, she also justifies her focus on Estella by arguing that the latter is "wiser, sadder, and funnier than Pip." Of course, going in the opposite direction (a vocabulary of "less") can also be an exigence-setting move. In part, Schor justifies her essay by indicating that she will deal with things "fewer critics have commented on."

Since Aristotle, rhetoricians have distinguished between common topics and special topics. The former are argumentative moves that many people resort to; the latter are moves specific to a given field. Three moves by Schor belong especially to the special topoi of literary studies. Even many undergraduate English majors know that literary critics often quote from a text to support their points about it. Schor continues this practice. In addition, as Jeanne Fahnestock and Marie Secor have observed, literary critics often try to prove their sensitivity to a text's language by weaving variations on that language into their own comments (93). Recall that near the end of the published version of *Great Expectations,* Estella acknowledges her "suffering" (499). Taking this cue, Schor refers to "insufferable" Pip. Similarly, she plays off the novel's final words—"I saw the shadow of no parting from her" (499)—when she claims to address "the real shadow that haunts the ending."

Schor's third discipline-specific move is her climactic assertion that Estella "writes her own novel." For several years now, literary critics have been enamored of the idea that literary texts are often self-reflexive: in other words, literature is often *about* literature. To a large extent, this idea was promoted by deconstruction, whose influence remains palpable even if its heyday has passed. It can also be argued, though, that such a notion serves disciplinary self-interest. Fahnestock and Secor note that "[T]o claim that any work of art is really about art itself confers dignity reciprocally on both artist and critic" (89). The field of literary studies seems newly important when literature becomes not just a category of texts but also their subject matter. In any case, Schor seems to assume—and rightly, I think—that much of her audience will like the claim that Estella "writes her own novel" because this type of statement is already so much in vogue within literary studies. Bear in mind that people outside the field may not find Schor's claim engaging or even sensible. Hence, it deserves to be called a special topic rather than a common topic. That is, it's a commonplace *within* but not *beyond* the discipline—something that literary critics can draw on as they try to make arguments that will persuade and interest professional peers.

I am proposing that graduate classes in English conduct the rhetorical analysis I have just demonstrated, applying it both to published scholarship and to students' texts. At the same time, these classes should bear in mind that no field is utterly homogeneous in its discursive habits. As Messer-Davidow, Shumway, and Sylvan remind us, "[D]isciplines are such by virtue of a historically contingent, adventitious coherence of dispersed elements," and "to study that coherence is necessarily to begin questioning portrayals of disciplines as seamless, progressive, or naturally 'about' certain topics" (3). True, particular factions within disciplines have been able to impose their agendas, often for a long time. But hegemony isn't the same as uniformity. As Gerald Graff has shown, literary studies has always experienced schisms, including challenges to each of its discursive regimes.

I realize that a focus on disciplinary conventions risks seeming to encourage disciplinary indoctrination. Were students to engage in the rhetorical analysis I propose, they may feel pushed to follow whatever protocols they find. Earlier I suggested that composition studies can contribute much to this rhetorical inquiry, but we should note that a great many writing instructors have accepted the academy's division of knowledge and sought to make their students good citizens of departments. If composition studies has often been labeled a "service" enterprise, one reason is its long compliance with disciplinary structures.

The prospect of disciplinary indoctrination seems to lurk, for instance, in the passage from David Bartholomae I quoted. When he calls for teaching "the commonplaces, set phrases, rituals and gestures, habits of mind, tricks of persuasion, obligatory conclusions and necessary connections that determine the 'what might be said' and constitute knowledge within the various branches of our academic community," he seems to endorse field-specific orthodoxies. As Susan Wall and Nicholas Coles point out, Bartholomae appears to have "a rather thin conception of student culture, of the material of their lives as this can be brought to bear on the development of a critical academic stance" (235). Hardly ever in his essay does Bartholomae suggest that students critically examine the academy's rhetorics. At one point, he does say that the most able student writers locate themselves "within and against competing discourses," so that they are "working self-consciously to claim an interpretive project of their own, one that grants them their privilege to speak" (158). With the term *competing discourses*, Bartholomae is apparently referring to the tension between students' previous discourses and the academy's forms of utterance. And in claiming that advanced student writers move against *both* these regimens, he does seem to put academic discourse itself in question. At the same time, though, Bartholomae seems complacent about the academy's power to grant certain people—and deny others—"their privilege to speak." In general, Wall and Coles are right to worry that Bartholomae's essay "can be, and in fact is now being, appropriated by those educators who want to argue for an unambiguously accommodationist Basic Writing pedagogy" (230–31).

Bartholomae's essay does note and endorse academic discourse's tendency to question commonplaces of everyday life, including those that have guided students prior to their entering college. He is right, I think, not only to value critical consciousness but to credit the academy with at least professing it. Furthermore, Bartholomae deserves praise for disputing the romantic, individualistic notion of "invention" and for promoting instead a concept of it that, gesturing toward classical rhetoric and poststructuralism, recognizes that writers must work with pre-existing discourses. Significant, too, is Bartholomae's subsequent change of heart. Even back in the 1980s, when he wrote "Inventing the University," he was far from being composition studies' most accommodationist scholar. Since then, he has grown notably more skeptical about academe, believing that it is bent on controlling students rather than truly educating them (see, e.g., "Tidy"). In fact, Bartholomae's skepticism reflects a larger trend within his field. While plenty of composition specialists still aim to produce students who would sustain, not disrupt, reigning scholarly practices, others are no longer so dedicated to preserving the academic status quo. They aim to help students critique disciplinary conventions and the ways power operates in the larger world.

The same agenda can drive graduate classes examining the rhetoric of literary studies. They needn't just help students adapt. For one thing, the instructor might include on the reading list articles that experiment with form. Furthermore, the students might be actively encouraged to try out new modes of scholarship themselves. Conceivably these would include various forms of electronic textuality, a medium that many graduate students know more about than their professors do. Probably students will expand the field's repertoire, too, if at times they are asked to write for audiences outside it. Given the bad press that literature specialists have received over the last several years, they need to invent new ways of persuading the public that their discipline is anything but parochial.

It would be good, too, if graduate courses in literature reviewed assorted methods of invention, such as those set forth by rhetoricians and composition scholars from ancient times to the present. Many graduate English instructors mock the romantic figure of the instinctual genius. Nevertheless, few discuss with their classes systematic ways to get ideas for writing, despite all the heuristic procedures that theorists of discourse have proposed. Above all, graduate students often need help discovering *issues* they might write about. Therefore, lately I have been spending more time in my graduate courses explaining various types of issues that literary critics and theorists might address. In part, I have drawn on the classical stases, a set of guidelines for delineating issues that a given subject conceivably raises. Specifically, the stases are questions of fact, definition, value, and policy. But

I have also attempted to identify for my students the kinds of issues I see being dealt with in present-day cases of literary scholarship. These categories include the questions established in the classical stases, but they include as well more specific questions such as "What significance, if any, should we attach to the patterns of imagery in a given text?" Needless to say, my purpose in bringing up various methods of invention isn't to overwhelm students with taxonomies. Rather, I hope to give them some resources for generating topics they might proceed to investigate.

Graduate students writing about a literary text tend to face certain additional challenges. For one thing, they wonder how best to acknowledge previous analysts of the text. In other words, they must decide how to appropriate past scholarship so as to make their own argument cogent. Another question they repeatedly face is how much "theory talk" they should include in their essay. Should the essay center mostly on the literary text, making theoretical comment here and there? Or, should their essay emphasize theory, using the literary work merely to elaborate a certain school of thought? In their courses, most graduate students do hear a great deal about theory, being repeatedly exhorted to reflect on the philosophy behind any act of practical criticism. Yet in actuality, much literary scholarship continues to explicate "primary" works of literature while minimizing theoretical pronouncements. Students hoping to succeed as writers in the field would benefit from exploring the apparent contradiction between its praise of theory and its enduring rhetorical habits. Faculty might tell students their own ways of dealing with this paradox. More generally, they might discuss how they have personally negotiated various conditions of a scholar's writing career.

To critique the disciplinary limits of literary studies, a writing-oriented graduate course in literature might compare the field's rhetoric to that of another field. Messer-Davidow, Shumway, and Sylvan make much the same suggestion in discussing ways to study how disciplines differentiate themselves from one another. They raise the possibility of examining "pairs of neighboring disciplines," with attention to the explicit and implicit ways in which these fields teach "what does and does not count as disciplinary knowledge" (2). Of course, how to define "neighboring" is an open question. Moreover, students can learn much from comparing two disciplines that are seemingly far apart. Nevertheless, the basic idea of juxtaposing two disciplines has merit. The process can especially illuminate these fields' respective rhetorics.

For example, as I have noted elsewhere ("Scholarship"), usually a work of literary criticism ends by implying that it has settled all the important questions about whatever texts it has discussed. Schor's essay on *Great Expectations* concludes with a most typical air of finality: "It is the desire for 'vision' that creates this novel; it is its creation of its own countervision that at once challenges and rewards other expectations" (557). On the other hand, scholarly texts in the social sciences, the sciences, and education often conclude by pointing out further research that needs to be done on their subject. Graduate English students might enjoy considering what this difference indicates about the priorities, procedures, and ethos of literary studies as a field.

Personally, I would like every graduate course in literature to consider the writing practices through which the subject has been "disciplined." I realize, however, that many English faculty will object to mainstreaming this kind of inquiry. For the time being, most English graduate programs will prefer to go slower, by arranging for certain specific courses to examine the discourse of literary studies at length. Each year, for instance, the University of Maryland's English department offers such a course for students beginning their dissertations. In the recent collection *Genre and Writing,* JoAnn Campbell presents another example, describing a graduate English course she taught called Academic Writing as Social Practice. Moreover, as I indicated earlier, introductory graduate classes seem an especially relevant forum for discussing literary studies as a discourse.

Departments should realize, however, that limited measures such as these may wind up making students hungry for more. As I can personally attest, Maryland's course at the dissertation stage now strikes many graduate students there as being too little and too late. They want more such courses, and they want them earlier. Indeed, it may be student demand rather than faculty interest that gets English graduate programs really pondering the "network of signifiers" that constitutes literary studies' "meanings, objects, and practices."

Notes

1. See, e.g., Bauerlein; Fahnestock and Secor; Levin; Macdonald; and Sosnoski *(Modern, Token).*

2. Also useful to consult is Patricia Sullivan's report on how particular students coped with writing tasks in the graduate English program at Ohio State.

3. Fahnestock and Secor provide additional examples of the appearance/reality disjunction as it shows up in literary criticism (84–86).

Works Cited

Aristotle. *On Rhetoric: A Theory of Civic Discourse.* Ed. and trans. George A. Kennedy. New York: Oxford UP, 1991.

Bartholomae, David. "Inventing the University." *When a Writer Can't Write: Studies in Writer's Block and Other Composing-Process Problems.* Ed. Mike Rose. New York: Guilford, 1985. 134–65.

———. "The Tidy House: Basic Writing in the American Curriculum." *Journal of Basic Writing* 12 (1993): 4–21.

Bauerlein, Mark. *Literary Criticism: An Autopsy.* Philadelphia: U of Pennsylvania P, 1997.

Campbell, JoAnn. "Alternative Genres for Graduate Student Writing." *Genre and Writing: Issues, Arguments, Alternatives.* Ed. Wendy Bishop and Hans Ostrom. Portsmouth, NH: Boynton/Cook, 1997. 265–75.

Dickens, Charles. *Great Expectations.* Ed. Janice Carlisle. Boston: Bedford, 1996.

Eagleton, Terry. *Literary Theory: An Introduction.* 1st ed. Minneapolis: U of Minnesota P, 1983.

Fahnestock, Jeanne, and Marie Secor. "The Rhetoric of Literary Criticism." *Textual Dynamics of the Professions: Historical and Contemporary Studies of Writing in Professional Communities.* Ed. Charles Bazerman and James Paradis. Madison: U of Wisconsin P, 1990. 76–96.

Foucault, Michel. *Discipline and Punish: The Birth of the Prison.* Trans. Alan Sheridan. New York: Vintage, 1979.

Graff, Gerald. *Professing Literature: An Institutional History.* Chicago: U of Chicago P, 1987.

Levin, Richard. *New Readings vs. Old Plays: Recent Trends in the Reinterpretation of English Renaissance Drama.* Chicago: U of Chicago P, 1979.

Macdonald, Susan Peck. *Professional Academic Writing in the Humanities and Social Sciences.* Carbondale: Southern Illinois UP, 1994.

Messer-Davidow, Ellen R., David R. Shumway, and David J. Sylvan. "Introduction: Disciplinary Ways of Knowing." *Knowledges: Historical and Critical Studies in Disciplinarity.* Ed. Messer-Davidow, Shumway, and Sylvan. Charlottesville: UP of Virginia, 1993. 1–21.

Perelman, Chaim, and Lucie Olbrechts-Tyteca. *The New Rhetoric: A Treatise on Argumentation.* Trans. J. Wilkinson and P. Weaver. Notre Dame: U of Notre Dame P, 1969.

Prior, Paul. "Response, Revision, Disciplinarity: A Microhistory of a Dissertation Prospectus in Sociology." *Written Communication* 11 (1994): 483–533.

Schilb, John. "Scholarship in Composition and Literature: Some Comparisons." *Academic Advancement in Composition Studies: Scholarship, Publication, Promotion, Tenure.* Ed. Richard C. Gebhardt and Barbara Genelle Smith Gebhardt. Mahwah: Erlbaum, 1997. 21–30.

Schor, Hilary. "'If He Should Turn to and Beat Her': Violence, Desire, and the Woman's Story in *Great Expectations.*" Dickens 541–57.

Sosnoski, James J. *Modern Skeletons in Postmodern Closets: A Cultural Studies Alternative.* Charlottesville: U of Virginia P, 1995.

———. *Token Professionals and Master Critics: A Critique of Orthodoxy in Literary Studies.* Albany: State U of New York P, 1994.

Sullivan, Patricia A. "Writing in the Graduate Curriculum: Literary Criticism as Composition." *Journal of Advanced Composition* 11 (1991): 283–99.

Wall, Susan, and Nicholas Coles. "Reading Basic Writing: Alternatives to a Pedagogy of Accommodation." *The Politics of Writing Instruction: Postsecondary.* Ed. Richard Bullock and John Trimbur. Portsmouth, NH: Boynton/Cook, 1991. 227–46.

Eight

Inventing Gender:
Creative Writing and Critical Agency

Molly Hite

In the United States the discipline of English is often more like three disciplines, each with its own faculty, value system, and budget. The area of study we now tend to call by the portmanteau name of literature-and-theory, which includes various kinds of cultural studies, media studies, gender studies, and Third World studies, has the lion's share of the prestige, to the point where it is what we usually mean when we speak of the profession of English. Unlike either of the other two specializations, it deals with the reception rather than the production of written, performed, or otherwise presented works. A second discipline, which will not directly concern me here, is composition, often the unacknowledged source of an English department's institutional power. The third of the disciplines of English is creative writing. Like composition, it aims at producing writing rather than consuming and interpreting writing that already exists. Unlike composition, it can have considerable prestige, although its relation to the lit-and-theory component of the department is often that of a charming but feckless younger sibling. A creative writing classroom is concerned with the same kind of object that concerns a lit-and-theory classroom: a piece of fiction or poetry. It theorizes this object very differently.

I emphasize that lit-and-theory is concerned with the reception of a culturally produced work while creative writing is directly concerned with cultural production, because these two relations give us different ends of the cultural text and entail different regions of ignorance. I am going to suggest that the founding assumptions of creative writing programs have generally kept the field in a universalist-humanist framework in which "the" subject ("the" author," "the" narrator, "the character, "the" reader) has certain kinds of economic and social privileges until proved otherwise. I am also going to suggest that the same assumptions favor particular kinds of writing styles and approaches that are somewhat different from the styles and approaches valued within the lit-and-theory camp. But I do not think that '80s and '90s-style lit-and-theory has simply got right what creative writing in its old-fashioned tenacity continues to get wrong. I am inclined to say that the ideological differences reveal problems in concepts of authoriality and authority taken for granted (or carefully avoided) in current practices of literary criticism, problems I can best indicate by mentioning the insistent student question, "Do you think the author did this on purpose?"[1] To abbreviate what could in another context be a very long discussion, lit-and-theory is insufficiently attentive to the processes by which writing *gets made.* In assimilating elements of critical theory into its own approaches, the discipline of creative writing might well help construct more intelligible theories about motivation, intention, and the individual and political unconscious in the making of cultural objects.

For the purposes of this discussion I am interested in fiction—both the study of fiction written by other people and fiction writing. Most of my own work is literary criticism that considers formally experimental twentieth-century fiction, and most of my teaching is in lit-and-theory courses on subjects such as modernism and postmodernism. My approach is generally feminist, and I also teach courses in feminist theory. Occasionally, however, I cross over into creative writing: creative as opposed to critical and theoretical, writing as opposed to reading and analyzing. The line is well marked, and crossing it makes me into a somewhat different sort of writer and teacher. The change occurs when I move into a discipline that defines fiction writing as an essentially creative activity.

In the context of writing programs, "creative" has traditionally been the sign of the natural. The standard workshop injunctions to avoid "forced" or "pretentious" phrases, to "find your own style" and to "write about what you know" all affirm the ground principle that good writing comes as naturally as leaves to a tree. At the same time, workshop procedure presumes that the natural is achieved only with craft and labor. Clearly, then, the natural is a *kind* of writing, comfortable because familiar, following certain patterns and models rather than others. In practice it is distinguished on the one hand from formally "difficult" work that challenges too strenuously the structural and stylistic conventions of the high-culture mainstream, and on the other hand from writing that has a palpable design on us or simply work that presents characters and situations perceived to be outside a particular norm of the representative. The standard of the natural thus places stringent limits on both the form and the content of workshop writing.

These limits have odd ideological contours. They foster a particular set of assumptions, even in classes taught by a feminist postmodernist. For instance, in one of my workshops two young men got into a jocular argument about whether there could be such an outré thing as a black lesbian poet. As far as I could tell, the question of possibility arose because this kind of poet would embody in her own person at least three separate deviations from the standard, or base model poet. Another instance: in at least two classes I had to impose a moratorium on the judgment "wordy," used to condemn stories that contained either long sentences or unfamiliar words. Both stylistic choices struck a majority of seminar participants as showing off, or at least as unnecessarily disrupting a story that could be told "directly," if the writer chose from a set group of familiar approaches.

The emphasis on the natural is of course at odds with the main theoretical tendencies in English departments from the 1980s through the present. In lit-and-theory classes, students tend to discuss the social construction of identity. In writing workshops the same students are encouraged to regard personal experience as an unmediated given and to "discover" their own "voices." The premises of the workshops thus carry on an older academic approach to works and authors. In 1989 Donald Morton and Masu'ud Zavarzadeh noted an alliance beween academic faculty committed to the supposedly apolitical tenets of bourgeois humanism and the faculty of creative writing programs. They commented, "[I]n a new political move, humanist scholars and critics are embracing creative writing programs as bastions of the inviolable human imagination, of solid because 'unique' style and of linguistic integrity—in short as the site in which the 'expert' subject can be saved" (160). This "expert" subject is not only the autonomous, self-expressive writer and the professor who can apprehend this writer's genius, but also the hero, the artist as a young man, and the protagonist who embodies "our" most secret and intimate desires—to kill small animals, to murder our wives, to light out for the territories, and so on. That is, he is the peculiar constricted embodiment of human possibility that those of us who went to college in the 1950s, '60s and '70s are most likely to remember as the subject of identificatory interpretations. He persists, of course. As Morton and Zavarzadeh observe, he is still a mainstay of many lit-and-theory classrooms and carries an even more evident political charge. And as Morton and Zavarzadeh do not observe, "he" is hardly ever "she." The inviolable human subject, the solid because "unique" style, and the standard of linguistic integrity are all gendered—gendered masculine, although of course various female subjects are invited, and even required, to participate.

Yet the writing workshop is also a potential site for the production of literature challenging exactly the presumptions of this kind of reactionary humanism—for instance, literature that explores and constructs various possible meanings of sexual difference as determinants of a given subject in a particular historical and social context. The writing workshop can be a context for *inventing gender,* in a narrative discourse that may well be innovative formally as well as thematically. If the criterion of the natural can restrict both thematic and formal possibilities, form and content are not separable elements during the process of writing. As a consequence, workshops designed to provoke a radical rethinking of the premises behind the construction of gender can make the writer conscious of the representational conventions that have made these constructions seem inevitable.

Notice that in a discussion about producing rather than reading literature, "the author" has to be a given, although what sort of given is another question. "The author" who is the postulate of such discussions must to some extent limit and control possible readings through an act of writing that involves a series of decisions, albeit decisions made within a determinate social and cultural context. In other words, a writing practice setting out to *contest* the ideology of the subject that Morton and Zavarzadeh identified as a tenet of bourgeois humanism—an ideology that posits this subject as "free," as they put it, to "collaborate within the existing social system, a collaboration that assures the continuation of patriarchal capitalism"—still requires a notion of agency and subjectivity, albeit a somewhat different notion, precisely in order to question the normative structures that this existing social system insists are freely chosen and natural (161).

My own analysis of creative writing as an institution differs from Morton and Zavarzadeh's in that I do not see criticism and writing as utterly different activities, with all the social consciousness bunched up on the side of theoretically-oriented critics. I am more inclined to attend to the considerable evidence that individual faculty in writing programs in the United States are at least as concerned with the circumstances of their students and as likely to be political activists as their colleagues in literature-and-theory. Moreover, not all fiction and poetry writing classes are conducted on the model of the traditional or "straight" workshop. The issue I do want to address is how during a period when the entire discipline of literary study was transformed, most writing programs remained resolutely untheorized—which is to say, resolutely committed to a particular unstated theory of what writing ought to be and how it necessarily gets produced. Part of the power of this theory resides in the fact that it remains for the most part unarticulated and thus in the realm of goes-without-saying, so that it tends to be assumed and transmitted without critical evaluation. I accordingly speak of an ideology of the writing workshop that is in many ways the same bourgeois humanist ideology that informed the discipline of English up through the early-to-mid 1970s and that now informs publications such as the *New Criterion*. A key feature of this ideology, of course, is that it denies it is one: it is the ideology that opposes ideology. Varieties of poststructuralist theory, including Marxist and feminist theories, actively contest this ideology, although in various ways and from the standpoint of various other ideologies.

If many writing programs as they are currently constructed share their preconceptions with the older humanist critical tradition vying for hegemony with theoretically-inflected literary study in departments of literature across the country, the historical reason for this state of affairs is ironic. Creative writing as an academic practice dates at least from the founding of the Iowa Writers' Workshop in 1936 by a number of faculty including Norman Foerster, a leading exponent of New Humanist criticism. The creative writing movement did not flourish, however, until the late 1960s and early 1970s, when writing programs proliferated throughout the country, styling themselves in opposition to the conformity-seeking, bureaucratic academy. In this respect they shared in some, though by no means all, of the ideology of the counterculture, including the New Left in its more romantic aspects.[2] This ideology helped foster a vision of the writer as by nature a seer. Somewhat paradoxically, the creative capacity of this writer was supposed to be manifested in the accuracy with which he depicted the preexisting and universally apprehensible ground called reality, which he perceived with special clarity and imitated using the conventions sanctioned by the real itself—that is, of realism. Despite this fidelity to the dictates of the external world, however, he was by nature a rebel and a solitary, someone whose inherent integrity led him to discover and sustain an individual "voice" capable of rendering the real accurately and unflinchingly. That he was supposed to "create" rather than construct or invent his fictions was thus a defining characteristic of the producer rather than the product, stressing his own Godlike independence of material conditions (creation, unlike construction or invention, carries the implication of *ex nihilo*) and placing him within a version of reality described by Pierre Macherey in terms of its implied allegiance to a philosophy of extreme voluntarism. As Macherey observed, "The proposition that the writer or artist is a creator belongs to a humanist ideology. In this ideology man is released from his function in an order external to himself, restored to his so-called powers. Circumscribed only by the resources of his own nature he becomes the maker of his own laws" (66).

This vision of the artist as solitary genius presumes a degree of freedom that can only arise from social and economic privilege. I have thus used the masculine pronoun throughout this description, in accordance with a proposition of the ideology, so evident as to remain largely unarticulated, that girls hardly ever grow up to be Satan or Prometheus. On the contrary, women figured in this romantic myth of the creative artist largely as blocking characters, representatives of the institutions that constrain individuality and stifle the outrageous yawp of the authentic writing voice. Morton and Zavarzadeh are correct to assume that a female student may under many circumstances perceive herself as autonomous and thus as freely collaborating with the existing social system. But their analysis does not take into account the ways in which even women of the upper middle classes resemble other socially marginalized students in being commensurately less able to participate in the ideology of the imperial subject, an ideology that in many respects constitutes itself by excluding them.[3]

I mentioned the young men in one of my workshops who regarded a black lesbian poet as nearly unthinkable. As this anecdote suggests, the implicit invocation of privilege in the creative writing classroom tends to mean that students are less self-conscious about classism, racism, and especially sexism and homophobia than are students in many lit-and-theory classrooms. Students who experience themselves as to an extent unfree, self-divided, or defined by their membership in a social or economic group—that is, as something other than the coherent, efficacious, unique subject of the humanist ideology—are under pressure in these workshops, where to be a writing subject is officially to have no specificity except the ultimate difference of personal uniqueness. As is usually the case, to insist on the fundamental uniqueness of the individual, as opposed to group membership, is tacitly to insist on one's membership in a particular group, the dominant one. Consider, for example, such (real) workshop comments as, "this story is about migrant workers so people can't really identify with it," or "this is a homosexual love poem but it's not offensive."

One interesting aspect of the ways the workshop stigmatizes such constructions of personal identity is that the terms used to dismiss overtly political writing, including writing concerned with minority characters who are treated as marginal to the dominant culture, are frequently the same terms as those used to dismiss structurally or stylistically innovative writing—writing that makes itself and its strategies visible to the reader. Both are likely to be called unpersuasive, implausible, or unrealistic. The fact that the same words can function as dismissals in two apparently different contexts suggests affinities between nontraditional content and nontraditional form. The realist narrative, evolving concurrently with bourgeois individualism, tends to carry certain kinds of ideological implications. One of the most ingrained of these implications is that protagonists of realist fiction *bring things on themselves:* they are in essential and even defining ways the captains of their own fates, the agents of their own destinies, however complex and ironic these destinies turn out to be. To challenge this premise as a writer is to produce a somewhat different sort of main character and a somewhat different sort of plot. Such ideological changes, such characters and plots, may ultimately entail a somewhat different kind of writing: conventionally "unrealistic," if not necessarily nonrealist or experimental.

The conventional judgment points up the affinities between the "unrealistic" and the nonrealist. To alter any of the acceptable conventions of representation is to call attention to these conventions *as* conventions, to point to their fundamentally artificial and arbitrary nature. Even narrative experiments that aim only to enlarge the scope of realist representation—to make realism in some sense more real—serve to defamiliarize conditions previously perceived as natural and thus as unchangeable.[4] The link between political and experimental writing here is that both tend to reveal the postulated natural order of experience as a construction, one among many possible, one that can accordingly be changed. If one role of a fiction opposing the dominant ideology is to expose this fact, another role of such an oppositional fiction might be to construct other possible configurations of the real. In a feminist context, both fictional projects might be termed inventing gender because they begin from an acknowledgment that sexual difference is *made,* in the same general way that a story is made. They might aim to participate discursively in remaking sexual difference.

Inventing gender in this sense involves students in feminist literary production in that it emphasizes the authorial subject as conscious, self-conscious, and self-consciously contextualized in social and cultural constructions of identity. In this situation, a student may be writing very different kinds of fiction than she or he would ordinarily produce in a workshop. To address conventions of representation directly is always, if only to a degree, to render dubious the category of the natural—and this includes the notion of writing as something that comes naturally and carries the instant credibility of the well-written, the easy-to-read, the work that flows. For a writer thus engaged in thinking about how her representation *invents* the natural, the question "What shall I write about?" is inseparable from the question "How should I write it?"

In feminist writing workshops, where the rubric of feminist theory helps ward off some of the most evident presumptions of the ordinary workshop, experimental assignments tend to generate more enthusiastic responses than in the "straight" classes. In this kind of class, theory elicits works of prose fiction. For example, I used the three questions below at different points in a feminist writing workshop. The initial two questions address considerations of content—the first dealing with characters functioning in certain highly formulaic kinds of plot, the second dealing with the premises of a non-natural alternative reality. The third addresses considerations of form, emphasizing the implicit teleology of narrative structure. The narratives that students produced, however, necessarily engaged both content and form, often in imaginative, innovative ways.

1. What happens when roles in genre fiction—for example, the romance, the gothic romance, the detective story, the police procedural, and the Western—are assigned to characters of the conventionally opposite sex, but the other genre conventions remain intact? Consider as cases in point the foul-mouthed female detective who regularly gets beat up, the female cop who embodies the most stereotypical racist, sexist, and homophobic cop attitudes, the male child care provider who finds himself menaced by two mysteriously potent and attractive women, the male nurse or secretary secretly attracted by an overbearing, dismissive female boss.
2. What sorts of inner life and interactions would be possible among member of a species undistinguished by sexual difference? Among members of a species with three or more distinct sexes?
3. Is it possible to construct a work of fiction with multiple climaxes? What could one do—if anything—to reinforce the implication that these multiple climaxes should be *read* as multiple and not just accretive excitations in the course of a traditional "rising action"?

The first assignment, which involved regendering the protagonist of a "genre" plot while retaining intact the other conventions of the genre, necessarily focused attention on these conventions and revealed the extent to which they themselves are gendered. For example, the tough female cop of the police procedural has to be described by a third-person omniscient narrator, but students discovered that in addition this narrator can do little reporting of such a cop's inner states—reflections, feelings, or other "subjective" experiences. Although characters in procedurals are far more complicated than, say, characters in classic Agatha Christie-style detective stories, where the emphasis is on plotting, the procedural relies heavily on dialogue to develop and convey character. The omniscient narrator may indeed report on a protagonist's attitudes, but these are more likely to be presented in terms that are universal. Cops in procedurals often brood about the nature of crime or of victimhood, about law and enforcement and the incapacity of human beings to make one or succeed in the other. Conversely, the menaced male child-care provider of the Gothic has to be far more subject to terrors, trepidations, and unnameable yearnings than conventions for representing embattled masculinity normally allow. Like the terrified and fascinated secretary or nurse of other set romance forms, he must brood over what the gendered other thinks and feels about him and maintain an artful passivity while trying to interpret the signals that the superior is sending. In other words, this first assignment called attention to ways in which extended representations of the "subjective" or "inner" life connote femininity, while the more laconic mode of reportage, conveying action, dialogue, or meditation on very large subjects, connotes masculinity.

The second assignment, advancing the premise of either a one-sex or a more-than-two-sex society, turned out to restructure the romance plot by violating the principle of complementarity that undergirds this plot. In the process of dismantling the dichotomy masculine/feminine, students who undertook this assignment discovered that they were exposing a whole scaffolding based on binary oppositions. (We had decided as a class to rule out more or less equivalent binaries such as butch femme.) The assignments produced a number of failed narratives and several more successful stories in which writers decided to redefine radically what romance might entail. My favorite detailed the development of a passionate threesome who shared an obsession with Monopoly.

The third assignment, which began with a formal question about the possibility of constructing a plot with multiple climaxes, proved impossible to bring off without some (parodic) reference to the sexual implications of both conventional and unconventional narrative structures, one indication of how entrenched this particular convention is to the entire Western notion of "story." One interpid student decided to take on the kind of writing with the most conventionally complete closure, the detective novel:

> Well, that's over," he said, pocketing the pistol. "Let's get everybody together and you can explain how this all happened."
> "No!" she gasped. "There's been *another murder!*"
> He pulled out the weapon and raised it wearily. "You just never quit, do you?"
> She cried, "Oh God! I see it all now!"
> "Again?" His arm felt unbearably heavy. "It's going to take me a while to aim," he warned her.

In general, the most radical examinations of subject matter produced radical innovations in form, and vice versa.

Other questions, analogous at least to the first two, could be formulated to deal with other kinds of specificity—race, class, sexual preference. The central device here, a foregrounding and questioning of representational conventions, politicizes the aesthetic realm, a strategy that could be extended to other kinds of questioning. My classes invented gender, and along the way did a lot of inventing of sexual preference. Other workshops might be focused on inventing class or race.

"Invention" in this context has the opposite connotation of "creation" in another important respect. Whereas the "creative" writing class characteristically encourages participants to write about what they know, relating their unique experiences through an authorial act aiming to expose their most inner and unsharable truths—"We are telling our terrible secrets," Amy Hempel reported when describing her fiction workshop with Gordon Lish—the theoretically-informed variant I have described, which for the sake of symmetry I will call the inventive writing class, demands reflection on the consequences of various narrative choices and thus emphasizes the gap between writer and written-about. The aim of even the most avowedly autobiographical writing in an inventive writing class can never be unmediated self-revelation, and the "self" thus revealed must always be acknowledged as to some degree a product of the writing. In a sense, writers in an inventive writing class are always writing about what they *don't* (yet) know.

The notion of agency implied in invention seems equally important for the *reading* of feminist writing. I have suggested that "straight" writing workshops share in bourgeois humanist assumptions about the nature of writing and the writer. These assumptions take an exceptionally damaging form when they are applied to women's writing, including those instances when they are applied to women's writing by critics who regard themselves as feminist but still adhere to humanism's "common-sense" dicta. Among these notions is the maxim that the artist "expresses" a preexisting self on the page, a metaphor that in the case of a woman writer is even more likely to imply that her writing is the product of squeezing out her insides like toothpaste from a tube. As Mary Jacobus has noted, both male and female humanist critics tend to conflate the author and her work, assuming uncritically that "women's writing is somehow closer to [women's] experience than men's, that the female text *is* the author, or at any rate a dramatic extension of her unconsciousness. The notion of invention may grant a measure of authority to the female author while acknowledging the importance of her marginality, her difference—that is, without collapsing her immediately into that ungendered, autonomous, universal, and heroic figure the creative artist.

Both as critics and as writers, as teachers of lit-and-theory and as teachers of writing, professionals in all the disciplines of English need to recognize that it is at least possible to invent things: to make them up. Among the things that can be made up is a whole range of selves rather different than those any given society has invented, and a whole range of texts that act and mean in a variety of ways. Because fiction can invent apparently natural characteristics such as gender, fiction can engage in the one of the fundamental activities of cultural criticism, which is to suggest that apparently natural characteristics can very well be otherwise.

Notes

1. As I write, the e-list of the International Society for Narrative Literature is once again engaged with this problem of authorial intentionality. Although New Critics and post-structuralists had a rare moment of unanimity in the assertion that the author and her purposes are irrelevant to the business of reading, it is impossible to separate reading so completely from writing. After all, no one can write, not even against the idea of authorial intention, without a certain faith that one's own intentions will condition the way the argument is received.

2. The notion of a writer that undergirds such writing programs is the intensification of an artistic identity described at length in the work of Pierre Bourdieu and, in a U.S. context, John Guillory.

3. In the spirit of gender-neutrality, they use the feminine pronoun as much as the masculine, e.g., "a subject who perceives herself as self-constituted and free" (18). My point is that the ideology is *not* gender-neutral, nor is, consequently, participation in it.

4. According to Maureen Howard, writing on the fitieth anniversary of the Iowa Writers' Workshop, the director Jack Leggett "allows that in judging the poems and stories of applicants, the selection committee avoids extremes, steering clear of experimental work . . ." (168). Phillip Brian Harper argues that such "extremes" are to some extent inevitable when the writer is that "extreme" individual the socially marginalized subject, and that in particular the decentered subject of postmodernist writing is in many respects not a nonrepresentational construct but an accurate representation of necessarily decentered social minorities.

Works Cited

Bourdieu, Pierre, *The Field of Cultural Production: Essays on Art and Literature.* Oxford: Polity Press, 1993.

Guillory, John. *Cultural Capital: The Problem of Literary Canon Formation.* Chicago: U of Chicago P, 1993.

Harper, Philip Brian. *Framing the Margins: The Social Logic of Postmodern Culture.* New York: Oxford UP, 1994.

Hempel, Amy. "Captain Fiction." *Vanity Fair* (December 1984).

Howard, Maureen. "Can Writing Be Taught in Iowa?" *New York Times Magazine* (25 May 1986): 168.

Jacobus, Mary. Review of Sandra Gilbert and Susan Gubar, *The Madwoman in the Attic. Signs* 6:3 (1981).

Macherey, Pierre. *A Theory of Literary Production.* London: Routledge and Kegan Paul, 1978.

Morton, Donald, and Masu'ud Zavarzadeh. "The Cultural Politics of the Writing Wrokshop." *Cultural Critique* 11 (1988–1989).

Nine

Profiting Pedants:
Symbolic Capital, Text Editing,
and Cultural Reproduction

Laurie A. Finke

Martin B. Shichtman

l'écriture médiévale ne produit pas des variantes, elle est variance.
—Bernard Cerquiglini

Christopher Baswell, in a paper delivered at the Thirtieth International Congress on Medieval and Renaissance Studies, in Kalamazoo, reflected on the "heroic age of text editing" of the nineteenth and early twentieth century, which saw the production of scholarly editions of major medieval texts such as *Beowulf,* the romances of Chrétien de Troyes, Chaucer's works, the French Vulgate Cycle, and Langland's *Piers Plowman,* as well as the creation of societies such as the Early English Text Society (EETS) and the Société des Anciens Textes Français whose purpose was to produce and disseminate affordable and definitive editions of manuscripts inaccessible to all but a handful of antiquarians. Those engaged in this project became powerful and prestigious members of literature faculties—Walter Skeat, R. W. Chambers, J. M. Manly, H. Oskar Sommer, Israel Gollanz, Gaston Paris, Joseph Bédier, Eugene Vinaver.

For reasons we would like to explore in this essay, by the late 1960s and early 1970s text editing had largely fallen into disrepute among literature faculty, no longer a certain route to tenure and prestige in the profession. Both Jerome McGann and Derek Pearsall lament "the rift between textual studies and literary criticism (especially hermeneutics) . . . that began to display itself in a serious way about fifty years ago and that has grown wider and deeper ever since" (McGann vii). Derek Pearsall conveys the consternation of most textual scholars and editors when he writes that the major advances in the field of Middle English literature for the past thirty years have been "in the work of interpretation, evaluation, comparative study, and literary history, and most scholars have been content to regard textual criticism as a matter for specialists, or at least somebody else's business" (Pearsall 92).

Baswell's response to the prominence in medieval studies of what Pearsall calls the "untextual reader" (94) is to argue that challenges to the dominant para-

digms of medieval studies from feminists, literary theorists, and other cultural critics are doomed to reproduce the very order they challenge if they continue to accept as finished the editorial work of the last century. He calls for a new monumental editorial project informed by a very different set of theoretical and
ideological assumptions. Baswell would seem to be in the vanguard of such a new
project. Yet his nostalgia for the heroism of his predecessors and his exhortation to
his colleagues to sacrifice instant fame and return to the archives—an exhortation
almost ritualistically rehearsed at meetings of medievalists—lacks an analysis of the
politics and economics of scholarly reputation. This essay will examine moments
in the history of editing medieval manuscripts. We will try to show why in the late
nineteenth and early twentieth century text editing could bring professional reputation and influence to its practitioners, why after World War II symbolic capital
ceased to accrue to philologists and medieval scholars, and, finally, why in the next
decade digital reproduction and transmission may recenter the academic enterprise
making text editing once again a profitable means of career advancement for the
medievalist. This essay, then, will explore the interplay among scholarly reputation,
symbolic capital, and academic self-fashioning.

It is not enough, we believe, simply to decry the hard times upon which
scholarly editing has steadily fallen in the last four decades and call for self-
sacrificial initiatives, usually on the part of graduate students or untenured colleagues. We must understand how the system of rewards and punishments within
the profession itself conditions the sorts of scholarly work that can profitably be
pursued by graduate students and the newest members of our profession. Charity
Canon Willard's call at a 1995 Christine de Pisan conference for her auditors to
set their graduate students to work on the unedited texts of the fifteenth-century
French poet will remain a hollow one until we understand why that particular
choice is no longer a route to tenure, or even survival in an increasingly competitive job market. Graduate students and the armies of untenured assistant professors and instructors seeking even a modicum of job security are all too aware that
the choices they make to pursue this or that scholarly project will have consequences for their employability. Maureen Curnow, whose 1975 doctoral dissertation is the only scholarly edition of Christine's *Cité des Dames* ever made (it remains to this day unpublished), has never held a tenure-track academic position.
The ink was barely dry on James Spisak's edition of Caxton's *Morte d'Arthur* when
tenure disputes drove him to seek employment with the federal government. While
we do not take exception with Baswell's argument that our fashionable new literary theories require us to return to the manuscripts and rethink the assumptions
on which the medieval texts we take for granted are based, we believe that such a
reexamination will only begin when the scholars who undertake such labors are
confident that they will not go unrewarded.

At the same time that medievalists like Pearsall are lamenting the disrepute
into which scholarly editing has fallen, the editors of electronic text projects are

describing their projects in hyperbolic terms: "the most fundamental change in textual culture since Gutenberg" (Delany 5); "advances on the scholarly business of critical editing will be at least equal to that of the recensionist method associated with Karl Lachmann on nineteenth-century (and later) editors, and perhaps as great as that of the invention of printing itself" (Robinson 280). Because those promoting the benefits of electronic text editing so often claim to stand on the shoulders of those giants who preceded them and speak, like Baswell, so nostalgically of the heroic efforts of their predecessors, before we can turn to the ostensible subject of our paper—the politics of reputation that may accompany text editing in the age of digital reproduction—we must examine the material and cultural practices of scholarship that attended the "heroic age of text editing" in the late nineteenth century and the circumstances that led to its decline in the twentieth century.

Friend and Gossip of the Dead

What Baswell refers to as the "heroic age of text editing" coincided with the professionalization of the university in the last part of the nineteenth century. In literary studies the vanguard was represented by German-trained philologists who promoted the systematic and scientific study of modern languages (Graff 55). As colleges and universities in the United States shifted their mission from training students in the classical languages to the study of modern languages, some method of instruction was required that would equal the rigor, precision, and status of the positivistic sciences that were rapidly becoming the standard against which scholarship was measured. Germanic or "scientific" philology served this agenda nicely. As Graff has written, the success of philology and textual studies in nineteenth and early-twentieth-century universities both in America and Britain was fed by several sometimes contradictory needs, including a "nostalgia for the past, especially the European past and the Middle Ages, at the same time it met the desire for facts, for accuracy, for the imitation of the `scientific method' which had acquired such overwhelming prestige." At the University of Chicago, the philologist J. M. Manly could describe himself in a 1909 article as "a humble follower in paths of science long known and well charted" (Brewer 192), while the American Chaucer editor Mark Liddel could write in 1902 that language and literature presented "a field for scientific study much like that of Economics or Ethics . . . provided one took the trouble to investigate the phenomena in a scientific spirit" (Brewer 200). The teaching of German philology even in the introductory stages of the American university curriculum was fueled by the presence among English department faculty of large numbers of German-trained philologists. By the end of the nineteenth century at Johns Hopkins University, every undergraduate's introduction to English was through the early forms of its language and literature. "'Initial courses in

Anglo-Saxon and Middle English were prerequisite to more advanced courses such as Gothic' and 'the ultimate Indo-European affinities of English,'" while at the University of Minnesota, English majors spent the first two years on Old and Middle English (Graff 100–101).

Even a cursory glance at the first volumes of the *Publications of the Modern Language Association* reveals the extent to which philologists' concerns dominated the professional publications in this country and how far those concerns are from those of the MLA today. In the very first volume of 1884–1885, a high school principal, Francis B. Gummere, published an article on the importance of applying the principles of Old English philology to the teaching of English at all levels, even the elementary (170). Of the sixteen articles published in Volume 15 at the turn of the last century, ten were on medieval subjects and four dealt with topics in linguistics and philology. One can easily imagine the fate of a six-page note on the Germanic suffix -*ar-ja* if it were submitted to *PMLA* today; in 1900 it was printed. The table of contents also includes two editions, a Latin text of an Arthurian romance called *Meriadoci,* and a French edition of *La Vie de Sainte Catherine d'Alexandrie.* If the influence of philology and textual scholarship were waning by the 1920s, it would not be apparent from looking at *PMLA,* which in volume 35 (1920) was edited by Carleton Brown; out of twenty-two articles twelve deal with pre or early modern literature, including an essay by Curry on Chaucer and one by Patch on the *Ludus Coventraie* and Digby *Massacres.*

The call to science that characterized the methodology of late-nineteenth and early-twentieth-century text editors stood in direct opposition to the sort of study described by James Russell Lowell in his 1889 address to the MLA, where he spoke of literature as a "mysterious and pervasive essence always in itself beautiful, not always so in the shapes it informs, but even then full of infinite suggestion" (Graff 88). Lowell and others who shared his frustration with literary study as a stockpiling of information could, however, offer little in its stead. Lacking a theory to inform their passion, they advanced only a rhetoric of vagueness, a celebration of subjectivity, which held few attractions when compared to the illusions of objectivity maintained by the practitioners of those technologies that made text editing possible. For those who studied philology and edited texts, the association with science simultaneously provided for the enhancement of professional reputation and masked the ambition for that reputation. They fashioned themselves as seekers of objective truths, who, because their quests were the only ones genuinely worthwhile—among other things, the truths they sought promoted good morals and nationalistic devotion—soon became the most powerful members of the profession.

Those who were less enthusiastic about the new philology certainly felt that the philologists and textual scholars with their German theories of manuscript recension and vowel shifts monopolized the mechanisms of professional advancement, often to their detriment. According to Graff, Stuart Sherman, a Harvard Ph.D. of 1906, blamed scholars such as George Lyman Kittredge, who joined the

Harvard faculty in 1888, for turning students into "zealous bibliographers and compilers of card indexes." Kittredge, he said, was "a potent force in bringing about the present sterilizing divorce of philology from general ideas," while Irvine Babbitt complained that he "'felt bitterly the way in which Kittredge and one or two others' had 'blocked his advancement' at Harvard" (Graff 66, 88).

But the politics of reputation rarely express themselves so blatantly. We might get a more nuanced look at the success of the major editorial projects of the nineteenth century by examining the reputations of those two most indefatigable of British editors, F. J. Furnivall and W. W. Skeat. In England, the scientific methods of manuscript recension were much slower to gain acceptance. As Charlotte Brewer writes, "There was a new surge of interest in England's medieval literature during the course of the 19th century . . . . But there was little corresponding interest in and discussion of the proper way to edit texts. . . . English scholars seemed to have a distrust and ignorance of systems of editing, just as they had a distrust and ignorance of the systematic rules established by the new philology" (Brewer 68). This is not to say that British editors never linked their projects to scientific positivism when it served their cause. Despite the fact that he did not actually use German methods of manuscript recension to prepare his edition of *Piers Plowman,* Skeat wrote in 1873 that "it is high time that a true critical school should be established, and a true scientific method of instruction and inquiry should be adopted" (Brewer 104).

Despite British antiquarians' distrust of fashionable continental theories of editing, the late nineteenth century nonetheless saw the completion of ambitious editorial projects in England, including the work of the EETS, which Furnivall founded in 1864 to enable the publication of manuscripts that had hitherto been accessible only to those few scholars who could read them, and Skeat's massive edition of the A,B, and C texts of *Piers Plowman.* During the forty years of Furnivall's leadership, the EETS published 140 volumes of edited manuscripts (DNB 63). The primary impetus for this project seems to have been nationalism, a belief that the nation's earlier literature holds the key to understanding its true identity and destiny. According to the *Dictionary of National Biography,* Furnivall considered it his patriotic duty to print from manuscript works that were otherwise inaccessible to his fellow Englishmen. In his annual report to the EETS in 1867, Furnivall explicitly outlines this nationalistic agenda: "[T]he study of the native literature has a moral effect as well. *It is the true ground and foundation of patriotism.* . . . We too are a great historic nation; we too have 'titles manifold'. . . . I call that man uncivilized who is not connected with the past through the state in which he lives, and sympathy with the great men who have lived in it" (Brewer 73). Skeat used the same patriotic appeal in his proposal for a three volume edition of *Piers Plowman* in Volume 17 of the EETS, appealing to "any one who remembers how the old poem had called up before him the picture of his forefathers' life, and shown him the earnestness with which they strove for Truth amidst the many corruptions of their time" (Brewer 108).

A third factor—along with scientific methods of pedagogy and blatant nationalism—that fueled editing projects in England in the late nineteenth century
was the Philological Society's plan for the New Dictionary of the English Language
(later retitled the Oxford English Dictionary). As Skeat explains in his memoir, *A
Student's Pastime*, work on an English dictionary based on historical principles
could not even begin until the large mass of manuscript evidence was made available in inexpensive editions to readers who often lacked the access or skill to read
the manuscripts. Furnival created EETS primarily to fill this need (Skeat).

The reputations of these two founding fathers of English editorial practice
have been carefully tended by portraits in the *Dictionary of National Biography* by
Kenneth Sisam (Skeat) and Sidney Lee (Furnivall), by a festschrift in honor of Furnivall's seventy-fifth birthday, and by their own memoirs and biographies. Contemporary accounts of both men tend to stress not the power and prestige these
two men must have wielded, but the unselfish nature of their labors in the vine-
yards of English literature. According to these accounts, they worked not for pe-
cuniary reward, but for their love of their subject. To be sure, both Furnivall and
Skeat were, in effect, amateur antiquarians; they were both trained as mathemati-
cians and neither were remunerated for their literary and editorial efforts, at least
until 1878 when Skeat, appointed the first Bosworth Chair of Anglo-Saxon at
Cambridge, finally received the £500 and a room of his own that Virginia Woolf
argues is vital to the life of the mind (Skeat). Furnivall's labors for EETS, the
Chaucer Society, Wycliff Society, the Shakespeare Society, Philological Society, and
the host of other literary societies he organized were apparently unpaid. Verses by
George Saintsbury in the festschrift presented to Furnivall on his seventy-fifth
birthday also stress the unselfish nature of his contributions to English literature:

> And not for place or pay,
> But all for the fame of the English, he wrought in the
>   English way
> And his sheaves they follow, as his wage, at the closing of the
>   day. (Miscellany 1)

Here Furnivall is depicted not as working for either "place" or pay, but, as a true
Englishman, for the glory of England. The "wages" he sought were only the volumes themselves, proof of English superiority. Furnivall was fashioned by the
rather cloying poetic tribute of Stoppford A. Brook, "friend and gossip of the dead"
(Miscellany 3). According to one anecdote in his DNB biography, Furnival's financial resources in the last half of his life were so small that when he was left nearly
penniless in 1867, his wealthy friends bought up all the personal property he had
disposed of and restored it to him (DNB). Skeat likewise was supported by his father for most of his life, even after he took up the Bosworth Chair at Cambridge.
The Dictionary of National Biography notes, while praising "his vast output . . . dis-

tinguished by accuracy in matter of fact, wide learning, and humanity," that most of it Skeat produced "without prospect of reward, out of devotion to his subject" (DNB 496).

What's at stake in this representation of the late-nineteenth-century British academy? Why disguise the power and prestige these men enjoyed as an unremunerated labor of love? A certain complacency attends the letters, memoirs, biographies, and festschriften that are now our only source of information about the personalities behind the editorial projects of the late nineteenth century. The style is no doubt intrinsic to these genres, as if the raw display of power or reputation would be in bad taste. At times this modesty topos could backfire, reducing amateurishness to mere ineptitude, as for instance when Sir Frederic Madden refers to Furnivall as a "jackanapes" who should not be allowed to edit any of the work of the EETS: "His style of writing is thoroughly disgusting, and his ignorance is on par with his bad taste" (Brewer 85). Yet even in remarks such as these we can glimpse some of the status these men enjoyed. This status was evident in the controversies about *Piers Plowman,* for instance, that followed the appearance of Skeat's edition, controversies that appear to have enjoyed the patronage of both men (see Brewer 219–26 for an account). Certainly both Chambers and Knott understood that it would be wise to secure Skeat's and Furnivall's approval and cooperation before undertaking their own editions of *Piers Plowman.* What men such as Furnivall and Skeat had was the power of technical expertise and unlimited access to that which is available only to a privileged few (the manuscripts). That power was, at least ostensibly, mitigated by the claim that their project was to make this inaccessible knowledge available democratically to all. But what precisely was it that was being made available to the general public? Was it the original manuscript evidence or the editor's reconstruction of the medieval author's original work as he [inevitably he] intended it to appear? Until the advent of digital technology, the answers to this question and the power to determine what kinds of texts were available to the general public (and hence what knowledge they would have of the medieval texts) were solely in the hands of the text editor.

Will the Real New Philologists Please Stand Up?

We will borrow Roland Barthes's distinction between the "readerly" and "writerly" text to characterize two different kinds of editing practices that will be instrumental in determining how manuscript editing will survive the transition into the digital age.[1] In *S/Z* Barthes writes: "Our literature is characterized by the pitiless divorce which the literary institution maintains between the producer of the text and its user, between its owner and its customer, between its author and its reader. The reader is thereby plunged into a kind of idleness—he is intransitive; he is, in short, *serious:* instead of functioning himself, instead of gaining access to the magic of the signifer, to the pleasure of writing, he is left with no more than the poor freedom to accept or reject the text" (4). Such a text Barthes describes as "readerly." The "science" of manuscript recension pioneered by German philologists was based on this core assumption, positing that the medieval author's original work could be recovered from the detritus of its readers, that authorial intent could be understood once all manuscript variants (the results of various readings of the text) were exhumed, examined, and analyzed by professionals trained extensively in language, paleography, and editing practices. What was needed was simply time, patience, and, if one is to look honestly at the scope of the most ambitious editorial undertakings—such as, for instance, *The Variorum Chaucer*—a nearly inexhaustible supply of money. As such, this practice—which we will call the readerly editorial practice—aimed to produce a "readerly" edition of a medieval "work," one in which the poet was the only source of the work's meanings, which were imagined as fixed and recoverable through specialized techniques.

Not everyone, however, was (or is) equally committed to this method. As Peter Shillingsburg has written:

> It is questionable . . . whether authenticated texts are what critics or close students of works of art need. . . . [I]f scholarly editing involves critical judgment, authentication is a critical activity. It follows that persons relying upon authenticated texts are relying, unquestioningly, on the critical judgments of other scholars—something scholars seldom do in other spheres of their activities. (Shillingsburg 4)

Furnivall, whose interests were more linguistic and sociological than poetic, was content to produce diplomatic editions of individual manuscripts (and indeed he was, and still is, criticized for this choice). His edition of the *Canterbury Tales* for the Chaucer Society printed parallel texts of six manuscripts without editorial intervention, a practice some of his critics disdained as merely "mechanical" editing (Brewer 82–83). Yet we might read in his method another kind of editorial practice that makes "the reader no longer a consumer but a producer of the text" (Barthes 4). In this method, which we designate the "writerly" practice, the text is produced, "opened out" as much by its readers as by its author. Such editorial practices are concerned with understanding how readers of medieval texts made sense of them, as well as with offering the manuscript evidence intact to contemporary readers, allowing them to reconstruct medieval texts based on their own understanding of manuscript evidence rather than the authority of an editor.

The core assumption of the "writerly" editorial practice is that medieval texts may not have been as tied to what Michel Foucault calls the "author-function" as nineteenth and twentieth-century texts have been. In "What is an Author," Michel Foucault describes the function of the author in the age of mechanical reproduction:

[H]e is a certain functional principle by which, in our culture, one limits, excludes, and chooses; in short, by which one impedes the free circulation, the free manipulation, the free composition, decomposition, and recomposition of fiction. . . . The author is . . . the ideological figure by which one marks the manner in which we fear the proliferation of meaning. (Foucault 159)

Through readerly editing practices, text editors, by positing the author as the sole source of signification in the work, have been able successfully to link their authority with that of the author-function, and to limit the proliferation, circulation, and meaning of medieval texts. But the notion of an independent, stable text is a product of nineteenth-century editing practices and aesthetics. As Bernard Cerquiglini suggests in the epigram cited at the head of this essay, manuscript textuality does not simply produce variation; it is itself variability, in Barthes terms "a difference which does not stop . . . articulated upon the infinity of texts, of languages, of systems (3). Each manuscript is a unique event, representing not only the labor and genius of the poet, but also the activities of its medieval readers (patrons, scribes, illuminators, compilers, book makers, anthologizers, book collectors) who produce significations of their own. Writerly editing practices could open up new possibilities for understanding the text not as a fixed and immutable "work," but as an open and permeable "text" (Barthes). In the past editors have been limited in how far they can go to create writerly texts by the linear format of print (the EETS edition of Layamon's *Brut,* Furnivall's *Canterbury Tales,* Skeat's *Piers Plowman* are examples of fledgling attempts to create writerly medieval texts in the print media). Hypertext publishing opens up a whole new set of possibilities for the production of writerly texts, texts that can put readers' production of meaning into play.

It may have been the very success of the readerly editing project, coupled with the success of literary criticism (especially the New Criticism) in the university (see Graff), that was responsible for the decline throughout the twentieth century in the status of text editing as a scholarly pursuit. Once inexpensive editions of canonical medieval texts became readily available for classroom use, once publishers had a financial stake in continued classroom adoptions of those editions, once New Critical readings had converted these texts to timeless "verbal icons," it was perhaps inevitable that readerly editing would no longer command the kind of prestige it had previously enjoyed. Indeed, the New Criticism had a stake in the obsolescence of text editing, not only because its adherents saw it as a rival for resources and scholarly prestige, but also because its critical tenets required a stable and unchanging text. Once that text—Brooke's verbal icon—had been produced, the New Criticism had a stake in its timelessness and immutability. The constant reediting of texts would only call this assumption into question, revealing the shifting foundations upon which readerly editing and New Critical readings alike were based. Criticism's successes in undermining the centrality of the editing project can be seen in the professional diminution of manuscript editors from the 1950s to the present.

It is hardly surprising that the poststructuralist critique of the readerly text which came along in the late 1970s (Barthess' *S/Z* was published in this country in 1974) further undermined the stability of readerly editorial practices, subverting the very notion of "scientific" objectivity from which the project drew its authority. But the reaction of medievalists was not to question the process of producing medieval texts for scholarly consumption, but to elide altogether the move from manuscript to critical edition. Even *Speculum,* in what can only be regarded as a belated attempt in 1990 to catch the theoretical wave, dedicated an entire issue to the consideration of what a "new philology"—one that had wrestled with the insights of poststructuralist theory—might look like. This "new philology," however, only served to position manuscript editing even farther from the center of medieval studies by ignoring it entirely. It failed to consider, as Baswell suggests, that the insights of poststructuralism or cultural studies might require a reexamination of the very critical texts the issue's authors took for granted. It failed to consider that hypermedia might contribute toward the realization of poststructuralist medieval textuality, at the same time reinvigorating text editing as both an exciting and prestigious scholarly pursuit. It neglected to consider the potential for writerly texts to be produced through electronic and digital media and for these media to serve as a kind of "reified" poststructuralist theory (Bruno Latour uses the phrase *reified theory* to discuss the way in which objects or artifacts can literally embody a particular theory).

If the rest of the medieval studies community was ignoring text editing, those involved in electronic editing projects are clearly determined to take back the prestige they have lost. Their claims for the significance of their work are both conceptual and practical. Among the most important claims is that the production of texts through advanced technology (which involves highly specialized knowledges) will offer revolutionary ways of providing democratic access to medieval texts. In this claim they do not seem so far removed from their nineteenth-century counterparts who also made claims about the potential for specialized knowledge to provide democratic access to the contents of medieval manuscripts. Kevin Kiernan contends, repeatedly, in his World Wide Web (WWW) introduction to "The Electronic *Beowulf,*" that "an electronic *Beowulf* will provide better access to parts of the manuscript than studying the manuscript itself." Peter Robinson, in his WWW discussion of "*The Canterbury Tales* Project: its Predecessors and its History," maintains that "so far as I know, [*The Canterbury Tales* project] is the first time anyone has tried to present so great a mass of information of this kind about a whole textual tradition in electronic form (indeed, in any form)." Hoyt Duggan who, in his WWW essay, "Creating an Electronic Archive of *Piers Plowman,*" notes that "[w]ork on Piers Plowman has traditionally been in the vanguard of Middle English editorial practice" and that his electronic *Piers Plowman* project based at the University of Virginia will provide "an innovative editorial archive that will take advantage of the electronic revolution in textual studies." Karl J. Uitti, in his WWW position "paper," "A Brief History of the 'Charrette Project' and Its Basic Rationale," argues that "[s]cholarship on both sides of the Atlantic stands to gain from collaboration [on the Charrette Project] in many ways—surely some unforeseen at the present juncture," and goes on to suggest that "[o]ur procedure might well also contribute to preserve the manuscripts themselves from the effects of repeated handling by scholars and students—from otherwise inevitable wear and tear." He goes on to add a moral imperative to the project, insisting that the lessons derived from electronic editing will not only revolutionize critical/scholarly practice but will become central to our training of graduate students: "the pedagogical implications of our experience should not go unmentioned. To continue to train students in Old French paleography and textual criticism without encouraging them to take full advantage of present electronic technologies—technologies with which the younger generations of today are far more comfortable than many of their elders—would, quite simply, be unconscionable."

As the editors of electronic texts undertake this task of recentering manuscript editing within the medieval studies community, they link their efforts with those of their predecessors in ways that often border on hyperbole. Hoyt Duggan, for instance, refers to Walter W. Skeat's "twenty-odd years of heroic labor"and George Kane's "magisterial edition" of *Piers Plowman*'s A-Text. In doing so, he links the new digital *Piers Plowman* project with the assumptions and values of the old, to the principles of readerly editing that guided those predecessors. Nor is he alone in doing so.

One need only read the manifestos produced by those involved in electronic editing projects to see the centrality of readerly editing practices to their conception of this brave new world of hypertext. In such a practice, far from having any intrinsic artistic or historical interest, manuscripts are the enemy, concealing the poet's true words, which the editor must painstakingly reconstruct. Manuscripts are, in Duggan's words, "defective and fragmented handwritten documents", "imperfect documentary matrices" from which the editor needs to recover a lost original. Technology, in the form of the computer, is visualized as a faster and more efficient means of accomplishing the same old ends. Robinson's WWW discussion of the *Canterbury Tales* project describes the difficulties encountered by John Manly and Edith Rickert, who, for their edition of the *Canterbury Tales,* "gathered copies of all the witnesses and collated them all, word by word, and then sought to arrive at a single text on the basis of their analysis of the witness relations emergent from the patterns of agreements they found in this collation." Their efforts resulted in the monumental eight volume edition of *The Text of the Canterbury Tales.* The project, which took many years to complete, required, in Robinson's words, "labors of Herculean length, intensity, and consistency " (Robinson 274).

Rickert died before the edition was completed, and Manly was ill in the later stages, dying soon after it was finished. Despite the exhaustiveness of their effort, however, no modern editor has accepted their text nor did they leave enough evidence of their procedure for later scholars to find what they did particularly useful. Their edition finally raises more questions than it answers. Robinson concludes from this example not that there is something intrinsically flawed in the readerly editing practice, but that "Manly and Rickert's failure was that they were simply overwhelmed by the immense amount of evidence they gathered." They didn't have a computer, which would have saved them a great deal of time and bother and been much more accurate than mere human compilers: "The advent of the computer, and its application to textual editing, offers ways past the difficulties both of analysis of so much material and of its presentation in an accessible manner. Computers thrive on the sorting, organization, and presentation of just such vast collections of data as this."

These manifestos are not, however, entirely without reference to the possibilities of a postmodern writerly editorial practice. Virtually all the position "papers" on the electronic editing of medieval texts at least nod to contemporary theoretical critiques of readerly editorial practice. All at least glimpse the potential—or perhaps the inevitability given the technology—of a writerly editorial practice. The promise of freedom from the tyranny of the authorized edition lurks somewhere in the discourse of the editors of the Electronic *Beowulf,* the Electronic Archive of *Piers Plowman,* the Charrette Project, and the *Canterbury Tales* Project. Duggan repeatedly asserts, almost as a mantra of liberation that "[e]ditors of electronic texts, unlike earlier editors of printed editions, need not suppress or conceal editorial disagreement nor impose spurious notions of authority. They may, instead, exploit editorial disagreement and embrace the provisional nature of scholarly editing." Uitti similarly argues "[t]he Charrette Project has eliminated the need for a simple binarism of text vs. variant(s)—a requirement, it would appear, for modern printed editions. On the contrary, even in the case of so careful and poetically self-conscious an author as Chrétien de Troyes it seems that textuality comprises variant readings.'" Robinson begrudgingly admits that future students of an electronic *Canterbury Tales* might construct their own version of "what Chaucer is likely to have written," but only after arduous labor: "To discover the history of the text, even for just the earliest manuscripts, one must . . . look at every witness. . . . Nor is it possible to settle the question for just one part of the *Canterbury Tales,* in isolation from the rest. . . . To settle, as well as we can, what Chaucer is most likely to have written for any one word in any one part of the *Canterbury Tales* one must look at every word in every one of these eighty-eight witnesses to the text." Robinson, like most of his colleagues in the world of electronic editing, takes back with one hand what he gives with the other: readers can construct their own "writerly" text, but only if they pledge their allegiance to the discovery of what "Chaucer is most likely to have written."

Thus, the promise of freedom from the authorized text—and from the authority of the editor—is never really delivered. These editors cannot envision a truly writerly text, though it is very likely that such a text is inevitably implicit in technologies that they promote. This reluctance to grapple with poststructuralist and deconstructive potential of digital technology is presented most vividly by Hoyt Duggan, who comments on the eclecticism of the Electronic Archive of the *Piers Plowman* project, reasserting (perhaps in vain) the priority of the readerly editing project:

> To call oneself "eclectic" in this sense also implies a belief in the possibility, as well as the value, of retrieving authorial readings from complex traditions of scribal transmission. Such a commitment ought to be taken for granted in an editor.

But, Duggan complains, this venerable scholarly practice with its assumptions about the ultimately recoverable poetic word has been undermined recently by more writerly editing practices borne of poststructuralist and cultural theory.

> [T]he erosion of epistemological and cultural confidence has reached such a stage in literary studies that fashionable theorists (and some practicing editors) are retreating to "best-text" (or "diplomatic") editing, the commonest of premodern approaches. The best text editor merely chooses a "good" early copy to reproduce, occasionally emending obvious mistakes but avoiding subtle decisions. . . . The recent popularity of the method, however, is categorical rather than pragmatic. Chaucer, for example, is assumed to be unknowably remote. Moreover, any attempts to recover his social and political perceptions are taken to constitute an elitist disdain for those of his scribes. We reject both the skepticism and the naive populism of such opinions.

Why editing practices should not be informed by recent theoretical discussions about authorial intention or textual indeterminacy is not entirely clear from Duggan's remarks. He cannot mean to claim that readerly editing practice is self-evident, merely the most practical means of creating usable texts. The readerly editing practices of manuscript recension, as we have argued above, are informed by their own theoretical assumptions, assumptions that contemporary theory calls into question and which deserve closer scrutiny both by those who produce medieval texts and those who consume them. Duggan asserts the priority of authorial intention over current interest in the cultural milieu of manuscript production and reading, including the influence patrons, scribes, illuminators, and reading publics exerted over textual production, dismissing these cultural studies as "naive populism."

By refusing to relinquish the imaginary claims of the author-function, the editors of these electronic texts assert their own authority and hence centrality to the project of medieval studies. Duggan's argument demands that readers now submit to the professional determinations of current electronic editors as they did previously to book editors such as Skeat, Chambers, Mitchell, Grattan, Kane, Russell, and Donaldson. However, it is entirely possible that the readerly editorial project may simply collapse under the weight of the technology's potential for managing variance, opening up spaces for more writerly textual practices. As Duggan argues: "Effective representation of manuscript variants is a particular strength of an electronic text, since it will, when complete, permit a reader to see every variant from every manuscript by the simple expedient of calling up the line in a base text (which might be the critical edition, the archetype, or any other manuscript) and evoking the other manuscript readings in different windows or by consulting the output of COLLATE. Such a reader can also call up digitized facsimiles of the manuscript(s)." The *Piers Plowman* project seems a good case in point. It is our belief that no matter how much manuscript evidence the computer can transcribe, sort, collate, and otherwise organize, it will never tell us finally what Langland (if such a person existed) "really" wrote. Instead, we are much more likely to learn a great deal more about the ways in which this poem circulated among medieval readers: who read it, why they read it, where they read it, how they read it, and how they adapted it to their own purposes. We will learn about the texts that were read alongside of *Piers Plowman*. We may finally decide to abandon altogether the critical fiction that *Piers Plowman* is a single work of art with a single lone genius as its creator. We may finally come to treat the manuscript as an artifact in its own right, as a reified set of social relations between writers and readers, producers and consumers of books, rather than a ghost of a ruin that never existed—the author's "own words."

Blinded Us with Science

Yet the rhetoric Duggan adopts is finally as much strategic as it is theoretical. Why would he want to align his project against the textual play of contemporary literary and cultural theory and with conservative notions of authorial control? Electronic text editors are determined to add substantially to the literary community's store of knowledge, and the promise of their labors is substantial. But the professional politics involved in this repositioning of the text editor in medieval studies—and the literary profession, in general—should not be overlooked. Those who control the new technologies of electronic text editing are already situating themselves for realignment in a profession that has long disdained text editing as a manual practice. The Early English Text society has undergone a technological reincarnation in the Society for Early English and Norse Electronic Texts. Despite adherents' claims that "three decades of literary computing have failed to have any substantial impact on the mainstream of literary criticism and scholarship" (Delany 22), we would identify three signs of this realignment.

Like the nineteenth-century editing revolution, electronic text editing has based its claims about significance on the prestige the sciences still command in the twentieth-century university. All the discussions of the coming revolution in electronic text editing celebrate the wonders of new technologies that link the literary scholar with science. At times the language of such discussions can be, for the computer neophyte, overwhelming. But even for those somewhat familiar with the discursive practices of information systems, these descriptions can be intimidatingly esoteric, suggesting that electronic text editors are pushing against the folds of the technological envelope to accomplish their goals. Kiernan, for instance, writes: "The equipment we are using to capture the images is the Roche/Knotron ProgRes 3012 digital camera, which can scan any text, from a letter or a word to an entire page, at 2000 X 3000 pixels in 24–bit color. The resulting images at this maximum resolution are enormous, about 21–25 MB and tax the capabilities of the biggest machines." Duggan notes that: "The 30 MB tif files may be necessary for some manuscript pages, those with erasures or complicated stains. Such images may be doubled six times with a resulting image 32 times larger than the original. It should go without saying that 30–40 MB are expensive in terms of storage and slow to call to the screen and manipulate." Uitti and his collaborators, worried that tying the Charrette Project too closely to any particular word processing program might, given the rapid changes in computing, render its product quickly obsolete, decided that "our transcriptions would be from the start couched in SGML-TEI format, despite the ugly—even virtual unreadability—of this format." The language of these manifestos buttresses the projects' claims to scientific precision, to a certainty that seems alien to the textual indeterminacies of literary poststructuralism. Through the wizardry of computer science and graphics, medieval manuscripts, those "defective and fragmented handwritten documents," are rendered transparent, forced to yield up their secrets to the probing eye of the digital camera (on the scientific project of visual transparency, see Stafford 131ff). The project is not, however, without its own nearly Derridean ironies. The choice by the Charette project collaborators to use the SGML-TEI format for the manuscript transcriptions, for instance, achieves transparency, but at the cost of readability. The choice makes incompatible computer platforms transparent to one another, but, for the casual reader, the text will be opaque.

For reasons that will become apparent from the size, cost, and ambition of these projects, electronic editing projects have also begun to replicate the hierarchical structures of scientific collaboration. For most of the twentieth century, literary research was performed by individual researchers—theoreticians and scholars. Employment, tenure, and promotion rewards single author compositions—articles and books. Every medieval electronic text project, however, is collaborative. Should the academic community recognize value in these projects, a system of rewards for collaboration will need to be conceived. The most handy model for such a reward system also lies near to hand in the sciences where collaborative research has long been the standard and research teams are organized in hierarchies from graduate students and laboratory assistants up to senior researcher. We can already see how senior scholars in charge of major electronic text editing projects have begun to promote the efforts of their most promising graduate students and junior colleagues. Duggan, for instance, mentions "Sean Taylor, a doctoral student at the University of Washington, working under the direction of Professor Paul Remley," who "has virtually completed an electronic edition of R, and if his finished and revised edition is accepted for publication by the Society for Early English and Norse Electronic Texts, he has consented to incorporate its text in the Archive." Uitti points out that "[a] small group of Princeton University graduate students in Romance Languages and Literatures interested in paleological issues and furthering their computing skills began to transcribe several of the manuscripts in Word-Perfect 5.1 (DOS) or Word for Macintosh format. Their work has been (and has continued to be) closely supervised by Professor Gina Greco, of Portland State University (Oregon). While participating in practically all the various aspects of the Project, Professor Greco has assumed most of the responsibility for the accuracy of these crucial transcriptions." For both Duggan and Uitti, the success of initiates is essential to the ultimate success of their projects, for it is these initiates who will ultimately bring electronic text editing to its next stage of evolution and prominence. In the realm of academic professional politics, Duggan's and Uitti's reputations will be judged as much by the success of their protegées as by their own work.

Finally, like the sciences, virtually all of those extolling the significance of electronic text editing discuss the value of these projects in terms of their cost. The humanities have at last found a potential means of bringing large research grants into their universities, an accomplishment on which much of the prestige of the sciences (and particular scientists) rests. Every electronic editing project demands extensive resources for hardware, software, computer time and expertise, international travel and communication. All of their proponents disclose some concerns about finances; most have sought and received grant monies. Kiernan writes of early communications difficulties at the Electronic *Beowulf:* "The first published facsimile of this text was transmitted by phone from one UK to another, from the British Library to the University of Kentucky. These few words cost $55 in a phone bill, but at least they arrived intact, unlike the hand carried images at Gatwick (destroyed by airport security). They seemed to portend the start of something really big, expensive, and earth shattering." The Electronic *Beowulf* has thus far received extensive support from the British Library Digital and Network Services Steering Committee and the University of Kentucky. The *Canterbury Tales* on CD-Rom project has received support from the Universities of Oxford and Sheffield and the British Academy. Funding for the development of the computer program COLLATE, developed by Peter Robinson for the *Canterbury Tales* on CD-Rom project, and the collation program now used in most electronic editing projects, was provided by the Leverhulme Trust. Thus far, the *Canterbury Tales* on CD-Rom project has produced the Wife of Bath's Prologue on CD-Rom, which gathers together all fifty-eight witnesses, a word-by-word collation of each witness, digital images of all 1,200 pages of manuscript and early printed editions, transcriptions of glosses, descriptions of each witness, and spelling databases that contain every occurrence of every spelling of every word in all witnesses. Approximately 180 megabytes are needed for the 856 line poem. An individual purchasing this CD-Rom should expect to pay $240. Uitti complains, several times, that applications from the Charrette Project for funding from the National Endowment for the Humanities have proven unsuccessful. Financial assistance has, however, been supplied by the Princeton University Committee for Research in the Humanities and Social Sciences, Portland State University, and the Alfred Foulet Publications Fund. Uitti's expectations that a major electronic text editing project to circulate considerable amounts of real and professional capital can be recognized in his lament that "[l]ack of a major, over-arching Project grant has slowed our progress somewhat, however we have been able to move ahead over the years. Professor Greco has been able to spend several weeks each summer in Princeton, and has recently spent time at the Bibliotheque Nationale in Paris proof reading our transcriptions copy; I have traveled to the necessary European libraries (Paris, Chantilly, Vatican, and El Escorial) in order to secure digitizable (and quite legible) copies of the necessary manuscripts, as well as to inform interested colleagues (especially in France, Spain and Italy) of what we have been doing. We have been in a position to provide small stipends to our graduate student assistants." Uitti seems to see no irony in his project's pleas of poverty. The Electronic Archive of *Piers Plowman* may be the most openly entrepreneurial of all the text editing endeavors, listing no major source of financial patronage and instead noting that "SEENET (the Society for Early English and Norse Electronic Texts) and the University of Michigan Press plan to publish each of the eight diplomatic editions of manuscripts CFGHmLMRW as it is completed. The initial version of The *Piers Plowman* Electronic Archive will also be published by SEENET and the University of Michigan Press, with periodic updatings of the Archive as more manuscripts are added. Printed books remain a very efficient means for conveying texts, especially for class use. Eventually we will produce a traditional printed version of the critical text with full introduction and explanatory, glossarial, and historical notes." Prices for these various versions of the Archive still have not been set, but is difficult to imagine how expenses will be recovered through the avenue of publication, especially since the editors worry about the availability of publication permission for digital facsimiles.

While none of these projects has to date received a major grant from either a congressionally mandated funding agency such as NEH or from private foundations, electronic editing projects are perfectly positioned to acquire a large share of the public patronage being lost from agencies such as the NEA and NEH in the wake of the culture wars. In their rhetoric, enthusiasts such as Duggan avoid any connection with high theory and its largly imagined associations with leftist politics. Text editing is nonpolitical and noncontroversial; it offers a degree of cultural certainty in that it seems scientific. In doing so, it positions the humanities to enter the competition for serious grant monies.

We may be witnessing the beginnings of a transformation in the culture of the academic literary community. Even at colleges and universities that downplay research functions, institutions where, historically, time and resources have never been found to advance the sort of endeavors performed by literary scholars/critics, funding has become available for those working on electronic projects. Major granting institutions, made nervous by threats from the likes of William Bennett and Lynn Cheney that the politics of literary scholarship/criticism over the past fifty years are responsible for the subversion of Western culture, may find comfort in financing seemingly apolitical electronic projects. Even as capital for Individual Grants and Summer Seminars/Institutes has greatly dried up, the NEH has begun a technological initiative. Those responsible for the Electronic *Beowulf,* the Charrette Project, the Electronic Archive of *Piers Plowman,* and the *Canterbury Tales* on CD Rom seem poised to promote their efforts as a new "heroic age" of text editing.

The Germanic philologists—and the text editors who closely followed them—the New Critics, the structuralists, and the poststructuralists—all monopolized new methods for approaching literary texts, new methodologies of reading, which resulted in their rise in the profession. All of these groups attached their new technology to a new kind of literary discourse that served to empower initiates and disempower all others. The status of the text editors of the late nineteenth and early twentieth centuries also derived from their ability to connect moral and nationalistic significance to their labor. Electronic text editors of the late twentieth century are the gatekeepers of a new and very expensive technology, they are the speakers of a language that is still largely unknown to most in the literary community, they speak of the moral imperative both to bring texts as well as technology to the scholarly community, and they have begun a process of international collaboration that may even change the way scholarship is conceived and rewarded. The electronic editing of medieval texts has opened the door to the production of "writerly" editions, opened the door to the liberating prospect of the text overshadowed by neither the author's authority nor an editor's. The editors of electronic medieval texts seem reluctant to relinquish this authority, but it inevitably will slip away from them. The question remains as to whether readers are prepared for our liberation. Are we ready to confront the world of difference and differences that electronic text editing offers us? Are we ready to reconfigure our scholarly/critical processes to address the challenges of the electronic text? Or will we return to the stability of the "work," the stability of the authoritative edition, so that we may carry on our practices as we have grown accustomed to performing them?

Notes

1. In this section and the next we address a number of electronic editing projects: the Electronic *Beowulf,* the *Canterbury Tales* Project, the Electronic Archive of *Piers Plowman,* and the Charrette Project. Unlike print, electronic publishing is such a dynamic medium that, almost certainly, by the time this article is printed, many of the details we use to illustrate our argument will have changed—perhaps even dramatically. The technologies driving these projects will evolve as will their costs. As project directions shift, so too will personnel. We cannot even be certain that the web sites we reference will still be in the same place, or even in existence. Perhaps the dynamism of the medium will subvert or, at least, problematize the theoretical underpinnings of the projects, as well as the promise of stability held out by the print medium.

Works Cited

An English Miscellany, *Presented to Dr. Furnivall in Honor of His Seventy-Fifth Birthday.* Oxford: Clarendon Press, 1891.

Barthes, Roland. "From Work to Text." *Textual Strategies: Perspectives in Post-Structuralist Criticism.* Ed. Josue V. Harari. Ithaca: Cornell U P, 1979. 73–81.

———. *S/Z.* Trans. Richard Miller. New York: Hill and Wang, 1974.

Baswell, Christopher. "Seeking Marginality." Forum on the Future of Erudition. International Congress on Medieval Studies. Kalamazoo, Michigan. 4–7 December 1995.

Brewer. Charlotte. *Editing Piers Plowman: The Evolution of the Text.* Cambridge: Cambridge U P, 1996.

Delany, Paul, and George P. Landow. "Managing the Digital World: The Text in an Age of Electronic Reproduction." *The Digital Word: Text-Based Computing in the Humanities.* Ed. Paul Delany and George P. Landow. Cambridge: MIT Press, 1993. 3–30.

Donaldson, E. Talbot. "The Psychology of Editors of Middle English Texts." *Speaking of Chaucer.* Durham: Labyrinth, 1970.

Duggan, Hoyt. "Creating an Electronic Archive of Piers Plowman." http://jefferson.village.virginia.edu/piers/tcontents

Foucault, Michel. "What is an Author?" *Textual Strategies: Perspectives in Post-Structuralist Criticism.* Ed. Josue V. Harari. Ithaca: Cornell U P, 1979. 141–60.

Graff, Gerald. *Professing Literature: An Institutional History.* Chicago: U of Chicago P, 1987.

Kiernan, Kevin. "The Electronic Beowulf." http://www.uky.edu/~kiernan/eBeowulf/main.htm

Latour, Bruno. *Science in Action: How to Follow Scientists and Engineers Through Society.* Cambridge: Harvard U P, 1987.

Lee, Sidney, "Frederick James Furnivall." *Dictionary o f National Biography,* Supplement 1901–1911. Ed. Sidney Lee. Oxford: Oxford U P, 1912. 61–65.

Maas, Paul. *Textual Criticism.* Trans. Barbara Flower. Oxford: Clarendon, 1958.

McGann, Jerome. "Introduction." *Textual Criticism and Literary Interpretation*. Ed. Jerome McGann. Chicago: U of Chicago P, 1985. vii–xi.

Patterson, Lee. "The Logic of Textual Criticism and the Way of Genius: The Kane-Donaldson *Piers Plowman* in Historical Perspective." *Textual Criticism and Literary Interpretation*. Ed. Jerome McGann. Chicago: U of Chicago P, 1985. 55–91.

Pearsall, Derek. "Editing Medieval Texts: Some Developments and Some Problems." *Textual Criticism and Literary Interpretation*. Ed. Jerome McGann. Chicago: U of Chicago P, 1985. 92–106.

Robinson, Peter M. W. "Redefining Critical Editions." *The Digital Word: Text-Based Computing in the Humanities*. Ed. Paul Delany and George P. Landow. Cambridge: MIT P, 1993: 271–92.

———. "Introduction: Chaucer's *The Canterbury Tales* on CD-Rom," http://www.cta.dmu.ac.uk/projects/ctp/desc2.html

Shillingsburg, Peter L. *Scholarly Editing in the Computer Age: Theory and Practice*. Ann Arbor: U of Michigan P, 1996.

Sisam, Kenneth. "Walter William Skeat." *Dictionary of National Biography*, Supplement 1912–1921. Ed. H. W. C. Davis and J. R. H. Weaver, Oxford: Oxford U P, 1927. 495–96.

Skeat, W. W. *A Student's Pastime*. Oxford: Clarendon, 1896.

Stafford, Barbara Marie. *Good Looking: Essays on the Virtue of Images*. Cambridge: MIT Press, 1996.

Uitti, Karl J., "A Brief History of the 'Charrette Project' and Its Basic Rationale," http://www.princeton.edu/~lancelot/

Willard, Charity Cannon. "Christine de Pizan and the Art of Warfare" *Christine de Pizan and the Categories of Difference*. Ed. Marilynn Desmond. Minneapolis: U of Minnesota P, 1998. 3–15.

Ten

A New Kind of Work:
Publishing, Theory, and Cultural Studies

Ronald Schleifer

The Interdisciplinarity of Knowledge

Some years ago, when I had my first essay accepted for publication, the president of my university sent me a letter congratulating me, as he said, for my "contribution to knowledge." At the time I was struck by his description of my work—the essay was, after all, a rather humble rereading of Conrad's *Under Western Eyes*—for while I was greatly pleased to know it would appear in a scholarly journal and pleased, also, that President Sharp took the trouble to write me a note, I had never imagined that the analysis of the role of the narrator in that novel could be described as something added to the store of our "knowledge." I begin with this anecdote because it seems to me that the *institutional* reception of literary theory and cultural studies—in the publication of work in journals devoted to the study of theory and culture and in books and book series published by scholarly presses—calls for the transformation of the idea of "knowledge" that we inherited from Kant and the Enlightenment and that was later institutionalized in the establishment within higher education as part of Western modernism in Europe and America in the second half of the nineteenth century.

In some ways, the transformation called for attempts to reexamine what Gerald Graff has called positivist notions of knowledge that were part and parcel of the professionalization of higher education in the late nineteenth century ("Point of View" 1992: A56). This professionalization, institutionalized in the establishment of research institutions in the United States and Western Europe,[1] was the fulfillment of Enlightenment ideas of knowledge, faculties, and atemporal truth. Such a fulfillment, as I argue in *Modernism and Time,* created problems of abundance in addition to age-old problems of scarcity and dearth. The new professionalization of knowledge—the establishment of modern languages as legitimate areas of study within higher education, the explosion of institutional scientific experimentation, and the new research libraries and disciplinary scholarly publications—was both the fulfillment of Enlightenment notions of transcendental and atemporal truth and a sign of a crisis in the orderly organization of knowledge.

This, in any case, is the global argument of Bruno Latour's rereading of Enlightenment "knowledge," *We Have Never Been Modern.* "When the only thing at stake was the emergence of a few vacuum pumps," he writes, they could still be subsumed under two classes, that of natural laws and that of political representations; but when we find ourselves invaded by frozen embryos, expert systems, digital machines, sensory-equipped robots, hybrid corn, data banks, psychotropic drugs, whales outfitted with radar sounding devices, gene synthesizers, audience analyzers, and so on, when our daily newspapers display all these monsters on page after page, and when none of these chimera can be properly situated on the object side or on the subject side, or even in between, something has to be done. (49–50)

Latour is describing the world of "interdisciplinary" studies—whether we call them transdisciplinary "theory" or more simply the "cultural" study of large social and intellectual formations—and such work, I believe, necessitates the rethinking of "knowledge" and the vehicles of knowledge in books and articles in the humanities. This is most clear (for work in English studies) in the widening of the purview of literary studies beyond aesthetics; but it is clear in the "invasion" of the cognitive sciences by computer science and artificial intelligence, new transdisciplinary work in ecology, genetics, and even law, and other seemingly transgressive cross-disciplinary work.[2]

In the discipline of English, the interdisciplinary work of "cultural studies"—as opposed to the accumulation and study of positive philological "facts" or aesthetic "experience"—follows from the advent of literary theory as a legitimate aspect or subdiscipline in departments of English, even if the concept and function of culture and culture studies in disciplines such as anthropology is very different. One director of a university press suggested to me that the relationship between literary theory and cultural studies—what he calls multiculturalism—is in fact antagonistic rather than complementary, but while there have been some heated debates between people who work in one or the other of these areas, it seems to me they are closely aligned. What the concept of culture has done for English studies is to make aesthetics—and Kantian notions of disinterested experience and knowledge—a problem. "Knowledge" itself, in its Enlightenment scientific definition as the *accurate, simple,* and *generalizing* description of experience, has come into question even while it remains the most articulate and "reasonable" description of the collective enterprise of scholarship. Aesthetics itself is inscribed in this description under the category of "simple" (see Schleifer et al., *Cultural and Cognition* 22; and Schleifer, *Analogical Thinking*), as is Kant's harmony of the faculties of practical reason, judgment, and pure reason.

As I argue in *Analogical Thinking,* the power and importance of what has come to be called "theory" in literary studies in the last two decades—and even the very "violence and irrationality of the attacks on theory" that Hillis Miller numbered among the phenomena that indicate the "triumph" of theory in his 1986 MLA Presidential Address (285)—is, in fact, linked somehow to widespread reconsiderations of the nature of knowledge and cognition. This is clear, I think, in the transformation and conflicts in philosophy since midcentury. Perhaps the most compendious account is Martin Jay's *Downcast Eyes: The Denigration of Vision in Twentieth-Century French Thought*, which examines the reconsideration of the distinterestedness of eyesight—positioning the subject of knowledge *outside* the world that is comprehended—in relation to more interested relations to knowledge. But even someone as far from literary studies as Norbert Wiener argues that the disinterested mechanical world we have inherited from the Enlightenment— reaching its fullest articulations in the mathematical physics of Newton and Newton's philosopher, Kant—calls for transformation when light and vision become a problem for knowledge, rather than its ground, in Einstein's involvement of the observer with the observed. "In the theory of relativity," Wiener argues, "it is impossible to introduce the observer without also introducing the idea of message, and without, in fact, returning the emphasis of physics to a quasi-Leibnitzian state, whose tendency is once again optical" (30).

Such reconsiderations of the subject of knowledge in philosophy and science have transformed scholarly editing—and what *counts* for scholarship more generally—in the humanities more markedly, perhaps, than in other disciplines. W. K. Wimsatt's use of the term *theory* in literary studies in 1949—perhaps the earliest articulation of the contemporary meaning of the term—opposed itself to Kantian disinterested aesthetics: "Literary theorists of our day," Wimsatt argued, "have been content to say little about 'beauty' or about any over-all aesthetic concept. In his most general formulation the literary theorist is likely to be content with something like 'human interest'" even though "disinterestedness, we remember, is something that Kant made a character of art" (228–29). With the term *theory*, Wimsatt was attempting to replace the aesthetic focus on the disinterested affectiveness of art by focusing, to some degree or other, on the relationship between literary meaning and interested writers and readers: it makes understanding and not the world, while its object examining understanding—and the phenomenon of "knowledge"—outside of categories of aesthetic subjectivity. (For a longer discussion of this phenomena, see Schleifer, *Analogical Thinking* chap. 4.)

Scholarly journals in English studies founded in the last generation—*Critical Inquiry, New Literary History, Representations,* and even my own work as editor of *Genre* (not to mention self-proclaimed interdisciplinary journals open to English studies)—have reflected, in one degree or another, this change in focus, just as scholarly presses, in the burgeoning of published work in literary theory and cultural studies as well as their marked unwillingness to publish literary criticism that focuses on single authors or even exclusively on "literary-aesthetic" problems (see Germano and Pfund) have also reflected this transformation. In my own case, from the beginning of my tenure as editor of *Genre,* the journal has treated criticism and theory as other genres of discourse and, as such, as suitable objects of the same kinds of analysis that scholars brought to canonical texts. But the most striking manifestation of theory and cultural studies in our journal—which, I hasten to add, I only now see in retrospect as I step down as editor after more than twenty years—has been, above all, a kind of de-aestheticizing of literary analysis, a treatment of literature as a phenomenon that places neither the subject nor the object of experience outside of or detached from other, more quotidian phenomena. I can see this in the publication in *Genre* issues on "nonliterary" genres, on the function of "power" in Renaissance literature in the first articulation of the New Historicism, and articles on homologies between paranoia and literature, on moving beyond structuralism, on gothic sexuality, on intersections of discourse and photography. Genre itself is a category of understanding that can, as in the work of Mikhail Bakhtin, comprehend literature in relation to the political and social and to situate even "aesthetic" discourse and the understanding of literary experience within contexts of other *kinds*—other *disciplines*—of experiences, understandings, and values.

In other words, what overrides the distinctions and disruption between literary theory and culture studies that have often, and quite contentiously, been pointed out is the tendency of theory, like cultural studies, to transform the study of literature to the study of larger discursive formations that breach the canons of generalizing wholeness and simplicity of Kantian knowledge and art. In this way, most uses of the term *theory* lead to the striking phenomenon of the past two decades in which "theory," as Martin Kreiswirth and Mark Cheetham noted, "more and more, appears . . . on its own, without delimiting modifiers, either before or after. No longer is the term wedded to antecedent adjectives, as in *critical theory, literary theory,* or *psychoanalytic theory.* No longer does it routinely drag behind trailing genitives—*of social action, of language,* etc." (1–2). This is so because theory has come to designate a kind of "post-Kantian" critique so that we can see now that even Wimsatt uses it this way. "The mark of 'theory,'" Gerald Graff and Reginald Gibbons argue, "is inevitable at a moment when once-accepted definitions, categories and disciplinary boundaries have become matters of debate and controversy" (9). Critique breaches the self-standing boundaries of knowledge: "[W]hile criticism . . . stands outside the object it criticizes, asserting norms against facts, and the dictates of reason against the unreasonableness of the world," Seyla Benhabib has argued, "critique refuses to stand outside its object and instead juxtaposes the immanent, normative self-understanding of its object to the material actuality of this object" (32; see also Schleifer and Davis' chap. 1). Critique, then, goes beyond the aesthetic wholeness of knowledge, questioning its seeming simplicity, its generalizing wholeness, and even the modalities of its accuracy.

It does so, as I argue in *Analogical Thinking,* by imbuing the rhetoric of the visual metaphor in the ancient term *theoros* with a sense of *discursive witnessing.* *Theorein,* Wlad Godzich argues, as an "act of looking at, of surveying, . . . does not designate a private act carried out by a cogitating philosopher but a very public one with important social consequences" (vii). The *theoros* were public legates—always plural—who reported on and witnessed verbally far-away events of public/social interest. Their work, I note in *Analogical Thinking*, was to bear witness for the community, to transform the private perception—the *"aesthesis"* of "the individual citizen, indeed even women, slaves, and children [all of whom] were capable of aesthesis, that is perception [which had] no social standing" (Godzich xv)—into a social and institutional fact. "Between the event and its entry into public discourse," Godzich concludes, "there is a mediating instance invested with undeniable authority by the polity. This authority effects the passage from the seen to the told" (xv).

Such a notion of theory, as I have said, calls for the transformation of "knowledge." Here, knowledge isn't simply, as Jürgen Habermas has argued, the visual, detached, above all singular "contemplation of the cosmos" (301). Rather, knowledge is a moment of an ongoing dialogue or conversation, preceded and followed by other moments so that the atemporal knowledge of Enlightenment ethos—truths existing once-and-for-all—no longer conforms *at all times* to the aesthetic category of wholeness and completeness. This certainly is Eyal Amiran's powerful argument in examining what he calls "the publishing imaginary." "Publishing," he argues, "is the imaginary of the academic system, the system's elevated conception of itself which readily substitutes for the intellectual world itself. It does not replace intellectual activity, but stands in for it symbolically." Moreover, such publishing "in the profession generally, is not a part of a larger process, an ongoing event, but its end" (94). In this argument, Armiran is focusing on the *visualization* of knowledge—his use of the Lacanian "imaginary" makes this clear—as something that, like the imaginary, is above all taken to be complete, a manifestation of a "logic of monumentality." Opposed to this monumental knowledge, he argues, is a "a new kind of work." "What's important about this new kind of work," he says, "is not simply that it might be interactive, or that it allows one to publish more of the senses than print technology does; rather, it is that the electronic media make non-traditional work, work that isn't finished in the normative way, interesting and useful in ways that print cannot" (98). Even "the finished work" of print and books, he suggests, is "never finished" but only "makes you feel finished" (99). Or worse, as I have seen: it makes people imagine that their participation in our profession is to get the "last word" on some subject or another rather than, as I imagine, to join a conversation that antedates their entry and will be going on when after they are gone.[3] I say "worse" because such monumentalism can become as egotistical and paralyzing as the Edward Casaubon's Enlightenment pursuit of the key to all mythologies in *Middlemarch*.

Literary Theory and Cultural Studies

The witnessing of theory, I am arguing, entails the polemical enactment of critique, the very questioning of the assumptions governing cognition, understanding, and disciplinary languages, as a social and transpersonal enterprise. In literary studies, it arose in the last decades of the twentieth century as the questioning of the assumptions governing the cognition and understanding of "literature" itself. But when literature is expanded to be understood as discourse, then the object of critique becomes the largest *local* sense of culture, "that complex whole" that E. B. Tyler defined in 1871 in the first "professional" definition of anthropology, "which includes knowledge, belief, art, morals, law, custom, and any other capabilities and habits acquired by man as a member of society" (cited in Davis and Schleifer, 38). The "active role" of theory, Roland Barthes has suggested—though I would widen the definition and call it the active role of cultural studies—"is to reveal as past what we still believe to be present: theory mortifies, and that is what makes it avant-garde" (191). For Tyler, as for Clifford Geertz, "cultures" are plural, and the study of culture always includes multiculturalism, so that the wider "active role" of culture studies is to reveal as local what we still believe to be universal. But this, as I have suggested, is the broadest and, I believe, the most lasting achievement of literary and discourse theory of the last two decades. In this way, the critical role of both theory and cultural studies, then, is the critique of the concept and phenomenon of knowledge itself and the *cultural conditions* for that knowledge—the form it takes, its authority, its function within the particular world in which it arises. Such a critique, I think, has greatly transformed the nature of editing scholarly publications in language and literature.

This is because literary studies, as Samuel Weber has suggested, is a privileged area in which a nonpositivist and un-Kantian conception of knowledge and culture can arise. "The object that defines this field of study—'literature'—," Weber writes, "has traditionally been distinguished from other 'objects' of study precisely by a certain *lack* of objectivity. And such a lack of objectivity has, from Plato onward, confronted the study of literature (or of art in general) with the problem of its *legitimation*, and hence, with its status as, and in regard to, *institution(s)*" (33). For this reason, "theory" has become an institutionalized "area" in literary studies, which includes its own canonical texts, its own more or less authoritative textbooks, its own scholarly journals or delineated places within previously existing scholarly journals, and its own "discipline" within the curriculum and faculties of higher education.

Whether or not cultural studies has or will adopt all of these *forms* of institutionalization is the question and problem of its definition more generally. It certainly already has canonical texts, textbooks, journals, but it is rarely even a subdiscipline within curricula. There have been some, such as Henry Giroux, David Shumway, Paul Smith, and James Sosnoski, that argued that the capacity of institutional disciplines "simultaneously to normalize and hierarchize, to homogenize and differentiate" (474) means that the very institutional formalization of cultural studies will aestheticize its critique and make it another version of disinterested knowledge. Still, several voices have offered alternatives to such a danger by pointing out that in the critique of theory as well as the specificities of culture the dream of the atemporal aesthetics of method—that great Enlightenment goal—might be at least occasionally abandoned. For instance, the Chicago Cultural Studies Group has suggested that we "rethink culture, not as a timeless set of categories and structures but as a mode of producing a social world, of making boundaries and connections" (531) and that we redefine the field of "cultural studies" as "critical multiculturalism" in which juxtapositions of differently contextualized critiques are necessary even while "critical intellectual work cannot simply be exported from one context to another" (536). Earlier, in a similar gesture, Richard Johnson offered a sweeping description of the large number of powerful continuities "wrapped up in the single term 'culture,' which remains useful not as a rigorous category, but as a kind of summation of a history" (42). The advent of the New Literary History in English studies marks most clearly, I think, an intersection of literary theory and cultural studies, in a kind of theory without method. Like Jacques Derrida's repeated disclaimer that he is not pursuing a "method," the New Historicism, as Stephen Greenblatt conceives it, "never was and never should be a theory; it is an array of reading practices that investigate a series of issues that emerge when criticics seek to chart the ways texts, in dialectical fashion, both represent a society's behavior patterns and perpetuate, shape, or alter that culture's dominant codes" (Cadzow 535).

Bound up in these contrasting definitions is the controversy over the term itself, *cultural studies*. The volume published by the University of Illinois Press, *English Studies/Culture Studies*, uses the term *culture studies* rather than *cultural studies* in an attempt, as Ann Lowry suggested, to distinguish the work in America from the "cultural studies" of the Birmingham school. Such a distinction might also mark the difference (one way or another) from the localization of "culture studies" in departments of English rather than its institutionalization across disciplines. As Cary Nelson has argued, "cultural studies" might well require that traditional English departments open up membership to people with Ph.D.s *outside* of (aestheticized) literary studies. Yet distinctions both Lowry and Nelson articulate, like the controversies plaguing Chomskyan linguistics over the subtleties of notational systems for describing language, are based on a kind of Cartesian realism: that is, they are based on a rationalist sense of a universalist essence or method of cultural studies, a program that transcends local conditions and against which local institutions and knowledges must be measured. At the other extreme, others insist that the best term for this work is *multiculturalism* because it captures best the *local* nature of the knowledge it pursues, what Donna Haraway calls "situated knowledges" and others describe as the excitement in the *detail* in multiculturalism.

Still, all of these attempts to define culture and cultural studies to one extent or another are also attempts to avoid the *problem* of institutionalization. That problem is the danger of transforming local knowledge into universal knowledge, of transforming interested engagement at a particular moment, which calls upon the resources of intellectual and social life into the disinterested contemplation of something to be known, of transforming *culture* into methodological *theory*. It is the danger of generalizing "across cases," in Geertz's term, instead of generalizing "within them" (26). What complicates all of this is that what I am calling the resources of intellectual and social life *include* disinterested contemplation of something to be known. The problem, that is, is the powerful, real, and, under many particular circumstances, *useful* force embedded in the aestheticization of knowledge. Amiran suggests as much when he argues that the form of a *book* "makes you feel finished":

> It's the rare book that's memorable and worth keeping, as a book. That's normal, but the rhetoric of books ("$60 from Cambridge") says that it's not: it says that they're books. Book blurbs promise definitive and paradigm-shifting achievements. . . . These books can only promise such achievements because . . . they affirm, as Bourdieu has argued, the bound legitimacy of their fields, and fulfill the promise of autonomy and completeness made to the publishing imaginary. (99–100)

Thus, even cultural studies can call for neither abandonment of institutionalization (as Giroux et al. suggest) nor a transcendental list of do's and don'ts (as Nelson suggests). But most importantly, neither can it simply ignore the ways in which the motor of such institutionalization takes the forms of disinterested contemplation that can transform the *(theoretical)* critique explicit in cultural studies and implicit in multiculturalism into simply other institutions within the pluralism of higher education. Colleagues across disciplines see the term *cultural studies* in English departments as more or less informed appropriations of other disciplinary methods or areas; and one editor I know describes "multiculturalism" as simply comparative literature under another name. In any case, whatever it is called, the critical interdisciplinary work of theory and culture studies certainly cannot ignore these questions when faced with the need and difficulty of transforming these ongoing debates and controversies into published and relatively fixed texts.

Such texts, to one degree or another, take the form of "aesthetic" objects: whole, complete, and, within their own terms, self-contained. We all know the power of aestheticized knowledge—it is what we have been taught and, additionally, it more powerfully governs the dissemination of "knowledge" through the publication of books than the dissemination of knowledge in the ongoing "conversations" in local curricula, classroom teaching, and even, now in the age of desktop publishing, periodic publication. The aestheticization of knowledge is embedded in the traditional Enlightenment criteria defining "understanding" in terms of its coherence, simplicity, and correspondence to empirical "fact." Cognition seeks to universalize experience, to fit particulars within larger frameworks of understanding. In this way, "knowledge" is achieved. As Ernest Gellner has argued,

Enlightenment reason is, in fact, *against* culture: for Descartes, he argues, "liberation from error requires liberation from culture, from 'example and custom' as he calls it" (2). At the same time such understanding is *individualized*. Enlightenment rationalism is "profoundly individualist": "That which is collective and customary is non-rational, and the overcoming of unreason and of collective custom are one and the same process" (3). (Martin Jay describes this process in the use of "charismatic names in legitimating arguments" in the humanities 21).

This fact, more than others I think, locates the problem of the relationship of critical cultural studies to Kantian canons of knowledge: a transcendental conception of knowledge, a "view from nowhere" (Schleifer, *Modernism* 69–76), neverthless is defined against local collective vision. This is why Weber can argue that "if authors such as Derrida, Foucault, and to a lesser extent, Lacan, have been granted admission into the American Academy, the price they have had to pay has generally entailed the universalization and individualization of their work, which has thereby been purged of its conflictual and strategic elements and presented instead as a self-standing methodology" (41–42). The same can be said for Raymond Williams, Edward Said, bell hooks, and others: the combination of universalization and individualization is precisely the mode of the aesthetic as Kant describes it. (For a discussion of such a combination, see Eagleton.) Moreover, it calls for the *standardization* of knowledge implicit in Descartes: the standardization of movable type, universal (or at least translatable) concepts, and, in its more humble form, Samuel Johnson's standardized spellings. All of this makes knowledge itself, in Weber's term, "self-standing," and they make such self-standing *sites* of knowledge work at cross purposes, in conflict, and in ignorance.

Publishing Cultural Studies

The locus of these conflicts, for cultural studies as it has developed in departments of literature and discourse at least, are our classrooms, our curricula, our scholarly journals, and the publication of scholarly books. In these places, the "superimposition" of readings that Latour describes ("Visualization" 16, 20; see also Schleifer, *Analogical* chap. 4) take place, the contestation of cognition now understood, as not simply freestanding, universal, and forms of primary interpretation, but as also collective, polemical, and in their nature *as* knowledge always calling for response. Gaston Bachelard has called this "the polemical character of cognition" (cited in Weber xiii), a description of an understanding of interpretation not as the formal self-standing representation of phenomena, but as an analogical paraphrase of something that *already* signifies within another system of signification (see Schleifer, *Analogical* Introduction). Such a conception of cognition and knowledge implies that the function of publishing is at once central and marginal. Publication is authorizing and authoritative in its *underwriting* of understanding. Yet the publication of conflicts—if this, in part anyway, is what the critique of theory and the interdisciplinarity of cultural studies call for—exists by *undermining* authority in the many contested voices it presents. It undermines the authority of hierarchy implicit in claims of universalization, the authority of incontestable "fact" implicit in positivistic conceptions of the objects of knowledge, and the authority of simple experience implicit in individualized aestheticism. This is why, I think, that publishing cultural studies in the United States has taken form at first in periodic journals and scholarly book series. Such publication, like Geertz's description of the study of culture and Amiran's description of electronic publishing, is "intrinsically incomplete" (Geertz 29). Rather than the aesthetically complete description of the matter of fact at hand, for the interdisciplinarity of knowledge there is always something else to do. In an editorial in the first issue of *Signs* in 1975 Catherine Stimpson had said that "a journal is a series with a future" (cited in Schleifer et al. *Cultural Cognition* 237). By imagining editorial activity as *future* activity Stimpson allows for the truth and power of editing scholarly publications and, at the same time, underscores the element of its (sometimes polemical) relationship to other social institutions. "Editing Signs," Stimpson wrote in retrospect, "sets up special relationships to power. Our office has tried to embody certain feminist and egalitarian principles": "Those of us who founded the journal," she notes, "decided that if we were feminists, we ought to share our positions with others and establish the practice of rotating the editorship every five years or so" (cited in Schleifer et al., *Cultural Cognition* 237).

In these ways and others like them Stimpson and other journal editors—we attempted to institute similar structures at *Genre*—are attempting to develop *institutional* means to imagine interdisciplinary and collective forms of knowledge and authority, and, in fact, to *institutionalize* the incompleteness and the local nature of cultural studies. This can be done, in part, because journals exist in modes that are different from, and more or less more independent than the "monumental" publication of scholarly presses. Unlike university presses, with substantial overhead expenses for editorial and other services, large budgets significantly independent from the institutions whose names they bear, and often great pressure to make money, scholarly journals, even when they are owned by scholarly presses, are relatively low cost: editors volunteer their time, reviewing readers also volunteer their expertise, authors expect compensation for their work from their present or future employment institutions, and what small subsidies journals receive from their home universities are usually in kind—editorial released time, student assistants, free office space—and are seen, rightly I think, as legitimate parts of ongoing commitments. But most importantly, journals by their nature are periodic and *essentially* incomplete: one issue follows another, can correct what came before and, as I have always hoped as editor of *Genre,* can create the possibility of ongoing dialogue. As Ann Lowry has noted, the financial commitment libraries and individuals make to journals does not temporally coincide with publication, and this makes the risks of "de-aestheticized" knowledge—fragmentary, incomplete, and sometimes not conforming to received ideas of the *forms* of articulate knowledge—considerably less than those of book publishers. Scholarly journals, in short—like the more extreme example of electronic publication Amiran describes—are in a position, structurally and institutionally, to de-monumentalize knowledge and publication and to emphasize their collective nature. Periodic journals are structured, like the Greek institution of the *theoros,* to "witness" knowledge, repeatedly and dialogically .

The pressures on university presses are different from those of periodic publications, and in relation to them the "institution" of cultural studies takes different forms. At one level, cultural studies becomes a form of packaging: many of the editors and directors of university presses I have consulted have told me, as William Germano and Niko Pfund told Jeffrey Williams in their interviews (1998), that literary criticism simply will not sell any more, and that a very powerful marketing technique is the "fashionable" label of "cultural studies." "In recent years," one editor said, "the most traditional scholarly works have come to us describing themselves as work in cultural studies."[4] Another editor suggested that some presses are expanding their lists at breakneck speed in order to "capture" (in the most generous interpretation of this phenomenon) the local and "incomplete" nature of Geertz's "thick description" of culture. The explosion of lists is both good and bad: at its best, it rereads traditional and nontraditional texts, artifacts, and cultural formations through the lens of cultural critique, using the theory and multiculturalism I am speaking of to transform modes of understanding. At its worst, it is simply a marketing device, saturating the market with old wine in new bottles.

Other problems for university presses have to do with the evaluation of cultural studies. LeAnn Fields of the University of Michigan Press told me that traditionally "established" scholarly readers are no longer always the best evaluators of cultural and interdisciplinary work. The emphasis on "low" as well as "high" culture, the fact that cultural studies is asking us to rethink traditional foci of knowledge and scholarship, and to rethink, as well, the modes of "well-formed" arguments, often require "expert" readers who are at the beginning of rather than established in their careers. This is not just the case of the theoretical modes of knowledge that I have discussed; it also includes widening of multicultural "objects" of knowledge—television, popular culture, street talk, as well as more traditionally anthropological conceptions of cultural studies—"areas" that one editor told me could *only* be evaluated by relatively new scholars and that another told me has created the anarchy of the complete abandonment of common points of reference in evaluating scholarly work. One director asked me, more or less rhetorically, what, in this new world, *counts* as expertise? What *counts* as intellectual method or scholarly technique? Editorial boards of journals, with people joined together in explicitly acknowledged common goals, can and do discuss the nature of an authoritative argument—what makes a discussion convincing, whether or not the aesthetics of a beginning, middle, and end is a necessary part of dissemination and dialogue, the politics of choosing "objects" of knowledge. For a university press, constrained by financial considerations governing sales and review, scholarly oversight committees that do not also discuss publication policy, the necessity of single or, at best, double individual readings, and the sheer press of manuscripts that are circulating, such deliberation is much more difficult. Add to this the hefty books that result in the end of all, printed on paper guaranteed to last four hundred years (as I learned to my amazement years ago that the Printing Services at the University of Oklahoma prints all its books and journals), and the local nature of cultural studies seems to pale before monumentalism gone amok.

If presses as large, established institutions cannot pursue the conception of editorial incompletion I have described, nevertheless something approaching that can be seen in the many book series that have arisen in the last two decades. At their best, these series underline the incompletion of interdisciplinary knowledges: the ways in which study follows study in conflict and strategy. In the series I am associated with, "The Oklahoma Project for Discourse and Theory" (University of Oklahoma Press) and, lately, "NextMedia: Cross-disciplinary DVD-ROMs" (University of Pennsylvania Press), we consciously strive to get such incomplete and conflictual readings by seeking out cross-disciplinary studies that superimpose (in Latour's figure) disciplinary approaches that are rarely brought together in single volumes (in the book series) and superimpose the differing modalities of pedagogy and scholarship (in the electronic publications).

The lesson of theory and cultural studies for scholarly publishing can be seen in the very structure of publication "series" that emphasizes that scholarship is *textual* and *social*—that emphasizes, as I have, what literary theory and cultural studies share—and that this structure exists within the *institutional* formations of knowledge. Cultural studies and theoretical critique have taught us to recognize the interest embedded within "knowledge," the fact that the canons of Enlightenment reason (as opposed to the "errors" of custom and culture) serve ends beyond the invisible hand of universal knowledge. Moreover, they have taught us the collective nature of knowledge: that it is never free-standing but exists within cultural formations that are always interested, that the standardization of its forms affects the quality of its substance, and that the subject of that knowledge is not free-standing, standardized, but always exists in a historical situation. In other words, the rise of theory and cultural studies marks the process of redefinition of the faculties of higher education—the very disciplines that have governed our Kantian pursuits of knowledge. The forces arrayed against this redefinition—the very custom and culture of universal and individualized knowledge, and the standard published monograph—make this a troubled time in the academy: a time of opportunism, dead ends, and new weapons used in old battles of turf and resentment. But it is a time as well of new modes of understanding and objects of knowledge, a time of great excitement in the local details of cultural studies and the modes of critique of literary theory. It is my hope that in the midst of all this will emerge, here and there, intellectual communities where solidarity can accompany struggle so that new institutional forms of publication can respond to new senses of knowledge and new kinds of work.

Notes

In preparation of this essay, I have benefited from the conversation of Nancy Essig, director of the University of Virginia Press; LeAnn Fields, humanities editor of the University of Michigan Press; Kenneth Knoespel, former editor of *Configurations: A Journal of Literature, Science, and Technology;* Robert Markley, editor of *The Eighteenth Century: Theory and Interpretation;* the Editorial Collective of *Genre;* Ann Lowry, executive editor of the University of Illinois Press; Bill Regier, director of the University of Illinois Press; Bill Sisler, director of Harvard University Press; and Kimberly Wiar, humanities editor of the University of Oklahoma Press. I have also benefited greatly from the conversation of many other press and journal editors with whom I have discussed these matters, and from the particular advice of Robert Con Davis, Avrom Fleishman, Yvonne Fonteneau, and Melanie Wright.

1. A "professionalization" of higher education took place after the Civil War in the United States and in Victorian Britain. In the United States the first graduate schools and scholarly journals and presses at Johns Hopkins University and the University of Chicago were established in the 1870s and 1880s at the same time ancient institutions and scientific practices were transformed in Britain. In Britain, public service, a kind of "rational utilitarianism" (especially at Cambridge in the figures of Henry Sidgwick and Alfred Marshall), and the transformation of "the average Oxford and Cambridge don during the Victorian age from a celibate clergyman awaiting a college living in the church on which he could marry to a career-oriented, and usually married, teacher and scholar or scientist" (Perkins 127, 87) mark the transformation of high education in the late nineteenth century. The professionalization of science is especially important in this regard. For a fine account, see Bruno Latour, *The Pasteurization of France* (1988). Gerald Graff's *Professing Literature* (1987) and Chris Baldick's *The Social Mission of Literary Criticism* (1987) examine this transformation in disciplinary histories of English studies in America and England respectively.

2. Since there has been a great deal of talk about the ways in which both literary theory and cultural studies have attempted to stake out and "colonize" other disciplines with their own methods and vocabularies, I should note that other disciplines have also made gestures that also appear to transgress forms of knowledge. An instructive example is Herbert Simon's attempt to teach literary criticism how to do its work by means of cognitive science in "Literary Criticism: A Cognitive Approach." This essay, along with numerous— and often indignant—responses appeared in a special issue of *The Stanford Humanities Review* entitled *Bridging the Gap,* edited by Stefano Franchi and Güven Güzeldere (1994).

3. For a discussion of the "maieutic" function of editing and publication—the term is taken from Søren Kierkegaard and his repeated publications of polemical, pseudonymous

works—see Schleifer et al, *Culture and Cognition* 227–40. It is argued there, in a section called "Producing Knowledge: The Ethics of Publishing," that different *institutions* of editorial functions can help distinguish between monumental knowledges—discovered in particular authors' work by an acquisition editor, or constructed by an editor putting together a particular vision of truth—by means of the work of others, or, finally, articulated in a structure of impersonal disciplinary truthBand the "emergent cognition" of Kierkegaardian midwifery (238). Such a notion of "emergent" truth is of crucial importance to work in a discipline as far away from English studies and the electronic publishing Amiran is discussing as artificial intelligence (see, for instance, Holland).

4. Similarly, the conflict, as it has arisen, between literary theory and cultural studies, also marks editorial judgment. Thus, in his interview with Jeffrey Williams, William Germano uses the term *pizzazz* in order "to avoid the word theory because that [word] holds some history" (331).

Work Cited

Amiran, Eyal. "The Publishing Imaginary and Electronic Media." *Minnesota Review* 48/49 (1998): 91–102.

Baldick, Chris. *The Social Mission of English Criticism: 1848–1932.* Oxford: Clarendon, 1987.

Barthes, Roland. *The Grain of the Voice: Interviews 1962–1980.* Trans. Linda Coverdale. New York: Hill and Wang, 1985.

Benhabib, Seyla. *Critique, Norm, and Utopia: A Study of the Foundations of Critical Theory.* New York: Columbia University Press.

Cadzow, Hunter. "The New Historicism." *The Johns Hopkins Guide to Literary Theory and Criticism.* Ed. Michael Groden and Martin Kreiswirth. Baltimore: Johns Hopkins U P, 1994. 534–40.

Chicago Cultural Studies Group. "Critical Multiculturalism." *Critical Inquiry* 18 (1992): 530–55.

Davis, Robert Con, and Ronald Schleifer. *Criticism and Culture: The Role of Critique in Modern Literary Theory.* Harlow: Longman Group UK, 1991.

Eagleton, Terry. *The Ideology of the Aesthetic.* Cambridge: Basil Blackwell, 1990.

Franchi, Stefano and Güven Güzeldere, eds. *Bridging the Gap: Where Cognitive Science Meets Literary Criticism,* a special issue of *The Stanford Humanities Review:* 4 (1994). Available at *www.stanford.edu/group/SHR/4–1/text/toc.html.*

Geertz, Clifford. *Interpretation of Cultures.* New York: Harper Torchbooks, 1973.

Gellner, Ernest. *Reason and Culture: The Historic Role of Rationality and Rationalism.* Oxford: Blackwell Publishers, 1992.

Germano, William. "Editorial Instinct: An Interview with William P. Germano." *Minnesota Review* 48/49 (1998): 105–17.

Giroux, Henry, David R. Shumway, Paul Smith, and James V. Sosnoski. "The Need for Cultural Studies: Resisting Intellectuals and Oppositional Public Spheres." *Dalhousie Review* 64 (1984): 472–86.

Godzich, Wlad. "Introduction. Heterologies." Michel de Certeau, *Discourse on the Other.* Trans. Brian Massumi. Minneapolis: U of Minnesota P, 1986. i–xxi.

Graff, Gerald. *Professing Literature: An Institutional History.* Chicago: U of Chicago P, 1987.

———. "Point of View." *Chronicle of Higher Education.* (October 21, 1992): A56.

Graff, Gerald, and Reginald Gibbons. "Preface." *Criticism in the University.* Ed. Gerald Graff and Reginald Gibbons. Evanston: Northwestern UP, 1985. 7–12.

Habermas, Jürgen. "Knowledge and Human Interests: Perspective." *Knowledge and Human Interests.* Trans. Shapiro. Boston: Beacon Press, 1971.

Haraway, Donna. "Situated Knowledges: The Science Question in Feminism and the Privilege of Partial Perspective." *Simians, Cyborgs, and Women.* New York: Routledge, 1991. 183–201.

Holland, John. *Emergence: From Chaos to Order.* Reading, MA: Perseus Books, 1998.

Jay, Martin. "Name-Dropping or Dropping Names?: Modes of Legitimation in the Humanities." *Theory between the Disciplines.* Ed. Martin Kreiswirth and Mark Cheetham. Ann Arbor: U of Michigan P, 1990. 19–34.

———. *Downcast Eyes: The Denigration of Vision in Twentieth-Century French Thought.* Berkeley: U of California P, 1993.

Kreiswirth, Martin, and Mark Cheetham. "Introduction: 'Theory-Mad Beyond Redemption.'" *Theory between the Disciplines.* Ed. Martin Kreiswirth and Mark Cheetham. Ann Arbor: U of Michigan P, 1990. 1–16.

Latour, Bruno. "Visualization and Cognition: Thinking with Eyes and Hands." *Knowledge and Society: Studies in the Sociology of Culture Past and Present.* Ed. Henrika Kuklick and Elizabeth Long. Greenwich, CT: JAI Press, 1986. 1–40.

———. *We Have Never Been Modern.* New York: Harvester Wheatsheaf, 1993.

———. *The Pasteurization of France.* Trans. Alan Sheridan and John Law. Cambridge: Harvard UP, 1988.

———. (1988a) "A Relativistic Account of Einstein's Relativity." *Social Studies of Science* 18 (1988): 3–44.

Miller, J. Hillis. "The Triumph of Theory, the Resistance to Reading, and the Question of the Material Base." PMLA 102 (1987): 281–91.

Nelson, Carey. "Always Already Cultural Studies: Two Conferences and a Manifesto." *Journal of the Midwest MLA* 24 (1991): 24–38.

Perkins, Harold. *The Rise of Professional Society: England Since 1880.* London: Routledge, 1990.

Pfund, Niko. "Editor as Catalyst: An Interview with Niko Pfund." *Minnesota Review* 48/49 (1998): 119–39.

Schleifer, Ronald (2000) *Modernism and Time: The Logic of Abundance in Literature, Science, and Culture 1880–1930.* Cambridge: Cambridge UP, 2000.

————. *Analogical Thinking: Post-Enlightenment Understanding in Language, Collaboration, and Interpretation.* Ann Arbor: U of Michigan P, 2000.

Schleifer, Ronald, Robert Con Davis, and Nancy Mergler. *Culture and Cognition: The Boundaries of Literary and Scientific Inguiry.* Ithaca: Cornell UP, 1987.

Weber, Samuel. *Institution and Interpretation.* Minneapolis: U of Minnesota P, 1987.

Wiener, Norbert. *The Human Use of Human Beings: Cybernetics and Society.* New York: Avon, 1967.

Wimsatt, W. K. "The Domain of Criticism." *The Verbal Icon.* Lexington: U of Kentucky P, 1954; 221–32.

Eleven

What Hath English Wrought: The Corporate University's Fast Food Discipline

Cary Nelson

As I sat at my computer thinking about the future of higher education, I had before me the final version of a collaborative document with its stunned, startled gaze fixed on the past. It is the Modern Language Association's report from its Committee on Professional Employment, issued in December 1997. The report, which is the product of a series of discussion sessions, was assembled and drafted by Sandra Gilbert with assistance from her fellow committee members. The astonished gaze its collective author casts on recent history suggests the windswept visage of a profession no longer in control of its fate. Eyes bulging, the figure is nearly swept away by forces it cannot comprehend. In stark terror at their oncoming fury, it dares not turn to glimpse their destination.

The report gives us a reasonable—if economically and contextually impoverished—account of the recent history of the academic job market in the humanities. Its opening subheading, as one reader pointed out, introduces a passage in the text that refers to "the best of times at large contrasted eerily with the worst of times in academia." Of course the millions of underemployed or unemployed Americans, all those working at or near poverty-level wages, are not living in the best of times. We are not alone and as long as our disciplinary understanding of the national and global economy foregrounds us as exceptional victims the chances for meaningful solidarity, meaningful alliances, and significant change remain slim. But at least we are now symbolically committed to recognizing that our own house is in disrepair. Having argued for a time that jobless Ph.D.s were primarily ungrateful, its principal author now more or less announces, "I feel your pain." The proposals for action she and the others put forward in the final section of the report are, unfortunately, less generous. Yet after more than a quarter-century of denial, with this report English and the other literature and language professions have now condescended to admit that there is a problem.

I would like to review some of the report's strengths and weaknesses and in the process use it as an occasion to describe the wider implications of the history faculty members have hidden from themselves for decades.[1] I will argue that English as a discipline bears a special responsibility for making the precipitous decline of higher education more likely in the coming decades. That is partly because English departments have made the college teacher what standard economic theory calls an *elastic commodity*, one for which there are any number of substitutes. At the end of the paper I will make some predictions about where we are heading, based on the mounting corporatization of higher education and on the increasing assaults on both tenure and academic freedom.

One minor but characteristic feature of the report is its imaginary pairing of Association of Departments of English head David Laurence and Harvard University professor John Guillory as disciplinary seers. Up until 1995 Laurence could be encountered at MLA meetings heatedly insisting there was no job crisis; if there were one, he would add, it was wrong to speak of it, since that would discourage people from signing up for graduate study. Guillory's role has been more recent, first with his effort in the *ADE Bulletin* to infantilize graduate students by decrying their premature professionalization, then with his condescending regret at their increasing politicization in a paper presented at the 1996 MLA meeting. Their politicization and organized action is actually the only thing that might save the profession, and Guillory's effort to subvert it is part and parcel of the MLA leadership's steady attempts to undermine the Graduate Student Caucus and resist its initiatives. So it is more than a little ironic to have the CPE report hailing them as the profession's prophets.

On the positive side, however, the MLA has now effectively removed its imprimatur from its official posture of denial. And in one critical area the report recommends genuine action. It takes up the suggestion I have been making for several years—that the association investigate unfair hiring practices by individual departments—and urges approval. Of course, this recommendation will have to survive extensive review, but it could have real deterrence value if implemented effectively. But there is real doubt that the profession is willing and able to investigate complaints seriously. That doubt is reenforced throughout, because the report for the most part decorously avoids advocating the kind of activism we need and makes it clear the MLA will do little to highlight or criticize the educational practices of departments and institutions.

The MLA's importance in this area should not be underestimated. As the largest of our disciplinary organizations it has considerable leadership potential. It also has a deep structural responsibility for the present conditions of academic labor, as the professional organization representing the single largest disciplinary group of graduate student and part-time labor. So at issue here is not only the inadequacy of the CPE report but also the discipline's special culpability. Yet if I have been critical of the organization's reluctance to act politically I must also say it has perhaps been *the single most activist* large disciplinary organization. Most of the others are even more frightened of the public sphere, more unwilling to undermine faculty privileges and departmental autonomy. Thus, the MLA has been one of few such groups to defend NEH funding on Capitol Hill consistently and aggressively. One would think all humanities fields would have been in that battle for years, but such is not the case. The MLA also co-sponsored an important conference on part-time labor initiated by the American Historical Association in 1997, working closely with the American Association of University Professors, a group more experienced in articulating basic statements of principle, and the work of that conference should have major impact. Just by issuing its own report on the job crisis and by collaborating on the part-time employment report, the MLA in 1998 put itself ahead of most disciplinary groups. But the hour is late, much more needs to be done, and more than two decades of inaction will cost us very dearly indeed.

One relatively minor but telling example of an area where we need tough action is in the MLA's response to efforts to create *new* Ph.D. programs. Although many faculty members find it difficult to believe that institutions would attempt to establish new doctoral programs in the midst of the current oversupply of Ph.D.s—because creating new programs is much like throwing gasoline on an uncontrolled fire—there are always several such efforts under way. Often the pressure comes from above, from administrators who want to move up the hierarchy of rankings by institutional type, sometimes because that produces more state support. A number of doctoral programs were forced on faculty members on campuses in the Michigan state university system for that reason in the last decade. Sometimes departmental faculty resist these efforts but are overwhelmed by coldly unscrupulous administrators. A university president in Texas in 1997 urged his large humanities departments to start Ph.D. programs for the fist time: "The job crisis is over, and we have got to position ourselves to take advantage of the new job boom. We cannot miss this opportunity for prestige, impact, and visibility."[2] Departments who do not want to initiate new Ph.D. programs, he warned, would face penalties when next year's faculty salaries were assigned. When the history department courageously voted against starting a doctoral program anyway, one was imposed on them. Professional organizations such as the MLA should be leading the way to block new doctoral programs, and they should be doing so simultaneously on multiple fronts. Working on the supply of new Ph.D.s this way will not solve all our problems, but it is one necessary component of a comprehensive approach to the job crisis and can somewhat increase the employment prospects of the many underemployed Ph.D.s now seeking meaningful careers.

One reason we cannot simply attack the problem of supply is that our economic situation is far more complicated than that. Indeed, Marc Bousquet, former head of the MLA's Graduate Student Caucus, recently suggested to me that there really is no job market in English, and I agree. My own reasons follow:

1. Supply and demand are so thoroughly out of sync with one another that the product being marketed—the new Ph.D.—has become almost valueless.

2. Supply and demand in the higher education job system are not a function of need—or even dynamically interdependent—but are rather each independent variables shaped by quite different social and political forces.

3. The forces shaping supply and demand for new Ph.D.s are not exclusively or even necessarily primarily economic but rather cultural and institutional.
4. Supply has been artificially increased and demand artificially depressed.
This is not a simple economic relationship, though new Ph.D.s are suffering the classic economic consequences of dramatic oversupply.

Let's say, for example, that the country actually wanted to guarantee that all
college students could read texts critically and write well on their own. Many of us
have some idea of how much close attention and tutoring we would need to achieve
that standard. We'd need a hell of a lot more English professors than we have now
if we actually wanted to do so. The same holds for math professors, science professors, and foreign language teachers. If we wanted undergraduates to be knowl-
edgeable about art or music, well, once again, demand might match supply. Yet if
the need exists to hire large numbers of faculty, the cultural and political will to
pay their salaries is nowhere to be found.

Ph.D.s are produced in large numbers meanwhile, not because of a massive
demand for new faculty but because of an institutional demand for cheap graduate student labor and because of faculty desire to maintain the perks and pleasures
of graduate education. It's basically a pyramid scheme, most dramatically not only
at the Ph.D. level but also for the MFA in fields such as creative writing.

Bousquet and other members of the GSC would argue that there is thus really a *job system,* not a job market. Certainly they are right that there is no independent market for full-time academic employees registering supply and demand.
Rather, the job system we have is an interlocking structure of employment patterns, job definitions, salary constraints, hierarchized reward systems, training programs, institutional classifications, economic struggles, ideological mystifications,
differential allotments of prestige, and social or political forces. Together, all these
mechanisms produce an artificially restricted number of full-time jobs for Ph.D.
holders. Graduate students or adjunct faculty employed to teach introductory
courses at brutally exploitive wages are part of that job system; so are the dwin-
dling percentage of tenure-track faculty. They are all part of one system that severely limits the number of decent jobs for new Ph.D.s.

As a first step, then, we need to visualize new full-time tenure-track jobs as
one slice of a single employment pie in higher education. Such a pie graph may
help us realize that the system of employment is relational and interdependent. But
the whole job system has many other components as well. The mystification of humanities teaching that makes it seem just and reasonable for English professors to
teach four times as many courses as microbiology professors is part of the system.
All the elements of the system work together to regulate and normalize it. New
jobs are not independent functions of the number of students we need to teach or
the courses we are expected to offer. If the market for full-time positions flowed di-

rectly from those needs, then all our recent Ph.D.s would have jobs. So the MLA job list is a highly manipulated and contingent phenomenon. It is a small overdetermined segment of the job system.

Economic or cultural investment or disinvestment in one part of the system affects other parts either immediately or over time. Both the responsibilities individuals have and the benefits they receive are functions of this system. Even rewards for unique achievement are made possible and justified by it. That means we are all responsible, that our different status positions are interdependent. But many elements of this system are subject to change.

So it's not simply "the economy" that has given us a job crisis, as if the economy were our inexorable and monolithic fate; it's a host of social, political, and cultural forces, values, and constituencies that *can be acted upon,* that can be influenced and modified. And the faculty members who tell us otherwise—who spread disinformation out of their own naive ignorance and self-love—are culpable. Just as the faculty members who believe they bear no responsibility for institutional practices are culpable. Just as the faculty members who believe their sense of entitlement flows from nature not from differential forms of exploitation are culpable. Failing to acknowledge individual responsibility or to credit the potential for collective agency are just two ways the CPE report fails to view the crisis broadly enough. Both its narrow view of the forces acting on higher education and its recommendations for change have already been overtaken by events. What, then, has the committee failed to understand?

One succinct way of highlighting the problem is to point out a basic contradiction in the group's recommendations. Put bluntly, they cannot recognize the tension between their realism and their elitism. The report repeatedly urges us to prepare graduate students to teach in the real world, to prepare them for the jobs and responsibilities that will exist in the new millennium. "An offer from a two-year institution or a high school should not," the report remonstrates, "elicit the response (as it recently did from a prominent academic), 'Oh, well, it'll put food on the table while you're looking for a job.'" Instead, "the primary goal of graduate education should not be to replicate graduate faculty." Departments "will have to reimagine the size and shape of the graduate programs they offer and the directions in which those programs ought to evolve, given the range of educational needs our profession will have to meet in the twenty-first century." Part of the accompanying rhetoric is simply ignorant, as when they quote George Levine warning that "graduate programs will have to find ways to incorporate into their training 'the sorts of material that would serve students finding jobs at heavy teaching colleges.'" Here in River City, as in many other rural spots, we already do that; indeed, we've been doing it for decades. Our graduate students not only teach a whole range of lower-level composition, literature, and film courses; they also teach remedial rhetoric and composition for disadvantaged students. Indeed, they train at intensively tutoring remedial students. Short of practicing community college groundskeeping or high school lunch room monitoring it's not immediately clear what more our students should do to prepare themselves for the service jobs of the future. Certainly not all of them have set their dreams on the research track; some end up sick of their dissertations and hope never to see another major research project. Those who invest themselves in remedial tutoring seem to do it with great dedication; they believe the work matters and they are skilled at it. Whether any community colleges will be willing to pay for this kind of individual attention is the real issue, not whether our graduate students are qualified and interested in doing the work.

Where the real contradiction in the CPE report arises, however, is between its purportedly bracing dose of realism about jobs in the new millennium and its recommendation about graduate student teaching loads. The committee goes on to urge that graduate student employees teach only one course per semester. What the stern warning about preparing for the jobs that will exist means, quite simply, is hurry and set up what far too many faculty at elite institutions secretly think of as *the Rhet/Comp Droid assembly lines*. These dedicated "droids," so many literature faculty imagine, will fix comma splices, not spaceship wiring. But why give Rhet/Comp Droids extra leisure time? What are they going to do with time off? They beep and whir and grade, that's all. They're not training for research.

The University of Illinois' department offers teaching at two courses per semester and virtually every graduate student signs up for it. They need the money for living expenses. For years I have urged my departments to reduce the teaching load but retain the full salary. I want our students to have more time for their intellectual lives. But the JOBS OF THE FUTURE so confidently touted by the MLA will not have a major intellectual component, not *any* substantial intellectual component, let alone research time. That's not because they will be comp jobs, however, but rather because the instructors will be so underpaid and so overworked that they will have little time for reflection. So there's no reason to provide graduate students facing that sort of future with anything but job training and little reason not to extract the maximum labor from them while they're at it. Indeed, extracting the maximum labor at the lowest cost has been the aim of graduate training in English for decades.

Because I have the research-oriented Ph.D. in mind, my own politicking to lower the teaching loads of graduate employees has the aim of providing increased time first for seminar projects and then for dissertation research and writing. But do the Droids need to write dissertations? It's hard to see why many traditional faculty would think so. Of course, a number of people have been doing serious and intellectually ambitious work on rhetoric and technical writing for years, including political analyses of corporate writing, but the current premium on rhet/comp Ph.D.s, as opposed to M.A.s, in some corners of the job system is partly a product of mystification. In the assembly line comp course model, a Ph.D. has only limited pedagogical warrant. Meanwhile, demand for rhet/comp Ph.D.s now generally exceeds supply, but the profession will surely remain true to form and eventually generate an oversupply. I doubt if we are more than a decade away from that point.

All these forces will further undermine the value of the Ph.D., something we cannot defend without a better understanding of the dissertation's role in graduate training. What is at stake in writing a dissertation is not just preparation for future research. That is the general, very narrow, and, in my opinion, spiritually and culturally impoverished view that prevails. You write a dissertation to train you to do more such projects. If you are not going to do them, why write one? That seems as well to be Louis Menand's perspective on dissertation writing. In "How to Make a Ph.D. matter," Menand argues for a three-year Ph.D. with no dissertation or with only a moderately expanded seminar paper. Not only does he see dissertation writing as unnecessary; he sees it as culturally counterproductive, since it leads to inflated books that are little more than "articles on steroids."

But there is also a pedagogical reason for undertaking elaborate doctoral research. A person who writes a dissertation, one hopes, leaves graduate training with an understanding of the discipline based on deep, extended, even obsessional intellectual commitment. A person who writes a dissertation has ever thereafter a certain model of intellectual devotion, of in-depth study and reflection, as the only entirely appropriate and fulfilling way of coming to know anything well. It is that experience of thorough intellectual devotion that grants you the right to profess before a class. And every more casual intellectual encounter thereafter—every one of the hundreds of thousands of such casual encounters one promotes and requires as a teacher—is undertaken with knowledge of its inherent lack and limitation. You never thereafter believe the student who merely does his or her homework, whether carefully or perfunctorily, or who spends but a week on a seminar paper, has exhausted his or her potential or really traveled to the end of any intellectual journey. And as much as possible you try to embed echoes of more thorough devotion into the transitory work that actually occupies American classrooms. Writing a dissertation is thus part of the appropriate training in how to represent and transmit disciplinary knowledge. It also provides a model of intellectually committed writing, writing as a serious and extended undertaking that can inform the perspective of any composition teacher. Do we really want our writing teachers to have never written anything longer than a seminar paper? That is what pedagogy loses when we stop hiring Ph.D.s or grant the degree without a dissertation. And that is the bright new world the MLA report is unknowingly offering to us with such pride in realism.

Proposals to dumb down the humanities Ph.D. would have other negative consequences as well. Since no one is suggesting that physics or chemistry professors do not need to do dissertation research to get a Ph.D., the possibility of a two-tier credentialing and prestige system arises, with humanities faculty even lower in the professorial pecking order than they are now. Watering down the humanities

Ph.D. would help maximize the salary spread between disciplines, make it still easier to hire people without Ph.D.s to teach humanities courses, make humanities
departments less competitive in the battle for campus resources, and turn us into
less effective advocates in Congress and elsewhere. If all this sounds wonderful, I've
got a bridge I want to sell you.

Proposals such as Menand's are also often linked with the alternative career
model for the Ph.D., a plan almost every tenured faculty member thinks is the
greatest thing since sliced bread. Advocacy for alternative careers, which the MLA
is ready to embrace with giddy abandon, is without question the most cynical and
self-interested solution anyone has offered to the job crisis. When I visited the University of Arkansas a few years ago to talk about the job market, a senior colleague
rose to say he had little sympathy for people who viewed their failure to get an academic job as a disaster: "There are lots of things a Ph.D. can do. You could go
into the army." This was appropriately greeted with groans and protest from the
graduate students in attendance, and I doubt if even an MLA president will have
enough of a tin ear to call for that solution.

MLA presidents will no doubt instead pick glamorous, high-salary career alternatives with some creative component. Screenwriting is one obvious fantasy
they hope might bedazzle jobless Ph.D.s. This is the MLA's version of what Alan
Golding described to me as "the Michael Jordan effect." In other words, bring in
high achievers outside academia with Ph.D.s to inspire ghettoized part-timers and
grad students. You too can be a star. Why teach? Direct blockbuster Hollywood
movies. Run for the U.S. Senate. But no one needs a Ph.D. to become a director
or a screenwriter. An Illinois graduate student left for Hollywood some years ago
and became reasonably successful, but he bailed out long before writing his dissertation. Meanwhile, dangling T. S. Eliot's bank job before a new Ph.D.—dissertation and Routledge book contract in hand—is not likely to win any gratitude for
the MLA.

The MLA doesn't seem to realize that most of these folks have already chosen *not* to be Horatio Alger. The organization's leaders might counter that Elaine
Showalter, 1998 MLA President, earns just about as much writing journalism for
Vanity Fair or *People Magazine* as she does teaching for Princeton. Good for her,
but has she quit her job? Journalists' pay checks are not quite so secure. Could
Showalter have launched herself into high profile journalism on the way out of
graduate school? There are more than a few Ph.D.s who failed to get academic jobs
who are now employed at the other end of journalism's income spectrum and who
are not too happy about the time spent in graduate school.

Faculty members like the alternative career model *for other people* for several
reasons: it holds the promise of sustaining large graduate programs, along with
their faculty perks; it gets complaining graduate students out of their hair; it allows
faculty to combine their contempt for commercial employment with a hidden
conviction that Ph.D.s who don't get academic jobs are not as good as those who

do. But no graduate student who loves reading literature and being in the classroom wants to be told cheerfully that insurance companies are hiring.

There is good reason to design terminal M.A. programs with alternative careers in mind, since the skills we teach *do* have wide applicability. Furthermore, M.A.s have generally not yet fully internalized the classroom professor identity, so the likelihood of psychic damage is much less. Such programs should include courses and work experience linked to the alternative career, an option easier to realize at metropolitan campuses. We'll have to design appropriate curricula and hire appropriate faculty. But offering an alternative career to a talented Ph.D. is a cynically self-interested move. Furthermore, it offers no programmatic answers for the profession. There have always been some jobs outside academia where the Ph.D. is a valued credential—including jobs at foundations and government agencies—but there aren't enough of them to justify maintaining doctoral programs. Nor are we likely to convince anyone, especially state boards of higher education, that literature or history or anthropology departments are the best places to train film directors or advertising magnates. We're not going to win formal public consent to turn humanities Ph.D. programs into alternative career mills.

Yet that is far from the only misreading of the future built into this document. When the MLA committee members imagine the future of higher education they think of full-time jobs with higher teaching loads, more service courses, less time for research. Well, folks, those were the good old days. That degraded future is already past. Late capitalism has more exploitive working conditions than those in store for us. What's worse is that English more than any other discipline has helped pave the way for the alternative academic workplace and the full proletarianization of the professoriate. About this, the MLA's committee had not a clue. The future is one of part-time work dominated by corporate managers. Some of those managers will have Ph.D.s; indeed, that may in the long run be the only full-time job market for the composition Ph.D. The rest of the M.A.s and Ph.D.s will do piece work. Academic freedom will be nonexistent. Salaries will hover at the poverty level except for those who work past distraction. And English departments have helped make this brave new world come true.

Confident for decades that literary studies opens Heaven's Gate, the discipline is about to learn it has been praying in a corporate lobby. English has in fact been an unwitting corporate partner in a project to defund, defang, and deform higher education as we know it. How has this happened? How can I make these claims?

English, I would argue, is the discipline most responsible for laying the groundwork for the corporate university. I refer to our employment practices. For English departments above all have demonstrated that *neither* full-time faculty *nor* Ph.D.s are essential to lower-level undergraduate education. What's more, we've shown that people teaching lower-division courses need not be paid a living wage. We can no longer claim that such courses have to be taught by people with years of specialized training. Like many departments, mine puts people in front of a composition class the semester after they earn their B.A. So the educational requirement to teach rhetoric is apparently a B.A., a summer vacation, and a week's training. A couple of years of graduate study, having completed M.A. course work and a proseminar in teaching, and they are then assigned "Introduction to Fiction" or other beginning courses.

Any research university that wanted to would be educationally justified in hiring such folks full-time at $3,000 per course. In the English department at Illinois two-thirds of the undergraduate teaching is already done by graduate student employees without Ph.D.s. We can hardly justify hiring full-time faculty with Ph.D.s by arguing that no one else is capable of teaching the courses, since we have already "proven" otherwise. Indeed, after an ethical decision to reduce the size of our graduate program, Illinois was forced to turn to graduate students *in other fields* to teach its composition courses. Illinois now hires more than a score of law students to teach introductory rhetoric. These "apprentices" are not even enrolled in the department's degree programs.

There is now some statistical support for these claims. Data from the 1993 National Study of Postsecondary Faculty, based on Fall 1992 hiring figures, is now available as a CD-ROM. More up-to-date figures will not be available for another couple of years, but they will hardly be heartening. Ernst Benjamin of the national office of the American Association of University Professors has assembled the raw 1992 data into charts and passed them on to me. English departments nationwide had the largest percentage (8.2 percent) of the part-time faculty work force. Four other fields with much smaller work forces overall (Law, Communications, Computer Sciences, and Psychology) used a higher percentage of part-time faculty— English used 52.9 percent, whereas Law used 65.3 percent and Communications and Computer sciences each used about 55 percent—but most of those other disciplines were employing moonlighting professionals who were supplementing full-time jobs for prestige or pleasure. Thus, colleges of law regularly hire community lawyers part-time; notably, 99 percent of part-time law faculty in four-year colleges and 79.8 percent of them in two-year institutions have the appropriate professional degree. Communication programs often hire local journalists part-time. A number of other disciplines, such as business and nursing, do the same with full-time practitioners in their fields. Taken together, English and Foreign Languages—the MLA's constituency—accounted for 11 percent of the part-time faculty in 1992. And they amount to a bloc of people working at slave wages—people who depend on their instructional income for their living expenses—that dwarfs other small fields such as philosophy, which accounts for but 1.3 percent of part-time hires.

Finally, a number of these fields, such as law, use their part-time faculty to train students in professional schools, not for basic undergraduate instruction. It is above all English and foreign language departments that have proven that full-time Ph.D.s are superfluous for at least the courses they offer for the first two years of the undergraduate degree. If we then consider what graduate students having completed all doctoral course work might teach—and what salaries we could hire them at—the picture becomes still more troubling.

Here and there across the country that picture is already being filled out. At Illinois, the large lecture courses once categorically (and self-righteously) reserved for faculty are now sometimes taught instead by advanced graduate students. Thus, the history and sociology departments sometimes have a graduate student give all the lectures in the 750-student Survey of American History or the 300-student Introduction to Sociology. Still other grad students teach the discussion sections. No faculty members are involved. It's a great opportunity for the graduate student lecturers, who may well deliver a fine course, often replacing faculty who are far less eager for the task, but it also further undermines the need to employ Ph.D.s.

Of course it is still English departments that have pioneered the mass employment of college teachers at subminimum wages. English department employment practices have demonstrated that most—or even all—of the undergraduate degree can be handled by severely exploited labor. Indeed, many courses are taught *at a profit*. The gap between the tuition paid by the students in an introductory course and the salary paid to a part-time faculty member to teach it (from $1,000 to $3,500 per course) can be considerable. Moreover, do you really need a library, a gymnasium, a chapel, an auditorium, a student union, or an elaborate physical plant to teach such a course? Proprietary schools such as the University of Phoenix, profiled by James Traub, have shown that we do not. As these forces come together in a moment of recognition, the corporate takeover of the profitable portion of the undergraduate curriculum becomes a possibility. As Arthur Levine writes in "How the Academic Profession is Changing," "high-technology and entertainment companies are viewing noncampus-based education as an opportunity"; we can look for "the growth of private-sector competitors." English has led the way in turning college teaching into a low-level service job; we are corporate America's fast food discipline.

It is worth calculating just what the hourly rate is for Ph.D.s paid between $1,000 and $1,500 per course, common salary levels at community colleges and proprietary schools. East-West University in Chicago, a four-year institution, paid $1,000 per course to part-time faculty in 1997. Assuming thirty to forty-five classroom hours, depending on the length of the term, assuming a rock-bottom minimum of two hours preparation time for each hour of classroom teaching, two hours a week of office hours, and a minimum of 75–100 hours of paper and exam grading per term, the hourly pay rate comes to *under* four dollars per hour. But this calculation makes two assumptions—that preparation involves reviewing familiar materials, not reading and researching new topics, and that paper grading includes no extensive comments by the instructor. Getting involved in either of these traditional forms of teaching, let alone more extensive tutoring during office hours, can cut the rate of compensation to three dollars per hour or less.

Some part-timers calculate their average pay at less than one dollar per hour. Others, struggling to find some dignity in their labor, prefer to put the best possible light on their working conditions. "Sure, in weeks when I'm grading papers," said one part-timer when I interviewed him in Cincinnati, "I earn less than two dollars an hour, but in other weeks it's not that bad." Meanwhile, ask yourself how many $1,000–$1,500 courses a person has to teach to assemble a reasonable livelihood? How much attention can students receive from someone teaching a dozen or more of such courses a year? Are subminimum wages for Ph.D.s to become the norm? Already in many places in the United States college teaching is the lowest paying job in the community. In any other legal industry these wages would land an employer in court. Full-time college teaching in a research institution may, as Stanley Aronowitz argues, be the last good job in America, but part-time teachers have the worst salaries of any employment category in the country.

Two things are clear enough. First, *paying faculty subminimum wages constitutes a genuine violation of professional ethics.* It must be characterized that way by everyone involved in higher education. Second, this kind of brutally exploitive salary structure represents the single greatest threat to quality higher education and the greatest temptation for corporations contemplating hostile takeovers of our enterprise. *It is not enough for organizations like the MLA to issue general statements urging fair compensation for adjuncts and part-timers.* MLA's report recommends that departments and institutions do "self-study" to determine whether their enrollment and compensation practices are fair. That's all well and good, but asking East-West University to look into the depths of its soul is really demanding they plumb the shallows.

The disciplinary organizations need to set minimum wages for part-timers and work to enforce them; there is no alternative. Full parity with full-time faculty is a necessary goal and a useful logic to deploy even if the goal remains distant. But the articulation of the principle alone will have little direct effect on the wages paid academia's exploited teachers. More direct and forceful action is needed from professional organizations.

Each discipline should publish an annual "Harvest of Shame" listing all departments and institutions paying less than $3,000 or $4,000 per course to instructors with Ph.D.s.[3] It is also essential that abstract institutional responsibility for exploitive labor practices be shared by those staff members who benefit from that exploitation. Thus, full-time faculty members and administrators from those schools should be barred from privileges such as discounted convention room rates and barred from advertising in professional publications. That means publishers could not advertise the books of those faculty in professional journals. I would also consider barring full-time faculty and administrators from such schools from publishing in journals published by professional associations and urging a ban on publishing in all university-sponsored venues. Other ways of highlighting faculty and administrative responsibility should be found for institutions not oriented toward research. Regional campaigns should condemn the institutions involved. And professional organizations, as Karen Thompson of Rutgers University suggested at the 1997 national conference on adjunct and part-time faculty, should also consider censuring institutions that treat part-timers unfairly by denying them all access to benefits such as health care. Finally, a major national effort must be undertaken to brand schools paying less than $2,000 per course to any instructor as rogue institutions that threaten the quality and survival of our higher education system.

There will be tremendous resistence among full-time faculty members toward any suggestion they should be personally penalized for their departmental or institutional policies. They will claim powerlessness, and however false that claim may be they will believe it. Some will argue with good reason that they are fighting to change exploitive practices at their own schools. Others will have so deeply entrenched a sense of entitlement that they will be convinced underpaid teachers are underpaid because they are inferior. Despite all this, I believe penalties must promote recognition of individual responsibility and accountability. Even the personal challenge built into the *prospect* of individual penalties for institutional behavior would be productive.

The only other argument mounted against an organized assault on part-time hiring practices is a particularly confused and defeatist one. I refer to the regular protest that some people *want* to teach part-time. First of all, no one wants to be paid $1,250 per course for their teaching. *Underpaid labor is devalued labor.* I would have fewer complaints about part-time employment if all Ph.D.s were paid at least $4,000 per course and had health and retirement benefits, increased job security, and proper grievance procedures. But the simple fact is that no power on our corner of the earth will enable us actually to eliminate part-time employment. The best we can hope for is to raise wages and benefits, stop the trend toward shifting still more full-time to part-time jobs, and perhaps alter the overall ratio of positions somewhat. But we are not going to be able to eliminate part-time employment in the academy. There will still be plenty of bad jobs out there. Voicing fantasmatic fears that the freedom to be exploited will disappear should not count as rational argument.

Indeed, the only sound reason to hesitate taking any of these punitive actions is if the numbers of schools involved is too large and the threat of censure thereby becomes ineffective. Based on the national statement on part-time/adjunct faculty published in the January/February 1998 issue of *Academe,* on resolutions debated by the MLA's delegate assembly, and on the ongoing accrediting challenge to institutions with excessive reliance on part-timers, it seems the profession is beginning to counter this threat on several fronts. We must now intensify this effort. For if we do not resist this exploitation, we will eventually find corporate-managed proprietary schools dominating the education market.

Numerous other changes in the intellectual and professional environment of academia would soon follow. Tenure of course would disappear. Yearly or term contracts with very narrow and vulnerable definitions of academic freedom are one certainty. The Pew Charitable Trust has recently given Harvard Professor of Higher Education Richard Chait a grant of more than a million dollars to develop alternatives to tenure, long one of Chait's interests. "One size no longer fits all," he cheerfully announces in a *Harvard Magazine* article about the granting of tenure; "the byword of the next century should be 'choice' for individuals and institutions." In what is a remarkably disingenuous scenario he suggests that "faculty so inclined should be able to forego tenure in return for higher salaries, more frequent sabbaticals, more desirable workloads, or some other valued trade-off." But of course exactly the reverse is the case. We will forgo tenure in exchange for lower salaries, no sabbaticals, and heavier workloads.

Most prospective faculty members will have less, not more, "choice" in Chait's brave new world. But "choice" is not the only slogan he cynically adopts; elimination of tenure and academic freedom, he suggests, will also help promote "diversity" in work arrangements. Meanwhile, other foundations linked to corporations, including the Mellon Foundation, are also mounting or supporting assaults on tenure. Some have suggested we measure the strength or weakness of current tenure policy by the level of public trust it elicits! Chait, on the other hand, has urged we decouple tenure from academic freedom and devise contractual guarantees for the latter. The proposals so far have been chilling at best.

The American Association for Higher Education has been a leader in seeking ways to restrict the intellectual freedom and independence of the professoriate. As part of their "New Pathways: Faculty Careers and Employment in the 21st Century" project, they have distributed Chait's work and that of others in a series of occasional papers that should be required reading for everyone interested in the future we face. In a 1997 AAHE working paper, J. Peter Byrne's *Academic Freedom Without Tenure,* prospective contractual guarantees of and limitations to academic freedom are expressed this way (the emphasis is mine):

> Faculty members have the right to teach without the imposition or threat of institutional penalty for the political, religious, or ideological tendencies of their work, *subject to their duties to satisfy reasonable educational objectives and to respect the dignity of their students.*

> Faculty members may exercise the rights of citizens to speak on matters of public concern and to organize with others for political ends without the imposition or threat of institutional penalty, *subject to their academic duty to clarify the distinction between advocacy and scholarship.*

> Faculty members have the right to express views on educational policies and institutional priorities of their schools without the imposition or threat of institutional penalty, *subject to duties to respect colleagues and to protect the school from external misunderstandings.*

It is the last requirement—to protect the school from external misunderstandings—that would have particularly amusing consequences in the corporate university. Imagine what caution these "guarantees" of academic freedom would instill in a faculty *none of whom had tenure,* but any and all of whom could be fired summarily. Moreover, once dismissed, the burden would be on faculty to file suit and seek to overturn an improper firing. In the present system the burden of proof in dismissing tenured faculty is on the institution, which must supply that proof in lengthy proceedings.

Imagine trying to defend your "reasonable educational objectives" in a court committed to upholding the institution's right to be protected from "external misunderstandings." Astonishingly, Byrne's proposal underwrites dismissal for any disagreement that produces public controversy, even for debates about institutional policies and goals. And his demand that we "respect colleagues" would obviously justify dismissal for a sharp disagreement with an administrator; of course, anything as aggressive as a campaign to oust a dean or a president would warrant immediate removal of a faculty member. Chait promises a revised set of contractual guarantees for academic "freedom" soon, but I would not expect much comfort from them.

Perhaps I may offer my own version of a faculty contract in the hypothetical corporate university:

MOBILe OIL
brings you
MASTERPIECE CLASSROOM THEATRE

The Corporate University's Principles of Governance:

1. The student consumer is always right.
2. Contract faculty will maintain a cheerful and friendly demeanor at all times.
3. Contract faculty will avoid challenging, threatening, or upsetting student consumers.
4. All courses will be graded on the basis of clear, universally achievable goals. Divisive notions of excellence and quality will play no role in evaluating consumer performance.
5. All products of faculty labor are the property of the corporation.
6. Termination without notice is available for faculty noncompliance or insubordination.
7. All faculty members are provided with course syllabi and textbooks without charge. Management is responsible for course content.
8. All faculty possess presumptive redundancy. The need for their services will be reassessed each term.
9. All faculty must submit an annual report detailing how they can better serve the corporation's mission.

10. Faculty members have full academic freedom to accept these principles or to resign.

If this is the world we are heading toward, the MLA's smug, cautious, and constipated recommendations will do nothing whatever to avert it. But in many ways this is the world adjuncts and part-timers *already* inhabit, and the MLA is that much more culpable for failing to address it, for limiting itself to stating vague principles rather than taking actions. This dystopian satire is no more than daily life for many academics, and those in tenured positions who feel sorry for themselves need to see their own working conditions reflected in this cultural mirror. Many part-timers have little freedom to design courses, no role in governance, no job security, no power to counter irrational student complaints, and are subject to summary dismissal for the most trivial, confused, or flatly inaccurate reasons. Some work in fear or resignation, knowing their livelihoods depend on not offending administrators or challenging their students. And they work for wages comparable to those in the worst illegal sweatshops in the country.

Thus, we may no longer be able to confront the job crisis for new Ph.D.s on its own. The multiple crises of higher education now present an interlocking and often interchangeable set of signifiers. Conversation about the lack of full-time jobs for Ph.D.s turns inevitably to the excessive and abusive use of part-time faculty or the exploitation of graduate student employees, which in turn suggests the replacement of tenured with contract faculty, which slides naturally into anxiety about distance learning, which leads to concern about shared governance in a world where administrators have all the power, which in turn invokes the wholesale proletarianization of the professoriate.

When Richard Chait, therefore, in an introduction to the New Pathways project, remarks, reasonably enough, that "technology threatens the virtual monopoly higher education has enjoyed as the purveyor of post-secondary degrees," we can and must recognize the implications along all the other cultural and institutional fronts his warning effects. But our own programmatic responses and strategies, adopted under pressure, can easily make things worse. Thus, whatever external assaults on humanities research, tenure, sabbaticals, teaching loads, and other elements of university life are mounted will be underwritten by disastrous compromises made in good faith by departments themselves.

English departments, for example, are compelled financially and structurally to hire non-Ph.D.s at a time when Ph.D.s cannot get jobs. Doctoral institutions also hire postdocs at teaching assistant wages—often out of the altogether decent aim of giving them additional years to get traditional jobs—and in the process undermine the status of the profession and the future job market by proving that Ph.D.s can be hired at half or less the typical current rate for new assistant professors. And the department that hires a new Ph.D. for $3,000 a course is placing itself dangerously close to the salary scale adopted by the schools hiring Ph.D.s for half that or less. Meanwhile, those with instrumental visions of higher education have no patience with the critical distance humanities faculty would like to maintain from their own culture. Their goal is to strip higher education of all its intellectual independence, its powers of cultural critique and political resistance.

Notes

1. We must say that, except in the U.S. Congress, we have never seen the mere appointment of a committee so elaborately celebrated. Here is a photo of the committee members accepting their appointments. Here they gather together for their first meeting. Here they are getting off the elevator. Here they are on the way to the 10 Astor Place restrooms. No matter what issues they have failed to address in their report, we are all to remember the rituals of appointment as a great accomplishment.

2. At the request of my informant, I have altered the rhetoric of this quotation and left the campus unnamed; the arguments put forward remain the same.

3. This suggestion would need to be worked out tactically, since the national list would be very large. The list might be assembled and distributed state by state to reduce the numbers and focus the disapproval on local conditions. One would also need to decide how much pressure to place on schools at the upper end of the part-time pay scale. The Art Institute of Chicago, for example, pays $3,000 per course. Obviously a "Harvest of Shame" that shows all institutions as noncompliant would serve no purpose or even be counterproductive. At the same time, one wants all part-time salaries raised. So one might need to set the figure so as to exempt schools at the upper end from criticism but warn that the minimum ethical salary would be raised each year.

Works Cited

Aronowitz, Stanley. "The Last Good Job in America." *Social Text* (Summer 1997): 93–108.

Benjamin, Ernst. "Variations in the Characteristics of PartTime Faculty by General Fields of Instruction and Research." *Working for Academic Renewal.* Washington, DC: American Association of University Professors, 1998.

Byrne, J. Peter. "Academic Freedom Without Tenure." American Association for Higher Education New Pathways Working Paper Series. Washington, DC, 1997.

Chait, Richard. "Rethinking Tenure: Towards New Templates for Academic Employment." *Harvard Magazine* (July–August 1997): 30–31, 90.

Gilbert, Sandra M., et al. *Final Report: MLA Committee on Professional Employment.* New York: Modern Language Association, 1998.

Guillory, John. "Preprofessionalism: What Graduate Students Want." *Profession 1996.* New York: MLA, 1996. 91–99.

Levine, Arthur. "How the Academic Profession is Changing." *Daedalus* (Fall 1997): 1–20.

Menand, Louis. "How to Make a Ph.D. Matter." *New York Times Magazine* (22 September 1996): 78–81.

Afterword

Richard Ohmann

I stumbled into graduate school fifty years ago, confused in the ordinary way. That is, I imagined Ph.D. work as a continuation of what gave pleasure in college: for me, reading great poems (primarily of the seventeenth and twentieth centuries), figuring out how they worked as formal structures, seeing what made them great, entering into their refined sensibilities, and writing papers about them that would show off my own. Disciplining began abruptly. I was directed to the Child Memorial Library at the top of Widener, and told by its grad student attendant that I would need to know the contents of all its books before I could hope to pass the dreaded orals. For F. P. Magoun's class I made and memorized Anglo-Saxon word cards, unclear why this was happening to me or how it would deepen my understanding of Yeats.[1] I learned from Douglas Bush's class in Victorian poetry that locating poems in a tradition of Christian humanism weighed in more heavily than spotting their tensions and ambiguities. (The New Criticism, which had thrilled me in college without my knowing its name, turned out to reside at Yale; at Harvard we were to take close reading for granted, and become scholars.) Likewise, Walter Jackson Bate showed in his driven, pacing lectures that all of English criticism (from Aristotle on) marched to the tune of "broad humanistic values." A contrapuntal tune in the chatter of my peers taught the importance of literary and professional anecdotes, of professional gossip, and of inflecting critical terms with just the right degree of ironic distance. My graduate chair taught me a sharper lesson about boundaries by declining at first to let me count a course from another department ("The Philosophy of Literature") for credit in English. I learned to disparage social science (see Wilson's essay in this book), lament the ignorant fecklessness of the freshmen we soon taught, think of literary culture as a saving grace in business society. In short, although nobody ever said, "These are the rules you must follow to practice English," I was vigorously recruited into a discourse, in both the ordinary and the Foucaultian sense, well before my first trip to MLA.

A perfectly ordinary story, I think—which, replicated a thousandfold by other stories of different but similar inductions, would bear out Shumway and Dionne's point about the disciplining power of disciplines, Wilson's about boundary conflicts, Russell's about "purification," and other themes that run through this volume. Disciplines constitute and sustain themselves through quiet pressures on daily conduct and on consciousness, as well as through official institutions and the formal regulation of careers.

Right, too, is the argument of the Introduction and the essays in Part I that every discipline is historically constructed. That history, for English and most academic fields, is brief enough. People of my age have lived through almost half of it. My college mentor was a student of Kittredge, who had no Ph.D. (because, as he put it, "who could examine me?"), but who was a student of Child, whose career began long before there was "English." I found the accounts (in Part I) of its formation, changes, and generations illuminating, a reminder that every discipline is a negotiated and conflicted process—something that *happens*, as E. P. Thompson said of social class—rather than a fixed entity. Yes, there were founding legends and ideological revisions (Harkin), purifications and demarcations (Russell), border wars with competing disciplines and practices (Wilson), subdivisions into specialties (Dionne), exfoliations into other disciplines (Russell and Shumway),[2] and intellectually telling shifts in core ideas and ideologies (Williams). But here, I want to subsume these in a longer narrative, from whose point of view English marked off a territory just over one hundred years ago and held it until . . . now? just yesterday? sometime in the near future?

I will return to those questions later. First, though, the story of English's foundation is fairly clear. Professorships, and then departments, called "English" proliferated only in the last quarter of the nineteenth century. Then, too, the English major and Ph.D. were initiated. The Modern Language Association and its journal date from 1883; only after 1900 did English become a more or less separate (and dominant) set of practices within them. Well before the National Council of Teachers of English split off from the MLA in 1912, English was recognized, and recognized itself, as a discipline—witness the publication in 1895 of *English in American Universities,* a collection of essays by its practitioners (ed. William Payne; D.C. Heath). The local condition of its possibility was the emergence of the modern university after 1870, with its specialized research and instruction, its departments, its Ph.D. programs, and its undergraduate majors. English found a place in these arrangements partly by winning its claims for modern literature as successor to the old classical curriculum, partly by adopting philology as its body of knowledge—and also because universities wanted or needed to require composition, the inheritor of rhetoric, and its teachers had to be housed somewhere.

The broader condition of its possibility was the transformation of entrepreneurial into corporate capitalism. The new economic system required far more educated managers and intermediaries in production and marketing, built more on research, and opened a space for professions in their modern form. Hence, the rapid growth and transformation of the old college into the new university, with its complex structure, professional schools, and array of arts and sciences disciplines. I let this ruthless simplification stand because the story is by now familiar, and because I want to return to the sort of disciplining that the new system enabled, and that is the subject of this book.

Since academic disciplines are professions (or subdivisions of one big profession, with a large measure of autonomy), I think it helpful to conceive their disciplining as aimed, however inefficiently, at the professional goal of winning and sustaining privileged conditions of labor: at control over its content and procedures, regulation of the market for it, exclusion of the uncertified from practice, control over admission of new members, public respect for its authority, good pay, and so on. All the episodes of "English" recounted in Part I make sense in this way, though of course not *only* in this way: other values play a part, ranging surely from a disinterested love of inquiry and of teaching young people, to a mean lust for petty power.

In sorting out their internal affairs, professions always exercise what Russell calls "purification": determining what activities will build the fortress of knowledge that authorizes privilege. In the case of English, that professional base quickly became the reverent but disciplined study of literature. With the laying of such a foundation often comes a distinction of the sort Harkin examines, between "work" that expresses the true "professional self" and the "job" in which one performs obligatory services. I would note that most professions informally divide into two tiers, one that does most of the "work" (academic medicine at the prestigious hospitals and medical schools), and one that shoulders most of the "job" (treating minor and unexciting illnesses, prescribing pills, handling paper work). One tier does most of the research and advanced teaching, while the other minds the store. In English, this distinction corresponds roughly to that between lit and comp. Purification always invokes heroes such as Child or Emerson (Shumway), creates honored special fields such as the "renaissance" (Dionne), and weaves justifying ideologies such as humanism (Shumway). The purified core of a profession can shift. Literary study replaced philology, and itself gave way for a while to "theory," as Williams notes, though with bitter resistance.(So, bookkeeping gave way to cost accounting, which in turn gave way to the theorizing of profitability and to corporate consulting or management.) But there remains a purified core.

Professions must also manage external relations. As Shumway and Dionne put it, a successful discipline "naturalizes its boundaries and legitimizes its right to exclude other disciplines from its territory." Medicine's triumphal consolidation a hundred years ago not only delegitimized herbal treatments, midwifery, and homeopathy, but drew its boundaries in such a way as to exclude other practitioners such as dentists, veterinarians, optometrists, and pharmacists, who were able to maintain legitimacy and organize their own (lesser) professions. Russell mentions the splitting off of theater, speech, linguistics, technical and business writing, and so on from English, usually by mutual consent. A discipline weaker than medicine must often maintain its boundaries defensively, as in the "border wars" Wilson describes between English and imperial social science, English and progressive education. And when boundaries become porous, a discipline is in trouble.

Like English, now. Nelson anatomizes the most obvious and painful symptom, our inability to sustain privileged conditions of labor for most new recruits. It is as if fresh accountants were consigned to seasonal work for H. & R. Block; or a majority of young physicians, after completing their internships and residencies, were forced to labor part-time in clinics and emergency rooms at $8.00 an hour, or leave the profession. Medicine is in trouble, too, but not *such* trouble. The leadership and senior practitioners of English and modern languages can't or won't calibrate entry to the profession with a job market that in Nelson's view does not even merit that name. If he is right that the forces behind supply of and demand for new Ph.D.s are chiefly institutional and cultural, then we have lost control of our institutions (compare medicine's analogous failure), and lost the battle to convince "society" that the value of what we do warrants greater support. It would be unseemly for tenured people in English to whine about their own lot, but they, too, apart from a few stars, have suffered increasing work loads, declining institutional power, lower relative pay, and a loss of public respect. Nelson's focus on the MLA and on Ph.D. programs shows how inattentive or sluggish or helpless (or all three) our chief organizations have been in facing the crisis.

To what extent does it stem from internal weakness or confusion in English? Certainly, purification strategies that worked well enough through the early 1960s have unraveled or come under attack since then. A number of the essays in this volume show that the marginalization of rhetoric, however useful in founding English one hundred years ago, has had unpleasant consequences in recent decades, running from the disciplinary lapse Schilb describes to the failure of most Ph.D. programs to prepare students for newly plentiful jobs in composition, and the establishment of rhetoric tracks or doctoral programs whose students now have an advantage in the job market over literature students. Other essays allude to internal disputes over what literary study should be, or "really" was. Around 1970 came poststructuralist theory, to unsettle the premise of the coherent and stable text that had underwritten both explication and historical criticism for some decades, and thus English's version of an ever-expanding body of knowledge, developed and tended by experts deploying secure methods. (See Schliefer, and also Finke and Schlichtman, on how electronic editing may finally chase the idea of the verbal icon from even that conservative branch of English.) The new theory eroded the discipline's ideology, too, by de-estheticizing literature and relinquishing its supposed difference from all other kinds of speech and writing. Although this seemed a bracing move at the time, it amounted to deconstituting the very *object* of English studies—much as if accounting theory were to discover the floating signifier in all financial data, and thus their identity with other signs. (Never mind that accounting's object *is* as malleable as the literary text: both disciplines need the working fiction of something fixed but opaque, that only they can rightly decipher.)

And of course theory opened the way to constructionism, which exposed the discipline itself as an artifact of history and social process. To do so is not to discredit it, Shumway and Dionne note, but makes it harder to defend to the lay public, who were used to accepting English as natural, on more or less the terms argued by practitioners.

Plainly, this upheaval at the center of the discipline affected its boundary claims, too. Theory's win justified letting English go to professional work on literally everything, from film to cheap romances to museums to hiphop to sexuality—an expansionist move already well underway for other reasons. It also put us into direct competition with practitioners of other disciplines, and in effect left us with nothing but high-wire artistry as our entitlement. That might have amounted to an advance for the field if (a) all in it had agreed on cultural studies as the work of the future; (b) people in anthropology, political science, art history, philosophy, and so on had flocked to amiable collaboration on a new level; and (c) administrators, trustees, journalists, funders, and voters had understood and celebrated the change as an exciting intellectual revolution. None of that happened, much. The upshot has been internal strife, resentment from neighboring disciplines and university administrations, and mockery from the Right as well as from media people enlisted in its culture wars. The English curriculum has lost its apparent if misleading coherence, has rapidly imported material and method from "outside," and has spilled over former boundaries into various interdisciplinary programs and multicultural "studies," as noted by Williams and Schliefer. Likewise research, to the bemusement of book publishers and MLA-watchers.

The decentering and the erasure of borders was driven by intellectual developments in English and neighboring fields. But it would be wrong to see that as the whole story, or even as the main story. At the same time, new populations of undergraduates were pouring into the university, quite apart from the turn toward theory. Some became graduate students and made their way onto the faculty, bringing with them ideas about literature and culture rather different from those around which English had organized itself. Also, many who were already apprentices or faculty members by, say, 1965 joined or sympathized with the civil rights, antiwar, feminist, and other broadly egalitarian movements of those years. No need to retell these events, beyond suggesting that the reconstruction of English after 1970 (or destruction, in the view of some) owes more to the playing out of this political and cultural story—including the conservative reaction to a "politicized" university—than to disciplinary events of the kind treated in this book. If the story has a moral, it's probably that disciplinary border tending and internal purification falter in times of social upheaval, though clearly that is less so for accounting or engineering than for such as English and sociology.

Further, the economic system began changing in profound ways about the same time. A crisis in profitability, debt, the foreign trade balance, and other of corporate capitalism's vital signs provoked responses that have now gathered into something like a new economic order: the dismantling of the old, stable, Fordist corporation in favor of a more mobile, borderless, "lean and mean" version; the proliferation of new products and services; the almost instantaneous movement of capital; the elaboration of exotic financial instruments; the intense cultivation of new markets, including especially the commodification of knowledge; and, closer to the subject at hand, the shrinking of the old core labor force, with high pay and benefits and job security, and its replacement by more casual labor. These changes have severely challenged the traditional university, driving it to cut costs, market its "products" in new ways, follow corporations in outsourcing and subcontracting, and generally privatize higher education—pressured the while by for-profit competition from proprietary universities, Internet providers, and corporations that train and retrain their own workers in internal "universities," of which there are now more than 1,500 (GE started the first, in 1955).

These developments have undercut professions, too, as business seeks to marketize their services and commodify knowledge of all sorts, including those that serve as intellectual capital for professional and disciplinary groups. I agree with Shumway and Dionne: "We may be on the verge of a new shift in higher education, one that will make disciplines as obsolete as the old classical curriculum." In a regime that has undermined medicine, law, and other professions stronger than the academic ones, worldwide (see Elliott-Krause, *The Death of the Guilds*), it is hard to imagine what strategies for redisciplining English could rebuild its former market shelter. More likely, it will experience a further erosion of its authority in and outside the university, continued marketizing of its "applied" work in writing instruction, and casualization of labor for new Ph.D.s, in spite of retirements and a recent upturn in the funding of higher education.

To leave it at that would be to encourage the sense of helplessness Nelson abjures. I agree with him that "the economy" is not "our inexorable and monolithic fate; it's a host of social, political, and cultural forces, values, and constituencies that *can be acted upon*. . . ." The kinds of action he proposes are worth pursuing; it would be heartless not to pursue them. But it's also worth keeping in mind that in a hegemonic arrangement of "forces, values, and constituencies," some people have more power than others to act consequentially. The actions of capital (to put it abstractly) fix the circumstances within which others can act. Capital will go on globalizing and casualizing labor and commodifying knowledge, in its own urgent interests. Political resistance is always possible, but had better be broadly imagined. Yes, support graduate student organizing, shame exploiting departments, trim Ph.D. programs. Also, explore alliances with other knowledge workers; support unionizing efforts by part-timers in every industry and worldwide; figure out how to bring knowledge and "intellectual property rights" under democratic control; learn from Seattle and the Boeing engineers' strike. It's a tall order, a project more ambitious than redisciplining English. Though that's worth trying, too.

Notes

    1. We recited Anglo-Saxon verse aloud in class, and when someone erred, Magoun would chasten us: "You mustn't say it that way; they'll never understand you."

    2. When I was at Harvard, a grad student in English could become an Americanist only by substituting American literature for the medieval period, as one of five fields on the oral exam. Harvard's landmark program in American civilization, dating from the 1930s, was small, and regarded by those in English as marginal.

Contributors

CRAIG DIONNE is Associate Professor of English at Eastern Michigan University and has published essays on Shakespeare and Renaissance literature. He is currently working on a book about early modern civic identity.

LAURIE A. FINKE is Associate Professor of English and Director of Women's Studies at Kenyon College. She is the author of *Feminist Theory, Women's Writing,* and editor with Martin Shichtman of *Medieval Texts and Contemporary Readers.*

PATRICIA HARKIN is Associate Professor of English at the University of Illinois, Chicago. Her articles on composition, rhetoric, and literary theory have appeared in numerous journals and collections. She is the author of *Acts of Reading* and co-editor of *Contending with Words.*

MOLLY HITE is Professor of English at Cornell University, where she teaches feminist theory, postmodern fiction, and creative writing. She is the author of a novel as well as numerous academic books and articles.

CARY NELSON is Jubilee Professor of Liberal Arts and Sciences at the University of Illinois at Urbana-Champaign. He is author of *Manifesto of a Tenured Radical* and *Repression and Recovery: Modern American Poetry and the Politics of Cultural Memory.*

DAVID R. RUSSELL is Associate Professor of English at Iowa State University and author of *Writing in the Academic Disciplines, 1870–1990.*

RONALD SCHLEIFER is Professor of English at the University of Oklahoma. He is one of editors of the series, "The Oklahoma Project for Discourse and Theory," and co-author of *Culture of Cognition: The Boundaries of Literary and Scientific Inquiry.*

JOHN SCHILB is Associate Professor of English and holds the Culbertson Chair in Writing at the Indiana University. He is author of *Between the Lines: Relating Composition Theory and Literary Theory* and coeditor of *Contending with Words* and *Writing Theory and Critical Theory.*

MARTIN B. SHICHTMAN is Professor of English at Eastern Michigan University. His books include *Culture And The King: The Social Implications Of The Arthurian Legend,* and *Medieval Texts and Contemporary Readers.*

DAVID R. SHUMWAY is Professor of English and Literary and Cultural Studies at Carnegie Mellon University. He is author of *Michel Foucault* and *Creating American Civilization: A Genealogy of American Literature as an Academic*

Discipline. He is one of the editors of _Knowledges: Historical and Critical Studies in Disciplinarity._

JEFFREY WILLIAMS, Assistant Professor of English, University of Missouri, Columbia, is editor of the _minnesota review,_ an editor of the _Norton Anthology of Literary Theory,_ and the author of numerous articles on the history and practice of theory in the discipline.

ELIZABETH A. WILSON previously taught English at Yale University. She is writing a book on childhood trauma.

Index

A
Abbot, Andrew, 6
Abrams, M. H., 118
  Mirror and the Lamp, The, 118
Academe, 207
Adams, Hazard, 60, 78n. 5
Adams, John Quincy, 35n. 1
ADE Bulletin, 196
Alfred Foulet Publications Fund, 175
Allen, Don Cameron, 92, 93, 94
Althusser, Louis, 14
American Academy of Arts and Sciences, 22
American Association for Higher Education, 208
  "New Pathways: Faculty Careers and Employment in the 21st Century," 208
American Association of University Professors, 197, 204
American Council of Learned Societies (ACLS), 60
American Economic Association, 61
American Historical Association (AHA), 61, 65, 75, 76, 196
American Philological Association, 55, 60
American Political Science Association (APSA), 61
American Sociological Association (ASA), 61
American Statistical Association, 61
Amiran, Eyal, 183, 188, 189, 192n. 3
Arac, Jonathan, 112n. 10
Aristotle, 21, 34, 143, 213

Arnold, Matthew, 59, 94, 105, 106
  Culture and Anarchy, 59
Aronowitz, Stanley, 206
Association of Departments of English (ADE), 196
Atlantic Monthly, 26, 31
Auden, W. H., 59

B
Babbitt, Irving, 59, 69, 105, 106, 163
Bacon, Sir Francis, 28
Bachelard, Gaston, 187
Bakhtin, Mikhail, 182
Baldick, Chris, 191 n. 1
  Social Mission of Literary Criticism, The, 191n. 1
Barnard, Frederick A. P., 47
Barthes, Roland, 165–166, 167, 184
  S/Z, 165–166, 168
Bartholomae, David, 14, 138, 144–145
  "Inventing the University," 138
Baswell, Christopher, 159–160, 161, 168
Baym, Nina, 110
Beard, Charles, 75
  Charter for the Social Sciences, 75
Benhabib, Seyla, 182
Benjamin, Ernst, 204
Bennet, William, 176
Berlin, James A., 32, 39
  Rhetoric and Reality, 32
Bérubé, Michael, 126–127, 131n. 19, 131n. 20, 131n. 22
  Public Access, 126